From Small Steps to Big Leaps

Vadim Muntagirov

Grosvenor House
Publishing Limited

This book is published by
Grosvenor House Publishing Ltd
Link House
140 The Broadway, Tolworth, Surrey, KT6 7HT.
www.grosvenorhousepublishing.co.uk

A CIP record for this book
is available from the British Library

ISBN 978-1-80381-385-1

INTRODUCTION

This autobiography opens a window on the uniquely individual life of one of the most celebrated dancers of our time.

Vadim left home aged 10 to enter full time ballet training, arrived at The Royal Ballet School via the Prix de Lausanne aged 16 with no English, was cast as Albrecht in English National Ballet's *Giselle* aged 19 and danced Siegfried in *Swan Lake* at The Royal Albert Hall to considerable acclaim less than a year after graduating. Since then, with an expanded repertoire as a Principal with The Royal Ballet and in parallel demand as an international guest, Vadim's early promise has translated into a stellar career. Nicknamed Vadream, he is hugely admired and very much loved by audiences at home and abroad.

Vadim's story affords a real insight into the intense work and level of commitment needed to rise to the top in ballet – and stay there. It enables readers to see the experiences which have shaped him, including the lasting effect of separation from his family, his rigorous early training, his discovery of a world beyond his homeland, and the unstinting support he has received in his adopted country as a student and during his years in the profession.

This is a book which looks 'behind the scenes' and 'beyond the interviews' to reveal what is involved in becoming and being a Principal dancer, including the privilege of working with many ballet luminaries, the more informal moments, and the many etceteras which come with the job.

But Vadim makes it about so much more than the daily 'ins and outs' as he shares his reactions, thoughts and emotions in a way which allows others to get to know him as a person.

FOREWORD AND ACKNOWLEDGEMENTS

In late June 2020, during the first pandemic lockdown, I had just performed *Dance of the Blessed Spirits* on the stage of The Royal Opera House. At that point, the future seemed particularly uncertain  and I was feeling low, not able to do what I live for and even wondering whether my dancing career might be over. However, inspired by the inventiveness of so many dancers who were using their spare time to develop other talents and explore new avenues, I thought that I would experiment with a book. Nearly three years later, this is the outcome!

Photo: Peter Smith

Of course, I couldn't have made any progress without a lot of help. My parents and other members of my family jogged my early memory; Linda Gainsbury gave me a framework, converted what I was saying into print and handled all the preparation and processes needed for self-publishing; Amber Hunt provided not only photographs but a variety of other assistance; Rachel Hollings and Grace Allwood enabled me to access images from my time with The Royal Ballet; and many amazing photographers have been extremely supportive. I am so grateful to them all and to everyone who contributed in some way.

I would also like to thank all my teachers, coaches, partners, colleagues and Directors and everyone who has invited me to dance or teach as a guest. Without them there would be no story to tell.

Footnotes:

i) Photographs which are not credited were taken by me or my family
ii) To see what lies behind the various QR codes, please scan with your phone. These link to posts on my Instagram account: @vadimmuntagirovofficial

FOR MY FAMILY WITH LOVE

A Tribute to Papa

All fathers are unique and very special to their families and I mention Papa a lot in this book. However, I wanted everyone to know how significant he has been in terms of ballet in Russia as well as to me.

Alexander Abubakirovich Muntagirov, was born on the 21st May 1955 in Pervouralsk. He trained in Perm at what was then called the State College of Choreography where he was taught by prominent teachers of the time. As a student, alongside his contemporary Marat Doukaev, he partnered both Olga Chenchikova and Nadezhda Pavlova and toured with Perm Ballet to Austria and Holland. Upon graduating with honours, he joined the ballet company in Chelyabinsk and danced all the leading male roles in the repertoire over a career of 24 years which included regular appearances at the Nureyev Festival in Kazan and, for ten consecutive years, tours with Vadim Pisarev in the USA.

In 1994, although he continued to dance, he was appointed Ballet Director at the Chelyabinsk Opera and Ballet Theatre, a post he held for eight years. Interestingly, as part of his strategy to develop the Company, he recruited many male dancers from the Perm School, including a number from outside Russia.

He was one of the founders of the annual Ekaterina Maximova Festival in Chelyabinsk and, because of his respect for Papa, the great Vladimir Vasiliev came to the city to produce his ballet *Cinderella* for free. During that period also, Papa was invited to stage *Romeo and Juliet* for the Romanian Ballet in Bucharest and spent half a year in Turkey mounting *Giselle* in Mersin.

In 2002, Papa decided to concentrate on teaching and the first approach he received was from Khanty-Mansiysk, a fast-developing city in Eastern Russia which was seeking to build its cultural profile and wanted its Professor of Ballet to have an already well-established reputation in the art. For his part, he was attracted by the new facilities and a portfolio of responsibility which involved teaching the history and theory of ballet as well as taking class. He was also able to appoint a supporting team, including trusted teachers from Chelyabinsk and a pianist.

His original official title was Head of the Choreography Department of the Khanty-Mansiysk University of Art and Culture, which was affiliated to the Moscow State University and had three sections: a residential school, a college, and an institute where young people could go on to study for a degree. From 2015, the institution focused in on its vocational ballet school/college provision and the framework for Papa's job in the re-named Cultural Centre became more like that of a senior teacher.

The 200+ graduates that Papa has nurtured over the years are to be found across Russia, not only as dancers but also as choreographers, ballet masters and coaches. But, in addition, he has regularly acted as a guest teacher in schools and companies around the country (and in the UK), a competition judge, and a festival organiser, and he has also been involved in many charitable activities related to dance.

I feel incredibly proud of what Papa has achieved, of his renown in the context of ballet in Russia, and of the public recognition and honours he has received. He is a People's Artist of Russia and he has also been awarded a First Grade Sergei Diaghilev Medal "for services to the arts" and the Knight of Dance Prize. In 2020 Vladimir Vasiliev travelled specially to Khanty-Mansiysk to present him with the Bright Past Award – a very notable accolade and a very memorable occasion.

Papa has been my inspiration and my guide and I am so happy that I am his son.

CONTENTS

PART ONE

STARTING POINTS [1990–2009]

After the Opening Night of Vladimir Vasiliev's Production of Cinderella in Chelyabinsk: Left to right: my sister Eleonora, Vladimir Vasiliev, me, Papa and Ekaterina Maximova

CHAPTER 1

A CHILD OF THE URALS

My City

In 1990, when I was born, the Soviet Union was several years into the political change, economic reform and restructuring associated with Perestroika. States and Republics were being established and regions such as that which centres on Chelyabinsk were being given a degree of autonomy. The city itself is in central Russia between the Ural Mountains to the west and the Siberian Plain to the east. It was founded as a fortress in the 18th century, became the centre of a local agricultural region and grew further with the coming of the Trans Siberian Railway in the 1890s. The higher areas are covered in forest but the Urals are also rich in minerals which led to Chelyabinsk developing as an industrial centre and benefiting from further growth when industry was evacuated eastwards after World War II. Although it also has significant educational, scientific, research, sports and cultural organisations, Chelyabinsk is not usually a tourist destination for people from outside Russia. Yet it is the country's seventh largest city with a population of over a million in 1990 and about one and a quarter million now.

My Family

My father (Papa, pronounced **Paa**pa), Alexander Abubakirovich Muntagirov, came from a nearby area (Pervouralsk), although he is half Tartar by descent, hence his patronymic. [In Russia, all children take their father's name in this way, so I am Vadim Alexandrovich. I am also Vadik to my family as almost every Russian name gets abbreviated for everyday use – even short ones like mine or Maria (Masha).] Papa's family had no background in ballet (his father worked in an iron foundry) but, as

3

a child, he went to a circus class. A former ballerina who came to teach there thought that he had the physique and way of moving which would suit him for ballet and she recommended that he audition in Perm. I get the sense that my grandfather, a former military man, might not have wanted him to become a ballet dancer but my grandmother took him to Perm and he was accepted for training there. After graduating with honours, he was given a contract in Chelyabinsk and rose quickly through the ranks to become a Principal Dancer at the State Academic Opera and Ballet Theatre and, later, its Ballet Director. When he retired from that position in 2004, he became a Professor at the University of Art and Culture in Khanty-Mansiysk.

My mother (Mama, spoken as **Maa**ma), Irina Fedorovna Kopeika came to Chelyabinsk by chance. She was born in Khabarovsk in far Eastern Russia, where her father worked in a submarine factory, but also has a Ukrainian ancestry. Dancing wasn't in her family either but she and her sister were taken to ballet class by my grandmother, trained in the local school and graduated into the company. There are companies everywhere in Russia and, as a result, ballet is understood and valued. There are no 'Billy Elliot' issues there: dancers are respected, celebrated and looked up to. However, my mother and her friends grew restless working in Khabarovsk because, they said, "Nothing ever happens here". So, one day, they pulled out a map, closed their eyes, and decided that they would relocate to wherever a finger landed. The nearest city to that point was Chelyabinsk and they were all successful in getting contracts there. At one point, Mama could have joined the Kirov — it was a case, as someone put it, of "taking up the opportunity to go to St Petersburg or cooking borsch" for her husband. She decided to stay in Chelyabinsk! Although she never had the official title of Principal there, as a Soloist and before my sister was born, she danced a number of leading roles, including Odette/Odile in *Swan Lake* with my father.

My parents married in 1981 in my father's home town. My sister, Eleonora, arrived when Mama was 29 and she took two years out before returning to dance Soloist and Corps roles.

Baby Me

It was rather different after I came along in 1990 because the nature of the Chelyabinsk ballet company was changing. One of the effects of Perestroika was a greater freedom of movement within Russia and beyond and this caused a lot of dancers to take the opportunity to leave. Consequently, my father had a very heavy workload and my mother had no option but to return to work quite quickly, when I was about 8 months old, because she was needed in the Corps. Having to cope with a baby as well must have been very difficult indeed for them at that time. Then aged 38, Mama was to dance for a further 10 years. Over the same period, Papa, who is two to three years younger than her, also continued to perform but, once he became Director in 2004, he first took on characters (Drosselmeyer; Espada etc.) as distinct from 'princes' and then concentrated on his managerial role alone. So, it was inevitable that, from babyhood onwards, I spent a great deal of time in the theatre – but I will come back to that shortly.

When I ask my parents about my very early childhood, they recall with horror that, when I was one month old and went to the clinic to be checked and weighed, the nurse dropped me and I hit my head on a concrete floor. Suffice it to say that Papa, especially, was very upset and angry. I don't think that there was any lasting damage. But who knows: it might explain a lot!!!!

It isn't like this any longer, but one of the advantages of being a dancer in the (then) Soviet Union was that accommodation came with the job, with the more senior artists getting a better choice of apartments. My parents had been allocated one in a typical Soviet, concrete block of 45 flats and we were on the top (9th) floor). It had three bedrooms, was near the city centre and was about 10 minutes' walk from the theatre. So, very convenient. I say 'was' but my sister lives there now with her husband, Yevgeny Mozharov, their student daughter Stanislava (Stasia) and their much younger child Zlataslava (Zlata).

At Home

Family Cuddles

My sister left to train in Perm when she was ten and we actually had only two/three years at home together. I don't really remember her as a 'big sister' figure but she would play with me when she was back from Perm and I used to look forward to those times. I also used to make 'pretend houses' from cushions and bed coverings and try to get her to join me inside. But I don't think that I was as nice a brother to her as I should have been. Mama tells me that, when I was still very little, she was chatting to another woman at the train station who commented, "You have two very sweet girls there". It was a reasonable misunderstanding as I had very long hair at the time. But then I punched my sister so hard in the stomach that the woman smiled, "Aaah, I guess that *that* one's a boy!" Similarly, I would tend to 'beat up' Eleonora in play and make her cry and I did silly things like drawing circles all over the writing in her girly diary. She would say, "Stop! Stop!" and pull her notebook away from me but I would be laughing because it was a fun game for me. A rather naughty boy, I regret to say! However, as children, we bonded strongly when trying to avoid Papa finding out if were unwell. We felt his love but he had no time for illnesses and we were both scared of getting told off.

Once my sister had gone, despite the family gatherings in the summer and at Christmas time, I suppose that much of my life was rather as if I was an only child. I had plenty of toys to play

6

with. Most of them were soft but my favourite was a stiffer, hero-type figure which had limbs which I could twist in various directions. I also had a cat, Sylvester, for my friend. Fortunately, at that stage, I hadn't developed the fur allergy which I now have.

Playing Houses with Eleonora

Loving my Friend

Owning the Sofa

Togetherness

I think that my parents were strict and very aware of the risk of spoiling me because other children seemed to have more fancy toys which they resisted buying for me. I wasn't allowed roller skates because skaters' legs have to be kept parallel and they were anticipating my need for 'turn out' as I developed. Riding a toy-sized bike and, later, a slightly bigger one was permitted, however. And I had a lot of clothes because of the cold – which, in Chelyabinsk, is extreme but somehow easier to tolerate than the wetter and windier climate in London. For a large part of the year, a typical outfit for a child in central Russia, is long, thin underpants under trousers, a T-shirt under a jumper and a padded jacket – all topped with a furry hat with warm ear flaps.

More generally, perhaps contrary to what people might think, there was no shortage of clothing, food or sweet things in the shops, well not that I was aware of in the local, corner shops I went to with Mama. There were also larger supermarkets but, looking back, I think that they were geared towards people who were richer than we were. The real markets were more our scene. Hundreds of lorries would turn up loaded with goods – I particularly remember the melons – and Papa could easily spend a whole day shopping there. Where he was born, there was a counter-style bakery shop which smelt amazing and would sell you as little as a quarter of a loaf of bread if that was all you wanted or all you could afford.

Some ballet fans in the UK will remember dancers from visiting Russian companies stocking up with electrical goods while they were on tour and, in particular, wheeling them away from the Coliseum or The Royal Opera House at the end of their run. In the 1980s and 1990s, Russian dancers did so because those sorts of items were in short supply. My sister is still using a microwave that my father took home from a tour in the USA! There were also times when workers, including dancers, couldn't be paid in money and were given food or furniture instead. In Russia, and in some other countries I believe, cabbage, which featured prominently in the payments, is also a slang term for a dollar, presumably because both are green. There is a funny story from when Papa was on tour in the USA. Asked in an interview about his salary, he explained, "Sometimes we are paid with goods, including cabbages". This drew a hugely surprised reaction because people thought he was saying that Russian dancers were paid in dollars. They were no less amazed when Papa told them, "Yes, really; I do receive some of my pay in vegetables". I suppose that those kinds of circumstances and stories seeped into me as a child and have made me appreciate and value what I am able to earn more than I might have done otherwise. Also, if I'm honest, I have felt driven to earn as much as I can while I can and, apart from wanting to help my family, to be careful about how I spend my money.

During my early childhood, I was always trying to creep into my parent's bed and sleep between them. I was also at my happiest when I was doing things with them – or, in the case of preparing a meal, trying unsuccessfully to copy Mama. I think that is why I was, and remain, a 'parents person' – if anything too attached to them. Our bond remains strong, even though I have spent a very small proportion of my life in their company. My mix of memories includes hysterical panicking because I thought, completely irrationally, that Mama was going to die but, conversely, I was equally capable of shouting, "I hate you" when forced to do my homework or to go to the dentist (who, by the way didn't use anaesthetic). I was certainly able to produce some high decibel temper tantrums.

In the Theatre

Early Practice for
The Nutcracker

Despite their demanding schedule, my parents never really left me on my own and, from the moment my mother went back to work until I went to school, my life was almost entirely framed by the theatre. I didn't really live in the family flat; I lived in the equivalent of an eight storey mansion. At first, I was just there in my pram but, once out of it, I would sit very shyly in the studio, preferring to stare at the pianist or play videos rather than to watch class or rehearsals. During the shows I would sometimes be in the auditorium (in the special lighting box near the stage), in the wings, or even in the orchestra pit. At other times, I would just

9

play all over the theatre with the children of other dancers. There were exciting places to explore and hide. Papa would also ask if we could go into the prop room and borrow something. So I was able to have imaginative fun with theatrical toys - a sword from *The Nutcracker* or even a pistol, for example.

The repertoire in Chelyabinsk at that time was very much the standard one in Russia with *The Nutcracker, Don Quixote, Swan Lake, Coppélia* and *Walpurgis Night* on repeat. The company also performed some children's ballets which people would laugh about now. I remember one of them featuring three pigs and a wolf eating together in a house and another about a boy called Onion, who built his home in the wrong place and interacted with a range of fruit and vegetable characters. My mother played a cherry and had two red ones wobbling about on her headdress.

Of course, my parents' lifestyle, and therefore mine, meant that I usually went to bed very late indeed and waking up was always hard. There is a very tender Russian word for son and Mama would use that every morning, followed by, "Wake up". What made getting up even harder was that it always seemed to be dark, often until mid-morning. This meant that most of my journeys on Mama's three-wheeled bicycle were made in what felt like night-time. This childhood regime was probably good training for a professional career as dancers are usually very late home after a show, are even later in being able to sleep, and have times when guesting abroad involves exceptionally early flights the following morning.

I suppose it was inevitable that, with dance going on all around me, I would try to copy moves almost as soon as I could walk. At first, I was just jumping and jigging around. Then Papa would make some suggestions accompanied by dramatic gestures – "Be Siegfried" - and I'd try to imitate him. It felt really good putting on the costumes he brought home and pretend I was the character. Sometimes, when I was dressed up and striking poses or pulling faces, Papa would say, "Show the death of Rothbart" and I would try to express his suffering with one wing. Maybe this was early acting practice for me.

Trying out Papa's Von Rothbart Costume

I don't remember wanting to be like Papa or any kind of steering or pressure on me to dance at that point, but I was flexible and I could make some sense of ballet movement. The other interesting thing, I suppose, was that, whereas I was resistant in other ways and my mother sometimes had to lie to get me to do things, I was much more compliant when my father demonstrated something and said, "Do this; do that" in relation to a sequence of movement, for example saut de basques. Even so, I can't claim that any passion or future dreams were developing inside me. There was no defining moment: dancing just began to feel a natural thing to be doing.

At School

Solo Football in the Street

Once I was in school, on nights when there was a show, I was collected and taken to the theatre afterwards. So I sat doing my homework in the dressing room occupied by Mama and five other dancers. That kind of arrangement was very different from that of my school mates but I never felt separated because of what my

11

parents did. I think it helped that the teachers, mostly women, were very supportive and talked about ballet in an interested and positive way. On other nights, I was allowed outside to play football beside the apartment block, but with close supervision which I can now see as being with an eye to the future. Almost every time I got kicked, Mama was calling, "Mind your legs" or "That's enough; we must go inside now" and I was either pretending not to hear her or pleading, "Let's stay longer, pleeeeeeease."

In the 1990s, it was possible for children to go to kindergarten when they were aged five but, because there was a lot of illness among that age group and as I seemed to catch colds frequently, my parents chose to wait until I was seven before they enrolled me in school. I went to a pre-school for a short time, where they started to teach writing, and then moved on to an ordinary school for pupils aged seven to 17/18 where I was for just three years. Children did not, and do not, change institutions between junior and secondary as they do in the UK and elsewhere.

My school was another concrete Soviet-style building. The classrooms were arranged very formally with pairs of desks for about 20 pupils in rows and the teacher was always at the front. The curriculum consisted of Language, Literature, Maths, History, Dance and Sport. The homework seemed to involve a lot of letter-writing exercises and Maths and the instructions were not always very clear to me. Mama and her colleagues had to put up with a fair amount of me crying with frustration, "I don't know what I have to doooo!" "I don't understand......I don't know what this means........" That couldn't have been very helpful for the dancers who were preparing to go on stage.

Chelyabinsk School

The early dance classes at school were called ballet but were really more in the 'slap chest, slap knee and jump' style which is traditionally associated with Russian folk dance. I really liked, and still like, that kind of dancing. It helps coordination but it isn't exactly a preparation for ballet. The school sports sessions – football - were good as well and we had men teaching us for those. In fact, I was very keen on football and took every opportunity I could for a game or for larking around with a ball, getting my legs covered in bruises in the process. I also participated in after school activities because staying on late made it easier for my parents to pick me up and manage me afterwards. But this extra time in school simply involved my staying in the classroom and doing more Russian language and literature. The inevitable boredom of this and the normal very formal lessons, each lasting 45 minutes, was lightened by friendships and fun within the class. Maybe it was this, alongside the times with my family, which brought out the jokey side of me which has never gone away. I also fell in love for the first time! At one point, I was put next to a girl called Lena (Elena) and she helped me with my homework. I must have liked her a lot because, when she invited me to her house to play console games, I asked Mama to buy me a single rose to give her. As was the case with all my other school friends, I lost touch with Lena when I left for Perm.

At the Dacha

Throughout my childhood, indeed into my teens, the very happiest of times were every summer from June onwards when, with at least 10 members of my father's wider family, we used to travel by minibus to Staraya Utka (which translates as old duck), a village near where Papa and his six siblings were born. There are a lot of villages in the Urals like this. They grew up originally because of metal mining, salt extraction and logging, but many of the factories fell into disuse and the population declined. Property was therefore relatively cheap and the wooden house which my father bought was in an old

The Village Area   Up a Bird Cherry Tree

Picking Blackcurrents   Soaking up the Sun
in Front of Our Dacha
in 2021

Russian style. It is a Dacha – a small summer home set in a vegetable garden. Many Dachas are in locations where all the properties are occupied for only part of the year but, unusually, ours is in an area where some three quarters of the owners are permanent residents.

Accommodation for my sister, all my cousins and me was a bit like I imagine it must be in the army because there were so many of us sleeping together. The adults slept in the big living room where there was a double bed and sofas and I remember the big stove in the kitchen which ran on wood and provided for heating as well as cooking. There was also an extra area which my family used for storage but where most similar houses would keep cows. A cowherd would gather them all together, very early in the morning after milking, and take them (and some goats) through the village up onto the mountain until around 6.00 in the evening when they would all come down and into their own byres to be hand-milked again. So, twice a day, we had cowbells ringing in our ears, poo splattered everywhere, and masses of attendant mosquitoes waiting to bite us. The reality of country life! The upside was that Papa only needed to walk a few steps to a neighbour's to buy milk which was so fresh that it was still warm when he brought it in.

The garden was full of all kinds of fruit and vegetable produce and we children would go and gather strawberries and crush them into the milk to make an amateur kind of smoothie. But, as if that wasn't enough, we would climb neighbours' trees to pick bird cherries, an activity which usually ended with us being chased away with a lot of screaming, "Off you go; that's stealing" and hands being waved as if to say, "Shoo, you terrible kids!"

We would also go foraging for mushrooms in the forest, bringing them back gleefully to be fried with potatoes. It was strangely emotional to watch the film *White Crow* about Rudolf Nureyev and to see him, too, going into the woods as a child and picking fruit there and in a garden,

 just as we did. There is also an episode in the ballet *A Month in the Country* – the one where the mother, the children and the tutor dance together – which evokes memories for me because of its joyful mood. But we had no tutor and no romantic intrigues to complicate our family time!

A Big 'Plaything'!

Then there was the exciting machinery........ Who needs small toys when there is massive tree-felling and slicing equipment to play on? Of course, access wasn't allowed as it was obviously highly dangerous, with razor-sharp edges exposed everywhere, so there were shouting guards to dodge and barking dogs to avoid. But some of the lorries were no longer used and, if we weren't caught, we could climb on them and pretend to be the drivers. The pedals would push down and the gears would change so, up high in the cabs, we could almost convince ourselves that we were moving.

We also needed to be inventive with our fishing. We didn't have a proper rod between us but a piece of bamboo, with some string dangling from it and anything we could find tied on for bait, was a good enough substitute to get some small catches. I think that we must have been quite 'wild' children as we would go out to play all over the village – on the grass or in the road depending on what we could find to create a game. Balls, of course, but a few sticks and a plastic bottle worked very well for our version of hockey. There were always, "Be careful!" warnings from the family, especially about the machinery and the wobbly piles of logs, but we were completely carefree. And that feeling of relaxation (a stark contrast with my time in Perm) and the massive fun I had with all my cousins will stay with me for ever.

Family is hugely important to Russian people – and I mean one's extended family, not just one's Mama and Papa and brothers/sisters who are obviously extra special – with relatives usually very interdependent and involved in one another's lives even if they are often argumentative. The mutual support between my father and his brothers in particular was very strong and, although Papa is the second youngest and has lived far away from them at times, he has always shopped as if to provide for all his family as well as for my mother and himself. There are now only four siblings as one of his brothers and his younger sister died relatively young. She was a circus acrobat and tightrope walker but the others had more sedate careers, one as a delivery driver, the others as teachers.

Our annual three month breaks also enabled me to spend time with my paternal grandmother (babushka) Polina, known as Baba Pola, who lived in Pervouralsk. [I didn't see my other grandmother, Kopeika Lida Semenovna, known as Baba Lida, until she was very old and had moved to Khanty Mansiysk so that my mother could look after her; and I didn't know my maternal grandfather Feodor.] It was Baba Pola who introduced me to amazing, thick homemade soups which I still enjoy. I think that she began to prepare food that way because she had to cater for my grandfather, Konstantin, who had digestion problems dating from World War II when the tank he was driving was caught in an explosion and ended up rolling on top of him. I have only one memory of him and that is of riding on his neck on the way to the shops.

The really super thing about visiting Ekaterinburg as a child was that my grandmother's dog, a Collie called Inga, would jump enthusiastically into my arms when I arrived, even though she might not have seen me for over eight months. I also remember sitting on her knee one day and her telling me, "One day, you will be a famous dancer and I will watch you on TV". I didn't believe her of course and it didn't come true because, very sadly, when I was ten, doctors wrongly diagnosed her stomach problem as appendicitis and she didn't survive the operation.

Water Sport with 'My' Dog   Trick Cyclist

It's only now I am looking back that I realise how little I actually know about my grandparents' lives but, being young and away from home, I never really asked the adults around me personal kinds of questions or thought about their ages. On one occasion, a mandatory form needed to be completed. "When was your mother born?", an official enquired. "1970", I replied because that date popped into my head (but that would have made her only 13 when she had my sister!). "When was your father born?", the man continued. "1942", I offered because that was another date which resonated with me for some reason – (it was during the siege of Leningrad!). The man looked up quizzically saying, "That's a very big gap" but he recorded the dates nonetheless. I did get my facts sorted immediately afterwards!

To the Seaside and Beyond

The smaller family unit of Mama and Papa, my sister and I also went for short stays at the seaside – mainly Sochi on the Black Sea, where the Winter Olympics were held in 2014. People who worked in some way for the country, especially teachers and the staff of cultural and sports organisations, could apply to be considered for free all-inclusive holidays in state-funded sanitoriums. Hundreds of these had been developed by the Soviet Union in coastal and country settings which were regarded as having healing qualities and where families could enjoy some rest and recuperation. They were very grand-looking buildings but the rooms were small and spartan, probably to emphasise the importance of communal activity. There was plenty going on in terms of group games and a range of treatments were available free. These were meant to be able to heal everything from arthritis to mould in the nose and options included breathing in salt in a cave, having massages, including ones under water, electrolysis and something called oxygen cocktails. But to me, as a child, it all felt more like a lovely holiday rather than anything medically therapeutic. Our family application was accepted most years but, if it was not, Papa would book us into a flat near the sea or a standard type of hotel, all of which seemed to have upbeat names, such as Victory or Sunrise, displayed on the building in large, brightly lit letters.

In the Sea at Sochi

Hugging a Lion in Sochi

In addition to family holidays, I also went to Sochi when the Chelyabinsk Company was on tour. I can visualise our having a private room on the train and still have the song about it taking three days and three nights to get there ringing in my ears. Once, when I was aged eight or nine, Papa told me, "You can work; you can give out programmes." This got me excited because work meant money – or so I thought. But it turned out that I was to do it for free and, when I saw the pile I was expected to carry, I said, "No way!" How I got away with that refusal, I don't know........

In contrast to Sochi, another tour I remember was to Astrakhan where it was very cold. I think to keep me occupied, there was talk of my having a pet. I immediately imagined something small and furry but, one day, I was given a shoe box with holes punched in the lid. I opened it up to find a tortoise, withdrawn into its shell and not very relatable. He/she ended up living a better life with one of my cousins than I could have provided.

With the Company Guesting
in Astrakhan

On Holiday in Sochi
with Eleonora

Postscript

As my career began to develop and because my family liked to spend their summers in Turkey, I returned to my home area only infrequently. Yet, when I went back to Staraya Utka and the surrounding countryside in 2021, it felt as if I had never been away and my visit seven years previously seemed like 'yesterday'. The natural, unspoilt beauty, the sense of peace, and the wild produce were there to rediscover and marvel at; but there had been changes over time. An ageing population was finding it more difficult to cultivate their plots and everywhere seemed quite overgrown, some houses had collapsed, others needed to be patched up, the woods had become more impenetrable and local industry had declined still further. Large, brick buildings which had been used to assemble machinery were derelict, around half of the big trucks were lying idle in various stages of disrepair and possibly only a quarter of the forest-based activity that there had been originally remained active. But nothing could detract from the area's very special qualities and those made me appreciate my childhood there even more.

Perhaps I should add here also that I have never guested with the Chelyabinsk company but I did dance there once in 2010 with a ballerina who was previously partnered by Papa. At the time, I was 20 and she was in her mid forties. I went back again in 2014 when I was given the *Bright Past* award which recognises the achievement of people from the city. I was one of 10 recipients, including a pilot and a musician. Some of them were famous and, as I sat waiting in the Drama Theatre, I almost thought that the honour was meant for Papa – after all, I was only 24 and my 'past' was a bit limited. But it was nice to know that I had made the city proud and to have the opportunity to perform the Cave pas de deux from *Le Corsaire* with Daria Klimentová. Otherwise, even when I was able to return home, it was mainly to the house in the countryside rather than to the flat; so, in effect, my familiarity with Chelyabinsk and connection with the city more or less ended when I was ten years old.

Except that.......in the wake of the Covid 19 pandemic, I spent more time in the city than I had done for over 20 years and was able to re-visit the scenes of my childhood, in the theatre in particular.

Having spotted my 2021 return on Instagram, a local ballet school invited me to teach a couple of sessions. Then, in 2022, I was able to take daily class with two veteran teachers and reconnect with some of the essentials of my initial training.

Best of all, I was able to renew my relationship with my sister in our home territory – this time as two adults.

CHAPTER 2

SIX YEARS IN PERM

A bit of background to begin with. I wasn't aware of this at the time but it explains why I was taught the way I was.....During the Siege of Leningrad in 1941, which was part of the Nazi's eastern attack in World War II, the ballet and opera companies of the then Kirov Theatre, together with the Leningrad Choreographic School, were evacuated to Molotov (Perm's name between 1940 and 1957). When the blockade was lifted in 1944, plans were put in place for a permanent theatre and school in Molotov/Perm and some of the artists and other staff chose to stay and become part of the new institution rather than return to Leningrad. Thus it was that the State Choreographic Ballet School opened in April 1945 under the direction of a former Kirov Ballet Soloist who had also taught In Leningrad. So it had been running for over 50 years when I went there.

Going and Arriving

Subconsciously, I knew that I would follow my father and my sister and go to train in Perm, but I don't think that it was mentioned specifically until a few weeks before I was due to start there. I did have an audition because I was seen by the Artistic Director when she visited Chelyabinsk. However, I didn't recognise it for what it was or understand its significance. In fact, at the time, it didn't feel any different to Papa making a rather coy me show other people how I could split my legs and move around. I have since been told that the notes made about me that day included a reference to my being a bit chubby around my thighs! There wasn't any other preparation (the medical check came later) or an opportunity for a visit to see what the school was like. Yet, when the moment came (end August/early

September 2000), going away for ballet training seemed a very normal thing for me to be doing and I was happy about that. Interestingly, although I didn't know this at the time, my parents were reassured by some signs - not just the way I reacted to them and in the theatre but also by my watching videos voluntarily and shadowing the movements I saw - that I was going to be interested in ballet.

I joined Mama in packing my clothes (including the dance uniform of black pants and vest and white socks and shoes), toys, some food and other necessities in a suitcase. As we closed it, I turned to her with a cheerful, "I'm ready to go" without any real idea of what lay ahead. The only thing I was sure of was that my sister (whose term had started before mine) was a senior student at the school and that, although she would be busy in her graduate year, she would be there to look after me if I needed her.

I feel quite ashamed that, over several years of interviews, I have said that I was alone on the train journey. I now know that my parents, who couldn't accompany me themselves because they had a show, had arranged for me to travel with other families from Chelyabinsk to Perm and for me to share a sleeper carriage with them. Maybe I didn't know the adults very well, maybe it was dark, or maybe the only thing I could think of was being separated from Mama and Papa; but my (distorted) memory is of a kiss and a hug from them and, then, of sitting by myself as the train pulled away and them waving to me through the window. As I lost sight of them, it felt as if a huge cloud of loneliness closed over me. I had never before had a night away on my own – not even in a friend's home – so the 10 hours on the train was a new experience in all sorts of ways. At least I had an upper bunk in the sleeper car. At the lower level other people tend to sit on one's bed and there is more than a risk of those above falling down onto the person below! Over the years, I came to enjoy travelling on those Trans Siberian Railway trains and I'm conscious of how little 'proper' rail travel I have done since.

The train drew into Perm early but, fortunately, my sister was there. Taking a taxi was too expensive, so we walked to find the tram which went nearest to the school – well, to the boarding house where about three quarters of the students (that is, those who weren't from the city) – lived. It was a five storey reddish brick building which looked as if it was a prison because the lower level windows were fitted with bars. The age groups and boys and girls were separated by floor so I was with the junior boys aged 10 to 15. At that stage, the top two levels had been upgraded and the third floor was a kind of 'luxury' area for international students (from Japan, Korea, Ireland and the USA, I remember) who were paying full fees to be there. Consequently, they had a room to themselves or shared with just one other person, the freedom to switch the lights on and off (a really big deal!), and the luxury of showers down their own corridor. Those of us in the rest of the building had to share just three shower cubicles for girls and three for boys in the basement, where there was also a long sink for hand washing our clothes as well as a heated drying room.

I arrived on a cold, windy and grey kind of day, typical of Central Russia, and I walked through the door in what can only be described as a daze. I knew that I had to say, "I am Vadim Alexandrovich Muntagirov and I have come to join the First Year". Then a housekeeper showed me to my room. She probably explained more to me than I was able to take in but I did understand that, if there were any problems, I should ask one of the five resident housekeepers and be sure to obey them over things like going to bed when we were told to. Someone from The West looking from the outside would probably think that those ladies, who all seemed to be very old, were quite fierce-looking.

That first night, I felt awkward with the other boys in the room and, during the night, I lay on my back in bed wondering what I was doing there. That recurring question, feeling homesick and lonely and wanting to cry (but not let anyone see the tears) would often overwhelm me in the years to come. Indeed, that feeling was so powerful and my memory is so etched with it that I have had to be reminded that I was very far from being left on my own.

Not only was my sister in Perm for the whole of my first year but my mother visited me about every two months and stayed over from Friday to early Monday so that she could be with me when I had free time at the weekend. My father was not able to come as frequently but, when he did, he used his previous connections with the staff to try to check up on my progress. But he wasn't always suitably dressed for the occasion. One day in the middle of winter, and I do remember this quite clearly, I was called down to meet him in reception only to find him sitting there in flip flops because his shoes had been stolen on the overnight train! In general, parents weren't allowed to observe classes, although Mama tells me that she, in particular, did manage to do so a few times because she was a professional dancer. I know now that there were no formal mechanisms for telling parents in person or through written reports how their children were getting on.

When my parents came to Perm, they used to stay in a flat owned by Andrei Valentinovich Kibanov whom they had got to know because he ran a stall in the basement next to the school which sold a range of ballet gear. This very kind man would also take me home in his car some weekends and I would have a nice time playing with his daughter (who was two years ahead of me in the school) and sitting on a comfortable sofa watching TV. The family also let me go with them to visit their relations. So, in a way, I was able to share in a normal family life, even though it wasn't my own.

Living

In terms of settling in and feeling at ease in my surroundings, it didn't help that, for the first two or three years, I was in a room which had probably not been renovated since the school opened. The floors were covered with lino which had holes in it, the paint was chipped, the walls were grimy, and the furniture was shabby. The mattresses had no substance and planks of wood had been put under them to stop them sagging. Each October, we would have to insulate our windows against the bitter winter cold. This involved dipping paper (off giant rolls) into soapy water and sticking layers of it against the glass and over the metal frames. Additionally, students whose beds were next to an outside wall needed to pin up a sort of carpet to reduce the cold. Mice would come most nights and try to raid our bedside cabinets for any food which might be inside. If their scratching at the wood woke us up we would chase and try to catch them in the dark. But, no matter how successful we were, it made no difference as they were pretty much everywhere – once even sitting on my sister's chest while she was asleep.

Initially, I shared with boys from Astrakhan and Ufa, but the group changed a lot as students were assessed out or decided to leave and others took their places. All 60 of us on the floor shared the wash basins and, although they could be fastened on the inside, the half-size toilet doors gave us little privacy. Combined with the showers being in the basement, that made me feel the constant need to get up early enough to avoid interruption or a queue. For 'safety reasons' the electric points were out in the corridor but this just meant that everyone bought adaptor plugs to avoid having to wait their turn and that probably created more danger than if every room had had its own socket.

Conditions improved hugely around my 5th Year when the renovation programme at last reached my floor. PVC double-glazed windows were installed, the new bunk beds, with brand new mattresses, gave us more space to move in our rooms and the flooring was renewed. Importantly as well, the refurbished toilets afforded much more privacy. It's good to see from more recent promotional videos that the living arrangements in the school have improved beyond recognition. The common rooms which were once so dingy and with old, worn sofas now seem bright, modern and much more spacious.

In my day, it was advisable to get to the living room as quickly as we could because, otherwise, there was nowhere to sit and no chance of getting anywhere near the TV or of being able to look over the shoulders of the boys who were lucky enough to have game consoles to play with. Even so, the older students (there was a five year age range on the floor) would occupy the sofas as if by right and boss the smaller boys around. Much of it was relatively harmless, issuing orders like "Boil kettle"; "Bring me tea", but there were some dominant boys who used horrible bullying language and did so a lot. No one ever stopped this behaviour and I seemed to be protected from the worst of it in my first year there because they didn't want to have to mess with my sister. One thing which involved us being ordered around was really more of a tradition than anything nasty. When an older boy blew a trumpet, we were expected to run into the living room and form a line. Each of us would then be allocated a solo to perform for the others. I also remember being invited to join the older boys in the foyer where they made up variations to cassette music. Later, perhaps as part of the wider overhaul, a table tennis table was installed and we had another diversion.

But I mustn't forget the real bonus - that every student had free entry to the theatre. The company's repertoire was classical in the main but I remember that they imported *Peer Gynt* with choreography by Ben Stevenson and Grieg's music arranged by John Lanchbery who, of course, adapted Hérold's score for The Royal Ballet's *La Fille Mal Gardée.* The more junior students had to go to watch ballets in a group but, from the 4th Year, we had individual passes. If we arrived without one of these, the receptionist would check our authenticity by making us demonstrate a simple ballet move, such as showing her the fifth position. I'm sure that being able to watch many performances was beneficial to me in a 'soaking it all in' kind of way, but the very best thing about having the access was being able to go to the theatre with my parents each New Year.

All of our meals – breakfast, lunch, an afternoon snack and dinner – were taken in the main school building over the road rather than in the boarding house. The menu was on a weekly cycle. Breakfast consisted of two tablespoonfuls of one or another kind of porridge with hot tea (coffee could be paid for as an extra). Chicken, fish, sausage and a sort of schnitzel, all with mashed potatoes, alternated for both lunch and dinner, with the addition of soup at lunchtime. The afternoon snack was a sweet piece of cake, boiled dried fruit, or a salad. Definitely no chocolate! On the surface, that doesn't sound too bad but, I suppose in common with all boarding schools everywhere, the food wasn't very appetising. There rarely seemed to be any treats but I do remember a lot of excitement when we heard that bananas were coming. They always ended up being the greenest possible ones which needed to be put on a radiator to make them anything like edible but they nevertheless had the effect of brightening the week.

The question of diet and quantity is a difficult one in a ballet school and I learned later that, while I was there, Perm had been involved in controversy over its strict approach to girls' weight and there had been accusations in a documentary that this had led to anorexia among students. The only thing that was ever said to me, I think in fun, was from a teacher who passed by when I was about to eat a super special jam pastry, saying "Well, if I were you, I would think twice about eating that". I don't recall any advice about diet being given to the boys generally, but I was always feeling hungry and probably not eating enough in relation to the energy I was expending. I wasn't on my own! Parents from different areas, in my case Chelyabinsk, would group together so that, if any one of them was visiting, they would collect up and bring food parcels for several students. My sister remembers the time when she arrived back in Perm with several bagfuls and opened a door to see a group of expectant faces, each hoping that she had something for them. It was possible to prepare or cook food on the ground floor of the boarding house but, if anyone did that, a hungry crowd would quickly gather in the hope of getting a share. It we wanted any left for ourselves, it was preferable to eat quietly in one's own room. However, even there, food wasn't safe: stealing snacks was as common as taking more valuable possessions.

Any money which we brought back with us or were given during the term had to be handed over to a housekeeper on arrival and requested if we wanted to go to the shops – something we had to do in a group of three or four. After school and on our one day off (Sundays), the ladies would also escort us to the park and allow us to stop off at the convenience store. Instant noodles were a popular purchase because they were cheap. We also stuffed ourselves with masses of bread. In my first month, I stupidly followed the recommendation of some older boys to put a lot of spices on my slice of bread and suffered the consequences. Terrible stomach cramps made me run in panic to the school doctor who thought that it was my appendix and told me it would need to be cut out urgently. I was in the ambulance by the time my sister arrived on the scene and, seeing my screwed up face through the window, persuaded them to let her go to the hospital with me. They had a look, said it was a form of food poisoning, told me that I should eat nothing but plain bread for a week, and discharged me. I don't know what I would have done if my sister hadn't been there to 'rescue' me as I was only ten, I had no idea where I was in a strange city, I didn't know where I should ask to go to, and I had no money on me. But, together, we made it back to the school.

I seemed to get ill with flu-like symptoms quite often while I was in Perm. It was put down to a weak immune system but I think that it had more to do with an inadequate diet and unsatisfactory living conditions in the boarding house. Anyone who was unwell was moved into an isolation unit where, during my six years there, I spent many miserable weeks. But there were things which were entirely my fault – like getting my hands caught in a door while chasing with other boys and then screaming so loudly that my sister heard me from several floors above. Finding ways to let off steam was essential and accidents will happen.......!!!

Having an early breakfast in the school itself meant waking up very early, getting washed and dressed and then packing a small rucksack with everything I needed for the day, including my ballet clothes because the changing room was in the school building. It was important not to forget anything as the boarding house was locked until 5.00pm, I think to prevent students' things 'going missing'. This meant, of course, that there was no chance of going and lying down on the bed – not that there were many spare moments.

I should perhaps add that, for long periods of the school year, not only was the temperature consistently at minus 30 degrees Celsius but our days began long before dawn and nightfall was well before our classes finished. All that darkness does have a limiting impact on daily life, even if one is accustomed to it, as I was. But there was an upside. Occasionally, if the thermometer read below the minus 30 mark, a housekeeper would open the door, wake us up and say, "Keep sleeping, boys. School is closed today". The happiest of news!

Training

A typical school day would consist of a morning of academics, daily ballet class, more academics after lunch, and further hours or more of dance or movement. After that, there could be evening rehearsals or we could stay to practise or to complete our homework. So, overall, the hours were very long. [We often tried to squeeze our homework into any gaps in the day in order to get more free time later, but that wasn't easy!] The morning lessons were: Russian language; Russian literature; Russian history; Geography (mainly about Russia too and taught by the Chief Executive of the school, Ludmila Dmitrievna Shevchenko); Maths; and Science. We also had Ballet History where we were told about Russian choreographers and legendary dancers but with some references to France, French language (for obvious reasons), and individual piano lessons to help us with our musicality. Theology and Make-Up were added for the more

31

senior students and Computer Studies were brought into the curriculum in my 5th year.

The teaching was very formal and, although students were at the school throughout their adolescence, I don't think that there was ever any reference to growing up or relationships. Also, although we would be shown videos, the teachers didn't talk to us much about what we were watching. So, all in all, our personal and ballet horizons remained quite limited. I know now that I didn't apply myself to my studies as much as I should have and there were times when I was fearful of being expelled because of my poor grades. So it was not surprising that, when my father asked one of the teachers how I was getting on, the answer was, "He would be better off sticking to dancing". I did go to the piano room at 7.00am to practise but I wish now that I had learned to play properly as it is so much more of a battle to improve as an adult. The same goes for French: I could be more at ease guesting in Paris if only......!!!!

Because how we lived and other things about the Perm school were so significant in relation to my time there, it's taken me a while to get round to talking about the ballet training itself! As I've said and as with most schools in Russia, this was based on the Vaganova method which is a very disciplined approach with a particular emphasis on posture, strong and clean movement, flexibility, expressive port be bras and epaulement, athletic but shapely jumping, and endurance. Another characteristic is that one's whole body is involved in every movement. This was never actually spelt out to us but it was obvious that, year on year, the curriculum was designed to develop these qualities, firstly by embedding the basics and then by adding more and more difficulty in the steps and sequences, all the time trying to make us perfect the moves by constant repetition and correction. Class, which was usually at 12.00 noon daily for me, was set so as to provide us with the necessary foundations and reinforce them again, again and again.

The system was that one teacher would take a group of 10/11 year olds for a year, concentrating on very simple things, then another teacher would have that group for the next three years (ages 11/12 to 14/15). A third teacher would then take over for the years up to graduation. That is why the CVs of Russian dancers often refer not only to the year they graduated but also to "class of......(name of professor)", the reason being that he/ she has been moulded by a particular tutor.

All the teachers in Perm were, I think, former dancers, but most of them were beyond the age where they could demonstrate the movements to us. The one who was, in effect, the Artistic Director for most of my time there was Ludmila Pavlovna Sakharova, whose reputation for slapping the girl students and yelling at them gave her a 'monster' reputation which extended beyond the walls of the school. But, in fairness, the school's reputation benefited from the passion she showed over her 30 years or so there and she nurtured many very distinctive ballerinas, such as Nadezhda Pavlova (Bolshoi) and Olga Chenchikova (Kirov/Mariinsky), who became stars not only in

First Year at the Barre   Mini Jumps for a Ten Year Old

Russia but also around the world. Of course, not all of the teachers were focused on ballet itself: we had character lessons, gymnastics, rhythmics, mime and, later, what was called modern dance. Each year group was subdivided into two groups for the boys and two for the girls which stayed the same, despite some comings and goings for five years. Partnering and, therefore, mixed classes weren't introduced until the sixth year (1st Year Upper School) but the fundamentals of 'playing a scene' or reacting as a corps de ballet member were also included, especially as performance time drew near.

I should probably explain about the 'gymnastics' as it is one of the more, dare I say, notorious aspects of Russian training and it runs across the years. In common with the academic lessons, these sessions involving the whole year group, boys and girls together, were held in a basketball hall adjacent to the school two or three times a week in my 1st, 2nd and 3rd years and less frequently subsequently. The teachers, mainly ladies, also trained ice-skaters and the exercises we were 'put through' were particularly designed to stretch us to the limits in terms of turn out and leg extensions, improve our jumping ability, and make our backs more supple. For example, we would sit on the floor with our legs bent in a 'frog' position and the teachers would brace one knee against our backs while at the same time pressing down on our knees. We also had to balance between two chairs while doing the splits so that our torsos could be pushed down past the horizontal. My bottom would touch the floor! These and other exercises could be painful but not as bad as the really 'hard core' procedure. This would involve our lying on a bench on our backs with another student holding one leg down while the teacher pulled the opposite leg up above our heads to such an extent that our pointed feet would go down below the level of the bench behind us. Sometimes, the boy holding us would let us cheat a little by disguising the fact that we were bending the other knee, but that exercise was never less than torture and resulted in many students crying out in pain. Once that was over, we would immediately have to do a lot of jumps, including

34

leaping over the bench, to help restore our muscle tone. The lessons would then conclude with us lining up to pass the teacher in charge who would make us lean forward onto one of her hands, breathe in and, then, as we breathed out, she would press hard into the middle of our backs. Each one of us was only allowed to leave once she had heard our backs 'crack', as if we were breaking in half. By the 4th year, our bodies were considered to have grown beyond the point where extreme stretching was useful and the emphasis turned to jumping with weights on our ankles, sometimes on a trampoline, as well as to lifting weights. But the earlier ordeal we went through in that hall remains so vivid that the sight of a basketball hoop, even in my dressing room at work, does not evoke the best of memories – and I say that as a great fan of the game.

As regards ballet itself, I was fortunate in my **First Year** to have a very pleasant lady teacher, Aida Petrovna Gorina. To begin with, I was more or less repeating what I had done in Chelyabinsk (a lot of tendus) but, in class with her, I was able to forget that I was homesick. She treated us as if we were little green shoots which needed nurturing in order for us to put down the correct roots and grow the sort of branches we would need to use in the future. Looking back, I can see that, through the class she set us every day, she was concentrating on how we should hold our torsos, proper alignment, strength, and control. She also began to build muscle memory and put together key movements such as tours en l'air - quarter turns then half turns properly prepared with the correct use of pliés, arms and head. Most of us already knew which way we felt most comfortable turning (I go left) and, although we had to practise both ways, there was no attempt to change that.

Quite a lot of the corrections were via physical contact to make sure, for example, that our shoulders were properly positioned, our bottoms were tucked in, and our hips were in the right place. This kind of approach is now frowned on, indeed forbidden, in certain quarters, but I don't think that I would have 'got it' as well through verbal explanations alone. And, even though she was instilling discipline, Aida Petrovna* was pushing and 'handling' us in the nicest possible way. [*In Russia, we refer to people by their first and patronymic names but, as students, we would acknowledge our teachers just with a respectful bow of the head.]

My **Second, Third and Fourth Years**, with Sergei Ivanovich Cherneyev, were a complete contrast. The teaching was still concentrated on building the base, using hours of exercise repetition – for example pirouettes fast and slow, fast and slow, fast and slow to get them clean and with our arms held properly – and increasingly challenging combinations to improve coordination and balance. However, Sergei Ivanovich's approach to instilling the skills and getting the best out of us can only be described as brutal.

He was very tall (perhaps two metres) and towered over us; he had a big bass voice, he smoked heavily; and he would shout all the time and bellow corrections at us in a frighteningly angry way. For added emphasis and to try to make us understand, he would not only prod or pull our bodies into the correct position but he would also smack so hard that some boys incurred internal bleeding. The lessons often had the added drama of him stopping the pianist, standing there still and silent for what seemed like ever and then pouncing like a mad man to give someone a correction.

I think that, even as early as my second year (my first under Sergei Ivanovich), I had had my card marked as someone with possible potential. I had a small head, a long neck, good feet, soft joints, and suitable body proportions with long legs; I was also flexible, I was showing that I could pick up combinations and absorb corrections quickly; and, maybe, I was trying harder and appearing 'to want it' more than many students. I was also getting chosen for roles in the school shows in addition to the Grand Defilé in which everyone was included. It was nearly always either

Coppélia or a children's ballet which translates as *Doctor I Have a Pain* in which a character called Vanya (Ivan), which I eventually played, helps a doctor to treat animals. It was a good sign to be chosen as a Monkey in the first year (which I was) and I enjoyed myself. Afterwards, I was skipping along a corridor when a teacher asked me if I was happy. When I replied that I was, he said, "Wrong answer!" and went on to tell me that I should always be unhappy because that was the only way I would keep on improving. That message really took root with me! Students usually progressed from being a Monkey to a Sea Horse but most boys were really hoping to dance as Bandits when they were

15/16 years old. The casting for *Coppélia* was similarly graded: Czardas at 16; Swanhilda's Cavalier at 17, and Franz in the graduation year. But I was either occupied with competitions or had left before any of those roles came my way. I was lucky as well to be a child dancer in the Waltz of the Flowers in *The Sleeping Beauty* with the Perm Opera Ballet when I was 12 and I got the impression that it was unusual to be picked at that age.

In Front of the Perm Theatre

Of course, the more tangible indication of how any student is doing comes from the regular assessments. In Perm, these happened in December and before the summer holiday break. We would prepare an appraisal class sequence for about a month beforehand, including centre work as well as exercises at the barre. We didn't perform solos as such because, as a key element of getting us ready for a ballet career, it was usual for each class to use an excerpt from a classical solo as the grand allegro. Initially, the Panels would be drawn from the teachers from the school but, subsequently, dancers from the company and other guests would join them. Indeed, the older one got, the more important the assessors became, including such famous dancers as Maya Plisetskaya, Ekaterina Maximova and Vladimir Vasiliev. There was always a lot of "whisper, whisper, whisper" among the assessors but it was never possible to read their faces or understand what was being said.

Second Year Class

Friends Off Duty

Once our group had had its turn, we would be sent back to the changing rooms and wait while the judges decided on each individual's scores on a scale of one to five. The waiting and being called back in to hear the results read out was beyond stressful. Being given a 1 was so bad that no one ever seemed to get that; 2 and 3 were also regarded as very weak (so much so that parents could be told that those students would have to leave); 4 was good and 5 was excellent. In the First Year and Second Year, I got 4+ which I'm told caused something of a stir as Nadezhda Pavlova (the Bolshoi Principal of the 1980s/90s I mentioned earlier) had *only* got a 3+ at that age. Subsequently, I was given, firstly, a 5- (which, apparently, was also 'quite something' for my age) and then a series of 5s or 5-s. I think that they used the minuses to make sure a student knew that, even though they had done well, there was still room for improvement. Having those good marks was more of an achievement for me in the 3rd Year than meets the eye since, almost as if by magic, I suddenly grew by 20cms and everything became harder: longer legs need much more strength to control them and lift them to the required height.

My assessment results also meant that my being in Perm became completely free. At the beginning, my parents had had to pay for my boarding and food. They tell me that, around the same time, they also saw me in a school performance and said to themselves, "Something is going to happen". They sensed as well, perhaps before I felt that myself, that a commitment to ballet was gradually growing inside me. That was why they let me get away without doing class in the holidays. Had I been struggling, it might have been a different matter!

Going back to Sergei Ivanovich,........ He made me work very hard, which is what I needed because I was a 'back row' sort of boy, not a natural fighter. He also had to deal with people who didn't really want to dance but were in the school because their parents had thought it a good idea to put them there. But, whatever our level of application, he was so seriously scary towards us that I was absolutely terrified of him. It was so bad that I would go to bed fearful of what the next day would bring and unable to sleep properly. Strange as it might seem, I accepted that as being normal for training as a ballet dancer and I didn't complain to my parents as I didn't want to let them down. In any case, I'm certain Papa would have told me to 'just get on with it'!

Actually, when I was 13 at the beginning of my fourth year, I did escape for a while because I transferred to the Bolshoi Ballet Academy. My father had ambitions for me to study there and he asked some friends to take a look at me. Their positive response led to us travelling to Moscow in June 2003 for me to audition with the Director (Marina Konstantinova Leonova). Because I was older, this required me to demonstrate various combinations and turns as well as basic exercises and I think that I was being watched by several teachers.

Coincidentally, as things were to turn out for me, this was when The Royal Ballet was appearing at The Bolshoi Theatre. The

Company danced a mixed programme, Swan Lake, a Triple Bill, and Mayerling and ended the tour with a combined Gala with Bolshoi dancers. From high up in the historic theatre, Papa and I were able to see the first night of the Triple Bill, which comprised Sir Frederick Ashton's Scènes de ballet, with Ivan Putrov as the leading man, and Sir Kenneth MacMillan's *The Judas Tree,* with Irek Mukhamedov as The Foreman. The last work was Macmillan's *Gloria,* led by Carlos Acosta. It seems extraordinary that that performance should star dancers with whom I would later cross paths in many kinds of ways.

I was accepted into the Bolshoi school and started in the September in the class of Andrei Alexandrovich Alferov, who worked very hard with his group and went on to be the senior teacher there. But things did not go well. The syllabus and some of the expectations were unfamiliar to me as the Bolshoi style is somehow more about 'bigger' movement and expression than the Vaganova one; but I think I could have adapted to that. What I couldn't take was what I can only describe as the 'city arrogance' of the boys in my room, the boarding house and my class. Most of the time, they didn't talk to me, but when they did, it was to ridicule me for not being 'cool' enough and be generally spiteful towards me. I couldn't see a way of ever being able to adjust to that kind of 'culture' and I didn't want to. So I summoned up my courage to call Papa and told him how unhappy I was. He wasn't pleased (to put it mildly; but who could blame him!) and told me that I had to stick it out, especially after all he had done to get me there. But I knew that I had to be brave and I fought so hard that he came to Moscow, took me out of the school, and put me on the train back to Perm. That time, I *was* by myself!

There has never been any point in wondering how things might have turned out had I graduated from the Bolshoi school, because the fact is that I didn't. Indeed, after my 'trip' to Moscow, I was unbelievably happy get back to school in Perm. This was much to the surprise of everyone there who had never seen me do so much smiling, even though I was still being taught by Sergei Ivanovich.

In my **Fifth Year,** I entered the class of Yuri Mikhailovich Sidorov who was to take us for all the years up to graduation. By that stage in the training, we were spending more time on ballet with a focus on building up extra challenging combinations and improving our jumping. The character dancing got harder too but the most noticeable change was that, in the context of the ballet classes, there was more emphasis on improvisation and interpretation. For example, we would learn a group scene from a Perm repertoire ballet lasting 10 minutes or so and run through it with everyone taking on the roles involved. As I mentioned earlier, in the sixth year, we also began pas de deux work with the boys and girls being matched according to height. Initially, this was all about knowing how to stand and to support the girl in an arabesque and when she turned. Of course, again, there was endless repetition, which there needed to be.

Maybe because I was well into my adolescence by then, I felt less compliant than I had been previously and more inclined to question (if only to myself) why I needed to be doing a particular exercise. Yuri Mikhailovich's wife had taught my sister and she had progressed well but I found his way of teaching intimidating and very dispiriting. He would make a lot of loud insulting remarks. "You're like a cow on ice" was one he directed at me. There was no underlying humour: he meant it and that somehow felt more like bullying than all the shouting which had come our way from Sergei Ivanovich. There were boys who tried to fight back at the persistent rudeness but I don't think that they went as far as quitting. Several girls did leave because they understandably couldn't take the way they were being treated by their teachers. In those days, students either coped or they didn't. Unfortunately, mental well-being wasn't something which was spoken of or thought about.

It actually wasn't until I was 13 or 14 that I was realising more and more for myself that I wanted to be a dancer. I have heard people speak of 'having a calling'. For me it was a sense of falling in love with ballet, an 'I can't live without it', and a 'this is what I must do'. I let football fade but basketball was more compelling to watch and an added motivation for my ballet jumps. I was daring, just a little, to 'dream big' - of being able to make dancing my job and to imagine myself as being successful enough to have a fancy apartment and be able to take my parents around the world. My greater interest might have coincided with my maturing a bit and being able as well to interpret the unspoken signals from my teachers. Compliments were almost unheard of, but there were little things which helped me to feel more confident that I was on the right track – for example, the extra attention they gave me or putting me in the centre of the barre when anyone was watching class. I was also becoming aware of former students, such Marat Doukaev as well as the ballerinas I have already mentioned, who were celebrated in the school's museum because they had gone on to have very successful careers. I think I started to look at ballet videos properly as well and tried to learn from them. But, even then, I knew little of the dance world beyond Perm, Chelyabinsk and a few dancers I found exciting, including Mikhail Baryshnikov and Julio Bocca, whom we watched on film. But, in 2006, that and many other things began to change......

Looking Back

Reflecting on my experience in Perm (and as an occasional teacher now myself), I think that a certain amount of pushing is vital, especially when students are very young, but that having high expectations and creating a necessary sense of discipline need to be balanced with encouragement, explanations and feedback which, while honest, is not expressed in a hurtful way. I know only too well how easily students' self-confidence can be undermined and their personal development blunted.

Although many years have passed since I was in Sergei Ivanovich's class, I have continued to have nightmare flashbacks in which I am nervous, frightened, in pain and completely unable to find an escape from having to endure another year with him. I can connect with what other dancers sometimes describe as being traumatised by their training and I can see now where my persistent self-doubt and unforgiving self-criticism (or, put another way, my 'perfectionism' tendencies) come from. Yet, at the same time, I know that I owe my career more to that man than to any other influence. Notwithstanding all the negatives, I have him to thank for ensuring that I got the grounding at the right age, for making me be, as he put it, 'like a sponge', for my strong work ethic and, so I'm told, for my resilience. And his often repeated words, "Inside you have a hard-working machine but outside there is just a beautiful portrait" will ring in my ears for ever.

When I danced Solor in *La Bayadère* with the Mariinsky in March 2013, I heard after the performance that Sergei Ivanovich had come to watch and had sought to meet me. I very much regret that I didn't try harder to make sure I found him backstage because I would have wanted to say, "Thank you". He died nine months later so that was my one opportunity to express my gratitude, and I didn't take it. With hindsight, I can see that he was just trying to give us his everything so as to help each one of us make the very best use of our talent.

The bigger issue for me throughout the six years in Perm, and whenever I think about it, was not being able to live with my parents and benefit more from their company, influence and guidance while I was growing up. I did have the holidays of course and, while writing this book, my parents have put me straight on several facts – importantly, that they visited me regularly and ensured that I was included in a local family. But knowing that now doesn't change my deep-seated personal memories. Maybe it would have felt different if mobile phones had been in more common use at the outset but, when combined with how the school itself was, the persistent feeling of being away from Mama and Papa on my own was almost unbearable and remains very much with me to this day. But, had it been otherwise, I probably wouldn't have been as able as I have been to handle some of the aspects of my professional ballet career or to cope with life's unexpected challenges.

CHAPTER 3

AN 'ESCAPE ROUTE' EMERGES

Over the years, ballet competitions have grown in number and popularity among students and young professional dancers who might not otherwise be able to perform, be assessed, and be noticed outside their school or country, especially by Directors of prestigious schools. I was more fortunate than some in having had opportunities to be on stage in front of an audience, but I had not been put to the test outside Perm and among students from very different ballet disciplines and cultural backgrounds. Moreover, as I have said, my knowledge of ballet in a wider sense remained rather narrow and, initially, I wasn't really aware of the significance of having 'important people' watching.

Prix de Lausanne

The Prix de Lausanne was created for students aged 15 – 18 as long ago as 1973 by a Swiss industrialist who noticed a lack of financial support for young dancers wanting to follow professional level programmes. The Perm School had sent students to Lausanne on a number of occasions, but with no prize-winning outcomes. Therefore, when, at the start of my 6th Year in 2005, my father approached my teacher, Yuri Mikhailovich Sidorov, about the possibility of my being entered in competitions, he proposed the 2006 Prix de Lausanne as the starting point and agreed to prepare me.

The first thing to do was to submit an audition video. I recorded Franz's solo from *Coppélia* and some jump/turn combinations, but didn't think that I had much hope of being accepted. This feeling was much reinforced by Yuri Mikhailovich who lost no time in drumming into me that I had 'messed up' and what I was showing on the clip wasn't good enough for me to secure a place in the competition. He seemed visibly shaken when I was given a place, the more so because he knew that applications from Bolshoi students had been declined and I would be the only Russian competitor that year.

So we prepared my solos together: 1) something from a set list – we chose Albrecht; 2) a contemporary piece – mine was *Sarabande* by Jiří Kylián; and 3) a personal choice – I stuck with Franz. The other kind of preparation, that which might have helped me to be more aware of what it all entailed – foreign travel, different languages, how the competition was structured and run, and who would be there etc.- wasn't on the agenda. Because the Prix takes place early in the calendar year, I needed to stay in Perm and work intensively on my solos over the winter holiday. I did class every morning and then twice daily rehearsals. Mama came and stayed with me in the Boarding House for as much time as she could and, fortunately, because the international students didn't go home, the heating was on and food was available in the canteen.

Then it was time to pack, set off for the airport and board a flight via Moscow to Geneva. I should explain that, from aged 14 and in common with all young Russians, I had had an identity passport but, of course, I needed an international one to go abroad. Anticipating that the process can easily take three months, Papa had ensured that the forms were filled in in good time – in fact while we were on holiday the previous year. That left the Swiss visa, which the school sorted out, and then I was all set to go. I had flown a number of times when we went away as a family in the summer, but I had never been out of Russia before and I was both excited and apprehensive. I expected that Switzerland would not be the same as Russia but, from the moment we set foot in the Swiss airport, almost everything I could see, hear and breathe in was completely different. Just for a start, as we travelled to the hotel, there seemed to be exciting shops and the delicious smell of pastries everywhere. I was even able to buy a coca cola!

But then I found out that I would be sharing a room with Yuri Mikhailovich. I think that came about because the Prix pays competitors' accommodation expenses as well as for their travel and it would have been too expensive to book an additional bedroom. I couldn't question the arrangement, which I now understand to be common practice, and I didn't feel vulnerable in any way. Nevertheless, my teacher's snoring apart, the situation made me feel constantly on edge. There was no conversation between us – I guess there couldn't be as he was constantly dissatisfied with me and I was upset all the time because of that – and there was no internet access to divert me. I do think, too, that Yuri Mikhailovich chaperoned me so closely at other times that I might have missed out on socialising with the other competitors.

That might not be altogether fair of me because, not being able to understand or speak English or French (the two languages of the Prix) and being shy as well, I was not exactly well-placed to communicate naturally with other people. I do remember the occasion when a Japanese boy and I tried hard to understand one another and he asked me how much practice I had put in for my solos. When I signalled, "Twice a day, every day for two months," I think he gestured that he only rehearsed twice a week. Sergei Polunin and I managed to talk rather better together, obviously in our native language and, although our encounter was very brief, he recommended The Royal Ballet School, where he had been training for several years, and added, "Come to London; life is good".

On Day 1 of the Prix, we had to sign in, receive our number labels, and there was an introduction and a warm-up class. For the following three days, the routine was for groups to rotate through classical and contemporary classes and coaching sessions with the number of participants gradually being reduced from over 70 to around 20 by the semi-final round. The coaches were from the Prix, but there was only time for each of us to have about 15 minutes' attention on each occasion, so I remained reliant on Yuri Mikhailovich to keep me on the ball. The contemporary classes introduced me to a new range of movement and what seemed strange teacher commands – for example, when our shoulders were touched, we were expected to sink and sink and sink to the ground. At one point, we were asked to improvise for one minute in the direction of an imaginary Juliet and I had never had to do anything like that before: I was used to being told what to do most of the time. I think that the instruction was that we could be whoever or whatever we wanted to be and many of the boys who went ahead of me pretended to be animals of some kind. I stayed as a (very self-conscious) human and tried to act and reach out towards 'her' using familiar ballet steps.

I wasn't conscious of it at the time – I think that my mind was totally concentrated on doing what I had come to do - but all these 'preliminaries' were being closely observed by members of the Jury and several Directors who were associated with various scholarships. The official criteria for assessment were, I believe: artistry; courage and individuality; physical suitability; technical facility; and control and coordination. Thinking about this with the benefit of hindsight, I realise that the heads of schools in particular would have been looking for qualities – such as our physique, how we held ourselves, and our ability to concentrate and apply corrections, as well as how eager we were to learn – which would not necessarily be evident from our solos. I guess that, even when we were performing as individuals, they would have been expecting to see technical strength, artistry and musicality in the context of potential as a much as a 'finished product'.

Ms. Gailene Stock, who was in charge of The Royal Ballet School (RBS) at the time, must have seen something in me that appealed to her because, during the week, she asked me if I would be interested in going to London. I think I sort of nodded, but her approach and Sergei's comment made me think I should put the RBS down on the official form as one of my choices: the others were Berlin (I'm not sure why) and the Vaganova. A kind of unreality surrounded that form-filling since the possibility that I might change schools as a result of the Prix hadn't surfaced before.

After class, Day 4 was occupied with the pre-selection for the Finals which took place formally in front of the Jury. We had had some contemporary sessions on the stage, but it was not until I came to perform my first classical solo that I realised what a challenge the steep rake would represent. A rake makes every move, even in the air, feel like learning to walk again and I hadn't practised for that, nor had I had encountered a stage like that before. As a result, dancing Albrecht, and even the Kilian piece, was far more scary than it would have been anyway and I knew that the quality I had been aiming for in my solos wasn't there. I was disappointed in myself; but what happened next came completely out of the blue. Yuri Mikhailovich strode across to me and punched me hard in the chest, bellowing at me, "We rehearsed three pirouettes and you only achieved two", and adding, "You stupid loser". There wasn't anything I could say so I just stood there feeling uneasy and embarrassed, but I could feel the shock waves among the people nearby.

Along with 11 others, I got through to the Finals on Day 5 and performed my Franz solo. It wasn't exactly bad but, looking at it some years later, I could of course see that it was a performance from someone who still had a lot of learning and work to do. The prize-giving ceremony came shortly after the final round and we were told to go and stand on the stage. On the platform was Maina Gielgud, a member of the Jury who was later to be one of my coaches at English National Ballet. Also in the arena was Benjamin Ella, who was not competing but had come with his parents who were accompanying another student. I didn't have any idea then that he would be my RBS room-mate just over six months later. I now know that these kinds of 'strange encounters' happen quite often in the ballet world but, in Lausanne, I was 'out and about' for the first time.

Although it was my initial experience of a competition, it hadn't really felt like one up to that moment. I was awash with new experiences, many of them bewildering, and all the Prix staff and other competitors were very friendly and supportive. That was just as well as several of us had no idea what was being said at the ceremony. It was like hearing a lot of words and then something like someone's name, at which point a dancer would be ushered forwards to receive his or her prize. As several people were called before me, I didn't think I had won anything but, suddenly, they were saying, "X xxx xxxx xx Vadim Muntagirov", followed by a round of applause. I didn't understand then what my award was but learned later that it was the Prix du President du Prix de Lausanne which translated as being second to Sergei among the boys and 4th overall when the girls were included.

I believe that monetary awards from the Prix mainly take the form of monthly instalments to support the recipients during their scholarship year. However, in 2006, some prize money was given to my teacher and we split it between us. The moment I got back to Perm I bought an MP3 player so that I could be like so many of the other Prix students and play my own music for my dancing. But there was a problem.......! The Perm School was expecting to have the money to cover various expenses. Luckily for me, I was forgiven for having spent some of my share, but I remember feeling rather aggrieved when I handed the rest of it over the school counter. I believe that my teacher had a bonus added to his salary in recognition of him having prepared me. Some time later, an engraved silver medal arrived for me in the post but the school itself did not acknowledge my success.

However, none of that really mattered as I had far bigger gains. I had had a glimpse of a different way of life (even more so because it was idyllic Lausanne): the houses were luxurious, the shops were enticing, people were wearing fashionable clothes and everyone around me seemed to have electronic gadgets. I know that this sounds materialistic but seeing all this flicked a switch in my head which made me start to dream of a life in Europe and made the urge to put space between myself and Perm even stronger. I wish, in a way, that I had been able to savour the whole experience of the competition more. But I do know that, despite being under my teacher's thumb and the Prix being highly organised, I felt somehow freer than ever before. I'm still not sure, though, even years afterwards, that I can see my time there in the positive light it deserves because, if anyone asks me what I recall about the Prix de Lausanne, I tend to mention first the horror of the room-sharing with my teacher, his shouting at me, and the raked stage rather than my more rounded memories of the week as a whole. But that perspective is limited and faulty – after all, it was that particular competition which was to provide my escape route from Perm and set my career on a completely new path.

But, first, there was another competition to prepare for..........

Arabesque International Ballet Competition, Perm

I think Papa would have liked me to compete in Moscow and I was quite keen to do so myself as I had watched a video of Denis Matvienko (the former Mariinsky and Bolshoi Principal) dancing there. But that event only happens every four years: one year I was too young, the next time I was already out of the country. On the other hand, the competition in Perm was a biennial one and the April 2006 timing was pretty much spot on for me.

To give it its full name, the Ekaterina Maximova Arabesque International Ballet Competition is designed "to promote classical knowledge, discover talent and promote international contact" and, over the years, it has boosted many dancers' careers – the record of winners contains several internationally well-known names. The Artistic Director and Chairman of the Jury, Vladimir Vasiliev, and his wife Maximova were the golden couple of the Bolshoi from the late 1950s into the 1980s, with Vasiliev having world-wide renown as one of the greatest

51

virtuoso dancers of all time, and their association with the competition lends it prominence. My father was invited to be a judge in 2006 but, of course, he was not allowed to mark me, vote for me, or be in the room when I was being discussed. I don't think I even saw him!

The year I competed, the Arabesque was open to dancers aged 15 to 28 but, subsequently, they created two age groups (13 – 17 and 18 – 25). This seems sensible because, in 2006, what I could offer aged 15 was being assessed alongside solos being presented by experienced professionals, such as the 27 year old Principal from Kazakhstan with whom I shared my prize.

Arabesque Competition
Nutcracker Prince Solo

The school entered me and I was again prepared by Yuri Mikhailovich but, this time, I needed to be ready to show no less than seven solos across the three rounds: for Round 1: the Albrecht and Franz variations I had used for the Prix de Lausanne; for Round 2 (for which the classical music had to be by Tchaikovsky): the Nutcracker Prince and the male solo from the *Tchaikovsky Pas de Deux;* plus Kilian's *Sarabande* which I had also shown in Lausanne; for Round 3: Ali's solo from *Le Corsaire;* and Basilio's solo from the *Don Quixote* grand pas. As competitors had to be selected to go forward from one round to the next, I had no expectation of being Ali or Basilio.

There were hundreds of competitors (mainly Russians back then) and, although each day was divided into four sessions, the first two rounds each took three days. This meant that the 20 or so students from Perm carried on with their normal training alongside their preparations in the school and commuted to the

Perm Tchaikovsky Opera and Ballet Theatre only when it was their turn to perform. Not at all like Lausanne in terms of organisation! I think that the Perm students must have been spread through the groups because we were having to share costumes and the wardrobe ladies needed to dry, if not fully clean, them between our performances. The fact that there were so many of us 'in it together' helped to reduce the pressure and to keep Yuri Mikhailovich at a more comfortable distance.

To my great surprise, I did make it through to the finals – well, after all, the stage was flat in Perm - so I ended up showing all seven of the pieces I had prepared. The first male prize was divided between Dmitri Semionov, who was then a Mariinsky Soloist but went on to dance in Berlin, and Ivan Vasiliev, who was in his graduate year and has since enjoyed huge fame in the Bolshoi and Mikhailovsky companies and internationally. Viktoria Tereshkina, also already a Mariinsky soloist in 2006, won the women's competition outright. I was announced as the joint winner of the Galina Ragozina Award (after a famous dancer from Perm) and was rewarded with a medal, the title of Laureate and a half share of the 60,000 rubles prize, which again went to the school. The records note that I also received a $1,000 in cash for being the best Perm school competitor that year, but that was paid to the school as well.

However, Papa fulfilled his promise of buying me a laptop if I did well and that was all that mattered at that moment. Back at the school, the precious computer was kept locked away and only available when I asked for it – just as well because the other boys were always saying, "May I have a go?" "Can I try?" and queuing for their turn. It's easy to forget what a novelty technology was back then, especially where I lived and trained.

6th International Vaganova Prix

In the light of how I did at the Arabesque Competition, I received an offer to join the Vaganova School but, as I will explain in the next chapter, 'things' were moving on by then. Meanwhile, in common with other Russian ballet schools, Perm could nominate students for the Vaganova Prix and chose me to go.

Along with Moscow and Varna, this is a competition which has entered the public consciousness outside Russia but, until 2016 when it came under the wing of the Vaganova School, it was only held sporadically. Nevertheless, the list of Laureates in earlier years reads like a roll call of Mariinsky, Bolshoi and international Principals, especially ballerinas − for example, Ulyana Lopatkina (1990), Svetlana Zakharova (1995), and Polina Semionova (2002). Most of the famous names are Russian but the Vaganova, also, is open to all nationalities. Students or recent graduates needed to be aged 15 to 18 inclusive and to have been receiving training in vocational ballet schools. [I think that, after 2006 and until 2022, this Prix and the one based in Lausanne formed a partnership which served to encourage international entries in one direction and Russian applications in the other.]

In 2006, there were 64 competitors, all of us housed in the Vaganova Boarding House, attached to the school. The awards included Gold, Silver and Bronze medals and the prize of a one year scholarship to the Vaganova Academy. Natalia Makarova (with whom, of course, I had the privilege of working many years later) headed the Jury and I have seen a quote where she explains that, while she was looking for talent and potential, she also wanted to see artistic finesse and musicality.

The competition was much more regimented than in Lausanne but I was accustomed to that kind of environment. Proceedings began in the Mikhailovsky Theatre with a ballet class in a room dominated by a huge portrait of Vaganova. Round 1 consisted a classical class given by Gennady Selyutsky, a former dancer and coach with the Mariinsky and a Vaganova School pedagogue. His combinations were challenging in terms of jumping and turning and included sequences from well-known solos; but he treated us like proper dancers and made it very enjoyable. This time, I was fully aware that the judges were watching and marking us and I felt confident in being able to show them my artistic ability, positive attitude, and stamina. But it came as a complete surprise to see my name at the top of a 'scoreboard' which went up in the theatre foyer at the end of the day!

This was amazing but it did put pressure on me to maintain my standard with my *Don Quixote* solo in Round 2 and, even more so, in Round 3 when the audience for the final called me back for several curtain calls after I had danced the extract from the *Tchaikovsky Pas de Deux*. They were obviously happier with my performance than I was with myself. I wasn't as fazed over the raked stage (yes, again!) as I had been in Lausanne but, having been inspired by a video of Julio Bocca competing in Moscow, I had attempted a version of the manège with double assemblées and I wasn't entirely sure that I had carried it off.

Nevertheless, I ended up with three awards; the Gold Medal, the "Hope of Russia" prize and the scholarship. I couldn't go to the Vaganova School as, by then, I was in the process of enrolling with The Royal Ballet School and receiving the 'hope' prize was a bit awkward. After saying 'thank you' I couldn't very well add, "Actually, I am leaving Russia in less than three months' time". It was especially nice afterwards that the Mikhailovsky Theatre Director, Nikolai Nikolaevich Boyarchikov, who had previously been the Artistic Director at the theatre in Perm, came over and wished me well. "Please come back to Vaganova," he said. "Thank you. Maybe next year," I replied – and, at that moment, I meant it.

Reflections

Thinking about the various reasons why such competitions exist, the three events I was entered for over those five months in 2006 did indeed bring me into contact with different situations and new people, some of them influential, and I am left with the honour and kudos of being listed as a winner. Somehow, however, winning feels more like an added bonus because, in common with so many other students I'm sure, the experiences I had were invaluable in terms of my personal development and future career. The lessons learned from concentrated hard work with a target in view and the added stress of being judged helped to toughen me up. I saw how other students danced, my horizons were widened, and my options were opened up in unexpected ways. It is no exaggeration to say now that the Prix de Lausanne changed my life.

CHAPTER 4

THE LEAP TO LONDON

The Preliminaries

After the Prix de Lausanne, candidates are given a month to decide which year-long scholarship or other 'offer' to take up. The crunch moment came for me in the middle of preparing for the next competition. One thing I was sure of was that I wanted to leave Perm. Having a glimpse of how things were done elsewhere had made me even more dissatisfied with the facilities and I wasn't looking forward to having Yuri Mikhailovich as my teacher for another two years. On top of that, my eyes had been opened to how the world looked beyond Russia, for real not just on television, and I was letting myself imagine what it would be like to have a slice of the life I had seen.

I've already mentioned that Sergei (Polunin) had made encouraging remarks to me about The Royal Ballet School (RBS) but, about six months earlier and completely out of the blue, Papa had received a phone call from Thomas Edur, who was then a Senior Principal with English National Ballet. It sounded as if he had been asked to put in a good word for the RBS, which was seeking to attract more students from abroad, and it created a bit of a mystery at the time. However, the recommendation lodged in my parents' minds and seemed to help them to view the London option positively. Did we know anything about the teaching at the RBS? No! Or the living arrangements? No! Did we think about the implications of my not knowing a word of English? No! Or the pros and cons of the RBS in relation to my future career? No! I think that I was just riding on a dreamboat and thought, very naively and mistakenly, that the training would be much the same as I was used to and that, if I had (sort of) managed at the Prix de Lausanne, I would be fine.

The decision-making process was basically a case of my saying, "I want to go to London," and my parents responding, "Then we'll reply that that's your choice".

The staff in Perm were not exactly pleased at the prospect of my leaving and offered me a private room with my own electricity plug if I stayed. But I was determined and I think that my parents were relieved to see me so obviously keen to go to the RBS. I have the sense that they had some lingering guilt about sending me to Perm but there I was, completely of my own accord, pushing to set off into the unknown and they were happy to adjust for me. At that point, it did not occur to me that I might not return to study further or to dance in Russia and I don't think that Mama and Papa thought about that possibility either. Maybe even the Perm school was under the impression that I would come back.

There was a lot of paperwork to get done, including information about my health and, inexplicably to me, something about body parts donation; but Papa filled in the forms and sent them for translation in Moscow. There was also a visa to be applied for, so it was all quite complicated.

The Journey

As far as I can remember, we had the usual kind of summer holiday with all the family gathered together in the dacha. By then, my parents were based in Khanty-Mansiysk but Mama was there to help me pack, anxiously adding everything she could think of, including food supplies, to my case. Then, with a relative at the wheel, I set off with both my parents on the four hour drive to Ekaterinburg.

All too quickly, I was at check-in and found myself needing to come up with a sob-story to avoid paying extra for my luggage as it was 10 kg overweight. Then, suddenly, after some 'goodbye hugs' and a promise to call my parents as soon as I arrived,

I was walking through the control area by myself. Part of me was excited about flying off into a big adventure, part of me was stressed about managing the journey on my own (including transiting in Prague with unfamiliar signage), and part of me was numbed by the unreality of it all.

I arrived at Heathrow the same afternoon and, although I don't know how I managed it, I navigated the complexities of the passport queue, baggage reclaim and customs area without incident, to be greeted at the exit by my Guardian. All Royal Ballet School students aged under 18 have to have a nominated adult to look after their welfare. Mine was a practising lawyer well-known in Russian ballet schools for sponsoring talented students. In Perm, he was a trusted benefactor, providing scholarships for boys and funding prizes. On hearing that I was going to the RBS, he suggested to the Perm school that he could look after me in London, as he had a flat and his brother and sister were there. This offer was passed to my parents who gratefully accepted the recommendation. I had met him briefly when he presented me with a prize that summer, so it was a relief to see a familiar face in the Heathrow crowd.

It was a lovely, sunny August day and we caught a black cab to travel up the M4 into Central London. My Guardian was talking to me in Russian as we went along but I think that I was too nervous to say much and, also, overwhelmed by everything around me. I was immediately struck by the fresh air. Yes, I know what everyone says about London but I had just left one of the most polluted cities in the world and it smelt wonderful to me, with the sky appearing bluer and the clouds brighter than I was used to. At the beginning of the journey, everywhere seemed green and spacious, then the buildings were of an unfamiliar shape and style, with lots of variety. I guess that people who regularly travel this route will be saying, "Whaaaat? The M4? You can't be serious!" But, that day, I really did feel that I had landed in a 'wonderland'.

Living

After about half an hour on the road, we drew up outside Wolf House in Barons Court W14. This was two large Victorian/Edwardian houses knocked into one to provide accommodation over five floors for the First Years in the Upper School and other students were arriving there with masses of domestic kit and food stocks. The House Parents greeted me, showed me the living room and took me up to my top floor room in the roof – hot in summer, cold in winter! – and there, smiling, was Benjamin (Ben) Ella saying and gesturing, "Hello. I remember you at the Prix de Lausanne; I'm new here too". I nodded a lot as he pointed to things in the room: a fridge, a kettle, an electric ring, a socket (just for the two of us!), where to put my clothes, and so on. Luxury! Ben was also motioning to try to get across to me that, alongside buying food, because we were self-catering, getting a sim card and putting money on my phone was THE priority. Ben was so kind, welcoming and helpful and I would have been at a total loss had he not been there and willing to go with me to source what I needed. Even so, it took me three days to have the means of ringing my parents – so much for my promise of calling them on arrival.

And so much for my thinking, on the basis of all the languages buzzing around me in Lausanne, that I would be able to cope without knowing any English. Back in Perm and at home, I had developed into a bit of an 'entertainer' – into pranks, poking fun (at myself too), and coming out with things which made people laugh. But, because I couldn't say anything, it was as if the person I was had been completely stripped away. This created a vicious circle because I was not only sending out the wrong kind of messages but, while living in Wolf House, I tended to behave in a way which exacerbated the situation – for example, avoiding the need to interact by isolating myself in my room. I might venture downstairs briefly to use the communal kitchen or to watch a video but then I would scurry upstairs to ring my parents or to talk to friends in Russia. But, without anything in common to bind us together, my former mates drifted away. With hindsight, I know that being in the midst of people using a language is the best way to assimilate it and that I needed to be dragged downstairs and made to socialise. But, as I said, I wasn't sending the right kind of signals and my obvious reluctance would have made it very difficult for anyone to intervene. Besides, Ben had introduced me to watching dancers on YouTube............

There was one occasion, however, when I was unexpectedly forced out, not only downstairs but into the street. I had taken to cooking toast at midnight, in the dark after lights out, and the bread caught fire, causing the alarms to sound and everyone having to evacuate the building. As we hurried out, I whispered and mimed, "Don't say" to Ben and I think I got away with it, although I must have been the main suspect.

Over time, Ben and I developed our own hybrid way of communicating, with both of us using words from one another's language mixed in with our own. We laughed a lot, especially when Ben picked a single Russian word from his dictionary and when I came out with one newly learned English word. Almost the very first phrase I learned was, "School – danger" which was Ben's helpful alert that trouble might be brewing. In fact, I was involved in an incident in my very first month. Dylan Gutierrez, (who went to San Francisco Ballet on graduation) produced some great tricks to rap music and posted them on YouTube. This did not go down well and he, Ben and I were summoned to the Director's office. I could tell that Ms. Stock wasn't best pleased as she was raising her voice and Dylan and Ben were crying but, as I didn't know what was being said, I stood there studying the pictures on her wall while all the drama was going on around me.

More generally, Ben was really good for me because he would make me say things, not just in the room but in the school and out and about as well. If I gave him a helpless look, he would respond with a firm, "You have to try yourself". Nevertheless, the language barrier made caring for myself for the first time an extra challenge. Everything I needed to buy was covered in Latin script rather than the Cyrillic alphabet I was used to. I wasn't very sensible either in the way I used my living allowance (from my Prix scholarship, then from sponsorship) as it was very tempting to buy some gadget or put money on my phone rather than budgeting for necessities. There was a row of shops in Barons Court with milk in plastic bottles, clean ripe bananas and shiny apples on display (all first sightings for me). But Tescos in Hammersmith was very convenient and, once I discovered Sainsbury's Basics (since discontinued), I tended to stick with that range. It was not only the cheapest but also of a better quality than Russian produce. Despite that, I often ended up having toast, cheese and a piece of apple for breakfast, lunch and dinner – or, if things got even more desperate, living on rice for a week or more. Not exactly an ideal diet for a trainee dancer. Sometimes, I handled my finances so badly that I would have no money left. I didn't feel that I could tell the school, so I would confess to my parents. Papa couldn't transfer any subsidy from Russia so, instead, he would ask the RBS for some of the following month's cash to be released to me slightly early.

The need for those negotiations were entirely due to my poor money management. But my personality change was something I couldn't control. Even when I was back in Russia for holiday breaks. I was quiet and subdued, I didn't initiate conversations or mess around and, as my parents pointed out at the time, I had become overly polite. For example, the larger family would buy boxes containing enough orange juice cartons for everyone. But, instead of grabbing one as I had always done, I was saying, "Please may I have one?" to which Mama smiled, "Of course you can, son. Don't be silly; you know you can help yourself. Why are you suddenly asking?".

Two shorter breaks from school during the First Year showed just how very kind the staff and other students were being towards me. Mr Martin Fosten, the Academic and Pastoral Principal, invited me to his home for a couple of days over half term. He pulled out a map to show me where we were going and we travelled there by overground train (a first in the UK for me). I don't remember exactly where we went but I do remember a large and happy family and a lot of delicious Chinese food. Then there was my classmate, Alex Arshamian (who went to the South African Ballet Theatre). He took me back to Manchester with him for another half term. It was so nice of him to do that, make me feel so welcome and give me the novel experience of family meal times with everyone eating together at a big table. The process in my family had been much more casual. There were many other RBS students who were able to go home for a day quite frequently and I envied them that normality.

As Wolf House was mainly for the First Years, I went with the flow in the Second Year and found myself in a nearby furnished flat with Tristan Dyer (who danced with The Royal Ballet from 2009 to 2019) and Giorgio Galli (who went to the National Ballet of Canada). Ben lived nearby with four other students, including Leticia Stock (who graduated into The Royal Ballet with him and Tristan) and I would spend quite a lot of my time with them. I don't think that anyone but me would have regarded our apartments as luxurious, but *I* did because everything – furnishings, equipment and linen – was provided and it was in an area of London which felt safe. Other students would say to me that it was best not to use the ATM across the road at night in case someone tried to take my money. But I would try to reply, "Just one person? I can handle that: I'm used to avoiding 10 people". It was the most fantastic feeling to be able to walk out onto the streets in the evening without being afraid of losing my money or my phone. And, because most people in that neighbourhood didn't draw their curtains, I could see how houses were furnished and decorated and how people were spending their free time. Another type of education.

The only slight disadvantage was the daily commute, although my very first journey from Barons Court to Covent Garden was a revelation. For a start, neither Chelyabinsk nor Perm had an underground system. But the real surprise was that the carriages were full of people of many different nationalities. Russia wasn't – isn't – multicultural in that way. I was watching everyone, trying to figure out how people behaved and unable to draw any conclusions, except that they had pleasant-looking facial expressions, not intimidating ones like I was used to seeing on public transport. On the way back – rush hour chaos! Covent Garden Station was packed and, as we could only get on the train by squeezing into non-existent gaps, we got split up. So both Ben and his parents spent the journey signalling to me above their heads at every stop, "No not this one; four more....." and so on until we were able to breathe again at Barons Court.

In the Third Year, everyone moved into the Covent Garden area (hurrah, no commute!) and students were responsible for finding their own accommodation. I shared with Ben, again, and also Jeremy Curnier (who was given a contract with Northern Ballet) and Benjamin Soerel (who went to Birmingham Royal Ballet initially). Mr. Meelis Pakri, about whom much more shortly, had kindly helped us find a flat in the Seven Dials area. The building contained a number of units, with a communal area at mezzanine level housing a kitchen and washing machine.

It was a good place to live because a lot of students would gather together in the evenings and, by then, I was beginning to feel more at more at ease in a sociable mixed group as well as being party to the boys' changing room banter. However, I still wasn't the most adept person at catering for myself. I always seemed to be hungry and, in place of toast, toast and more toast, I was succumbing to the temptation of the £4.50 pizzas available virtually next door to where I was living. That was fine when I was burning off all the calories in the studio, but not so good when I was forced to stop through injury ....

The Curriculum

The Royal Ballet School
Photography by ASH

My first sight of The Royal Ballet School itself was a day or so before term started when Ben's parents took us both to Covent Garden to be shown around. And WOW! The building was almost brand new: bright and light with superb facilities including proper dance floors and the Bridge of Aspiration connecting into The Royal Opera House to magnify students' dreams. It was unbelievable to be inside the school where I thought I wanted to be, especially after so many months of build-up, and I was walking on air and completely open-mouthed.

The following week, in early September, the school term started and I went upstairs to find myself in the midst of students greeting one another, laughing together in groups, and looking as if they were having a terrific time. I just looked at them rather enviously telling myself, "I *will* adjust; I *will* become as relaxed and happy as they are; just give it time". But, at that initial moment, the other students' confidence and obvious friendships were quite unnerving for me to see. The teachers, Mr. Meelis Pakri and Ms. Katia Zvelebilova were smiling and welcoming towards me but I felt very much the outsider.

As I stood there, I was struck too that I had no idea who the dancers and other people in all the photographs were. In Perm, I had had a sense of awe every time I went up the main stairs because of the famous artists who had walked before me and whose names and pictures I was passing, but none of the film clips I had watched before coming to London had introduced me to the equally illustrious British dancers, not even to someone as internationally acclaimed as Anthony Dowell (which now seems a really awful admission). Some time later, Mr. David Peden, the Second Year teacher, walked me across to a portrait of a beautiful woman and asked me, "Do you know who this is?". I shook my head to say "No", but I should have been shaking it in shame because it was Dame Margot Fonteyn. My ballet education in Perm was indeed very Russo-centric.

All the First Year students had timetables which included academics: A-levels, BTECs and also English for Speakers of Other Languages (ESOL). The English language group was, of course, very mixed but the other students from abroad had some basic English or could check their understanding with someone else from their own country – for example Shiori Kase and Ishigo Oguro would chatter away in Japanese. My English started at zero and it was difficult for the teacher, who tried very hard, to give me any individual help because she didn't speak Russian. Although I could access some assistance online there were no phrase books in the shops which translated Russian into English, only the other way around. I was also expected to attend some BTEC lessons but, as I couldn't really grasp enough to participate in any of the preparation for exams, I tended to sit in a corner with my PSP (play station portable) either using a translator or pretending I was doing that while actually passing the time indulging my love of basketball and playing other games. Not only seriously naughty but not exactly acting in my own best interests.

However, I did have another language through which I could express myself! Years later, in response to something I posted on Instagram, Ms. Petal Miller, who was to teach me subsequently, wrote, "*I remember an extremely quiet young man arriving at the RBS, not speaking a word of English and not knowing which way to turn or where to go in London. You seemed vulnerable and alone, Vadim – and then you danced"*. That was so true. When I danced, I felt able to be me – not at all inhibited. Indeed, I was secretly rather pleased that my inability to cope with the academics meant that, for the first time in my life, I was relatively free to concentrate on my dancing. "Yes", I thought, "This is what I have come to London to do!"

The performance elements of the curriculum included daily class with sessions for solos, pas de deux, traditional/folk dancing, contemporary dance, body conditioning, Pilates, improvisation/choreography, character interpretation and repertory spread across the weekly schedule. This incredible timetable and variety included many important elements which were new to me. I had not experienced Pilates before and found it more helpful in exercising different muscles than being told, as I had been in Perm, to go and use the exercise machines by myself. Then there was characterisation in the context of The Royal Ballet repertoire, with which I was totally unfamiliar. I remember, quite early on, that the group was introduced to one of the male roles in Kenneth MacMillan's *Gloria*. Most of the boys had come from White Lodge, knew the work and were quickly 'into it'. But, even with Ben's help, I was very slow on the uptake.

An overall, very noticeable difference from what I was accustomed to was the even-handed approach of the teachers. That was good, of course, because every student matters, but it made me realise that, in Perm, I had been treated a bit like a 'rising star'.

The First Year

In the First Year, I was really fortunate in having Mr. Pakri as my main teacher. Most RBS students from his era tell 'horror stories' about how strict he was; but, with my background of being taught by Sergei Ivanovich and Yuri Mikhailovich, his manner came across to me as the nicest and softest I had ever experienced.

I had been brought up in a system where, as someone put it to me, "If you don't get corrections, you should be very worried because the teacher doesn't care" or, alternatively, "If the teacher is screaming at you, you should be very happy because he cares about making you a better dancer". I felt that Mr. Pakri really cared about us all.

Although my ability to 'read' what was going on was limited, I think that many students were afraid of Mr. Pakri because he was honest. He was also a disciplinarian who rightly expected courtesy in the studio. I remember one occasion when he was concentrating on other boys and Ben, Dylan and I peeled off into a corner to see which of us could balance the longest on demi-pointe. Suddenly, our competition was interrupted by a very loud, "Get out, all three of you". But, although Mr. Pakri would tend to shout, "Get up!" at boys who were slouching on the floor instead of paying attention to the corrections being given to others, he would come across to me and tell me off quietly – although, of course, he still expected me to be fully engaged in the class and made that very plain too.

Besides speaking Russian, Mr. Pakri had another built-in advantage for me: he was himself a product of the Vaganova Academy. This made it easier for me to pick up on combinations, to apply corrections, and to accept the often harsh criticism of my efforts. He also gave me the sense that he knew how hard I was finding so much of being in the UK.

My need to feel I was progressing was helped in the pas de deux classes taken jointly by Mr. Pakri and Ms. Zvelebilova because they extended my partnering beyond what I had done before. Supporting the woman (I was paired with Anouska Wilkinson) not just in arabesques but in a variety of combinations and lifts felt very grown up. It always took time for every couple to feel comfortable with all the aspects of every move but, while that was happening, Anouska and I could work away on continuous improvement by ourselves.

The solo classes were less stimulating for me because everyone had to learn the same piece at the pace of the slowest and I was a bit impatient. That, and the content of the daily class, sometimes made me feel as if I was going backwards when I was desperate for more technical challenge. I even got upset over the grey/blue unitards because that uniform combined with white ankle socks made my legs look too short.

So there I was (once again!) crying down the phone to my parents, "I hate it here". (Sob) "How am I going to become a special dancer if everyone has to be the same?" (Sob) "I feel like a child." (Sob) "I want to be a man". (Sob) I was, of course, being over-dramatic but the confidence I had had about being able to adapt became very dented by the reality. Maybe I thought that my parents would let me escape, but they were having none of it and insisted, "You are in a different country now. You are on a valuable scholarship. You can't just catch the overnight train home this time". I protested, but they were right to be unmoved, "You have to do the one year. Just get on with it," they said. I think I tried, and one thing which helped was being able to hang around with the other boys after a class near the end of the day, with each of us 'showing off' some tricks to try to outdo one another. Being part of a group letting off some balletic steam was good therapy.

I was also one of the students chosen to perform at the mid year Solos Evening. Mr. Pakri stopped me one day and said, "You always want to do more jumps; let's see what you make of Solor (from *La Bayadère*) where you will have all the big jumps anyone could wish for". Of course, working on that solo with him was indeed everything I could have wished for and having the chance to dance in front of an audience in the Linden Studio was the icing on the cake. I was so grateful for that opportunity.

When I went home for Easter and saw my parents again after about eight months, I just blended back into family life. I was greeted with much needed hugs but no cross-examination about the RBS or how I was feeling. I think that they might have been almost afraid to ask! Nevertheless, that break made me realise that, although I was missing the virtuoso Russian training, coming back was not an altogether appealing option, that I would have cause for regret if I didn't make the most of my opportunities in London, and it was time to reset my brain. But I do need to confess that I never quite managed that. I had, and still have, a strong sense of what I want to do and an even stronger sense of what I don't want to do and that stubborn streak in me meant that my choices and my behaviour at the RBS were not necessarily the smartest.

The First Year was actually one which was full of 'treats'. Not only did we dance in Orange County, USA but I was one of a small group of students chosen to be part of a week-long exchange with the Vaganova Academy. I shared a room in the school's boarding house with Sergei (Polunin), who was in the Third Year, and the two of us ate and ate and ate. The British students didn't really take to the food they were offered. So Sergei and I devoured not only their soup and sausages but also some caviar. It didn't matter how much we tried to tell the others that caviar was a luxury which only rich people could afford, they were basically saying, "Yuk!" The related problem was that they then wanted to go and buy food from the corner shop, which would not have been a good idea for just a few of them on their own. So, to keep them out of danger, a very considerate group of Vaganova students went out for supplies instead.

The programme offered our party by the Vaganova Academy included watching a Mariinsky performance, meeting corps de ballet dancers, a museum visit, a city tour, and a shopping expedition in the Nevsky Prospekt. All of this was eye-opening for everyone, me included. But the classes were even more of a revelation for the other RBS students as they couldn't get over the way that sessions were run with "instructions being screamed at the students" (their words).

Of course, that was so normal for me that I felt completely at home, especially as one of the teachers was the much-revered Gennady Selutsky and it was such an honour to be taught by him again.

Towards the end of the First Year, I had the thrill of being selected by Ms. Miller, who had taken our pas de deux classes, to be part of her new creation *Suite Classique* to be performed in the school and in The Linbury Theatre across the road. I was paired with Shiori and the other couples were Ben and Leticia and Dylan and Ichigo. I had not been part of a choreographic process before and it was interesting that, while Ms. Miller came into the studio with very clear plans for the pas de deux sections of her work, for the solos, she worked with each one of us in building up the movement. On occasion, she would even go so far as to say, "What would you like to do here?" and this experimentation meant that our individuality came through when we performed the piece.

Then there was a series of RBS performances where I was second cast with Shiori and Leticia in the Peasant Pas de Trois from *Giselle*. Mr. Pakri and Ms. Zvelebilova taught us the steps and worked with us on the partnering with Ms. Stock keeping an eye on us and intervening with coaching points. We performed it first in Palermo and the opportunity to travel, to see another country and to stay in a fancy hotel brought with it several more completely new experiences for me. Several times while I was there I found myself drifting into dreams of a future where I was dancing around the world. Performances in The Linbury and for the School's Summer Performance followed, along with the Grand Defilé and I remember, as I stood waiting to make my entrance onto the main stage thinking, "This space is sooooooo big; I have to perform here really well". That same thought returned when I was waiting to perform *Dance of The Blessed Spirits* on my own during the 2020/21 pandemic.

I think our appraisals came towards the end of the school year. A panel composed of people from outside the school as well as RBS staff sat watching us in class, performing a solo and presenting a pas de deux. I understood that the visitors were important but not who they were and I only saw them briefly as our waiting and warming up area was in the studio next door. Afterwards, there was a debrief with Mr. Pakri, which felt awkward, even though it was in Russian, but the news was basically, "Well done; you can pass into the next year". Then I was called to see Ms. Stock, with Mr. Pakri as translator, and she offered me the opportunity to move in the Third Year, along with Dylan. She didn't rush me for an answer but the surprise freaked me out because I was fearful of another unknown and the possibility of being separated from the group I had got to know.

So it was for those reasons and my need to speak better English, rather than ones related to my training as a dancer, which resulted in my saying that I would prefer just to go into the second year. I remember not so much consulting my parents as telling them that I had decided to stay longer in London than originally planned. There were no financial implications for them as Ms. Stock assured me that I could be funded by The Rudolf Nureyev Foundation. Fourteen years on, the Foundation approached me to be one of its Ambassadors and, in 2022, I was invited to participate in a celebratory Gala in Nureyev's honour. It feels special to be able to help keep his artistry and choreography alive in people's minds, particularly as (almost unbelievably) I can now find myself alongside dancers who are unaware of him, his story and the importance of his legacy for male artists in particular.

The Second Year

Despite such a positive end to my first year, the Second Year did not get off to an auspicious start. The approach and expectations of my teacher, Mr. David Peden were entirely different from those of Mr. Pakri, with a strong emphasis on 'cleaning'. In addition, the combinations Mr. Peden set (and usually demonstrated himself), which seemed to me to be more complex, closer to the ground and with quick, very precise footwork, were also harder for me to remember because they were unfamiliar. It wasn't until later that I realised they were based on Ashton and MacMillan choreography which, of course, I came to love. As a consequence, and unusually for me, I was slow to pick things up – so much so that I was always in the last group to be given a turn. Then there was the corps de ballet rep. which also took a bit of getting my head around because I had never before had the responsibility of combining with others. Working on Wayne McGregor's *Chroma,* which we did at one point, was a very different kind of ensemble experience which, I'm sorry to say, took me back to my negative, "What am I doing here?" question – one which Mr. Peden would also ask of me if I looked as if I was complaining.

Overall, I wasn't coping at all well and started to make feeble excuses for missing classes. My absences mounted up to the extent that I was called to see Ms. Stock who pointed out (and I *did* understand her!) that I had missed a total of 30 days over the first three months and demanded that I should explain myself. I came out with utter rubbish about being unwell, going to the bank and so on – all of which goes to show that, while I was telling Ms. Stock that I was OK and saying to myself that I wanted to be a man, I was floundering and behaving like a silly child. It was one thing to be a touch selective in taking what I felt I needed but quite another, and totally disrespectful, to opt out and I remain full of remorse for that to this day.

My way of feeling better about myself and shaking off any discontent about things in general was to go back into the studios at the end of the formal day and, using a DVD, put myself through a Vaganova Graduate Year Class. As this included a lot of jumps, which were what I was craving for, I was gradually joined by a few other boys and we would end up experimenting until, eventually, the staff chased us out – well not before I had squeezed in just one more jump and one more pirouette.

Another filip was that we started to act as extras in Royal Ballet (RB) productions. My first appearance was as a walk-on aristocrat in *Giselle* - one of the men in big hats, heavy coats and gloves who come on with the Duke's party. The girls had had more opportunities to perform with the RB, for example as Snowflakes in *The Nutcracker* and as Wilis in *Giselle* and I think that they were daring to envisage themselves being part of the company when they graduated. I couldn't, at that point, nor in the Third Year when I was a static man in both *Ondine* and *The Sleeping Beauty,* make the same mental leap myself – indeed, until well into the Graduate Year, any ambitions I had were located in Russia – but being paid to appear with the RB was beyond amazing.

I must mention that Mr. Peden was the first teacher to make me laugh – really laugh – and he helped me to feel more relaxed. For example, I would say, "Please can I get some water?" and he would come across to me with his water bottle in his hand and circle round me as he took a sip. It was torture because I was gasping for a drink, but very funny too. With the whole class, he followed an amusing pattern along the lines of, "Right, we'll run through this and I'll buy you all tickets to Disneyland...........*if* no one makes a mistake". Then, after we'd all done our utmost, he'd say, "Bad luck – there was an error; no tickets!" Of course, we had the measure of his trickery but that was part of the fun. Years later, while taking company class with the RB, David was still using this kind of jokey approach, but with variations, and I was still smiling along with him.

In the lead up to the Solos Evening, I was again lucky enough to be chosen and Mr. Peden worked with me on finessing the *Don Quixote* solo. Soon afterwards, five of us were entered for the Youth America Grand Prix (YAGP) in New York. I hadn't heard of this competition previously (I wasn't really orientated towards winning prizes by then) but, even before it had preliminary rounds all over the world, it was a massive event with Senior and Junior Age Divisions for boys and opportunities to compete in pas de deux. The philosophy behind it is very similar to that of the Prix de Lausanne insofar as it seeks to give candidates the opportunity to proceed to top class ballet schools. That 'prize' didn't come into the equation for any of the RBS contingent as we had no intention of going elsewhere. Mr. Pakri travelled with us and was on hand to help us with the quite complex formalities. But, no, I did not share a room with my teacher this time! The RBS students doubled up in the hotel and I was paired with Ben.

The structure of the YAGP is also like the Prix, with classes, workshops and masterclasses in addition to the rounds of the competition, all observed by representatives of international ballet companies and schools. However, what I remember most is those of us from the RBS snatching moments in odd corners to be helped with our preparation by Mr Pakri before we had a 15 minute slot to rehearse on stage. As a result, we tended to hang out within our existing group rather than mixing with other contestants and, together, we had rather more takeaway pizzas than was wise. Because our focus had to be on the competition and, also I think, because security was tight that week for Pope Benedict's visit, we didn't really 'do the sights' in New York other than at a distance from our taxi – although I did catch a glimpse of the Popemobile! Nevertheless, there I was having a extra chance to be in another astonishing place which was again unlike anywhere I had seen before.

I danced Basilio's solo from *Don Quixote* solo in the first round and qualified for round two, where I performed Phillipe's solo from *The Flames of Paris*. The third element was a contemporary or character piece and I cheated a little with the Gopak. Some of us, including Ben and me, were then selected to appear at the New York City Centre Theatre in the *Stars of Today Meet the Stars of Tomorrow* programme. It wasn't entirely clear at the time that only dancers who were prize winners had been invited to perform so, after all the solos (I repeated my *Don Quixote),* we were standing on stage wondering what was going to happen.

It was a 'countdown' and Ben was called forward to be awarded the 2nd Prize, followed by the 1st Prize for me. The Grand Prix was awarded to Nobert Lucaszewski from Poland who had his first professional contract in Stuttgart before joining the Theater Hof. It's strange to think that, among the Junior Age Competitors that year, was Marcelino Sambé who was later to progress to the RBS and the RB. Even stranger, given the number of times I have since partnered them or been on the same bill as them, was the fact that Polina Semionova, Natalia Osipova, Roberto Bolle and David Hallberg were headline stars in the celebration Gala.

It was another busy year because, on our return, Mr. Pakri worked with Shiori and me to polish the *Le Corsaire* pas de deux which we had first prepared with him in the First Year. This time, it was for us to perform on the Second Year tour to the Palucco School in Dresden – another country, another different environment! I was in my element being the slave in those golden trousers and, seeing me rehearse, Ms. Miller called out to me, "You move like a tiger". That nickname stuck – hence the comments and animal emojis which have persisted on social media.

Napoli Variation 2008
Photo: Johan Persson/ArenaPAL

The *Napoli Divertissements* were chosen for the Second Year to perform in the Linbury Theatre and in the main auditorium, and the students were privileged to have Jonny Eliasen from Denmark to teach and stage it. I was familiar from videos with the male solo which has big entrechats six and double tours and was inwardly hoping to be picked for that. Unfortunately, that was not to be and, when the casting was announced, I let my body language show my disappointment. All I did really was to turn my head away and take a step back but it was enough to cause Jonny to comment, "That boy is not happy" and for me to feel very embarrassed. Jonathan Hanks was the lucky one and, of course, he did absolute justice to that solo. My role was within a group one, with a solo passage (2nd Male Variation) and dances which interacted with two or three Girls.

Alongside this, six of us (with Jonathan replacing Dylan) also had the opportunity to revisit *Suite Classique* with Ms. Miller and, again, the way she used us to develop the choreography with her helped me to feel more able to show the real me.

Of course, my English was improving by then and I was better able to express myself verbally and thus let more of my personality come through. However, the more I could communicate in English, the more I became wary of the potential traps. I was inhibited not just because of my nature but because, in Russia, it is regarded as disrespectful to say anything to a teacher: students are spoken to (or yelled at) but don't talk back and that etiquette is drilled into you from day one. The teachers at the RBS made themselves approachable but I was so afraid of appearing over-familiar that I got myself terribly hung up about the use of the word 'you'. In common with languages like French and Spanish, Russian has two words for 'you' – the one you use for a child or to someone you are familiar with and the one for people you don't know so well or who are more senior to you, and it took me ages to grasp that English has only one version and that, actually, I wasn't at risk of being rude to anyone.

At the end of the Second Year, I had injured my foot and ankle but I didn't want to show that I was in pain or to miss the end of year performances. So I danced on, using a spray to numb the soreness. It took the full two months of the summer holiday for the problem to resolve and I told myself, "Next time, you'd better watch it and look after yourself".

The Graduate Year

My Graduate Year introduced another teacher – Mr. Gary Norman, the husband of Ms. Stock, who brought a change of teaching approach from both Mr. Pakri and Mr. Peden. The combinations he gave for the barre (which included jumps) and for centre work were technically much harder, but the introduction of flashy sequences like the manège generated quite a bit of excitement within the group. As a teacher, Mr. Norman had a very pleasant and straightforward manner and I was able to understand him well, including 'getting' the odd joke which he would throw in. He not only gave clear explanations and corrections but his feedback also included compliments – just little things such as (to me), "You have a very good and high demi-plié" and, even, "You are a beautiful dancer". We all found his comments very motivating.

Perhaps I should divert briefly to explain a little more of what I mean when I refer a change of approach. One illustration could be the technique for double tours en l'air. We were taught two ways: firstly (my preference) to change one's feet over the moment one is off the ground; secondly to make the switch near to landing (which, in my view, runs the risk of catching one's heel and looking untidy). Other examples have to do with whether or not one's arms go through first position or 'straight there', whether feet in first position should be fully turned out or more relaxed, how far one's head should be angled to the side, and which way to look and how the arms are used when one jumps. These might appear to be very small differences but it can be confusing, not least for muscle memory, if one has been doing things one way for a year and expectations then change. It also matters – a lot - in terms of epaulement, coordination and presentation when all these kinds of movements are combined to make the bigger picture.

Another kind of change - in pas de deux partners - saw me paired with Elisa Badenes (who went to Stuttgart on graduation and was quickly promoted to Principal there) who had then just arrived at the RBS from Spain. Two classes a week were devoted to partnering and the challenges went up a considerable notch because we were being introduced to more demanding and higher kinds of lifts. Also helping us to master these was Ms Jacquelin Barrett who was teaching the Third Year Girls then but, quite soon afterwards, became Assistant to the choreographer Christopher Wheeldon. Overall, I felt comfortable adjusting what I did to present the girl well, but little did I realise how much I still had to learn about being the kind of partner professional ballerinas need.

A Studio Shoot for Don Quixote
Photo: Johan Persson/ArenaPAL

Before the Graduate Year Tour, at the end of January 2009, there was a preview performance in the RBS's Linden Theatre and Elisa and I danced the Grand Pas from *Don Quixote.* Unbeknown to me Wayne Eagling, the Artistic Director of English National Ballet (ENB) and Maina Gielgud, who was working with ENB at the time, were in the audience that night and approached me afterwards. But that is for the next chapter.........

The tour was to Salt Lake City (the centre of the Mormon Religion) in Utah, USA where we danced in a large Concert Hall venue. The city was another eye-opening destination, with houses and apartments widely spread out on the plain with mountains all around and, when we were there, snow everywhere. It could not have looked more beautiful. And what was more, some residents kindly invited us to their home for dinner, with the most massive ever portions of everything. I had never seen anything like their house itself – the spaciousness, the interior design, and the number of cars they owned were unbelievable. That night, combined with the fact that a very famous basketball team,

The Salt Lake City Stars, was based there made me feel that my dreams of what a life in the West could be like really were coming true.

In contrast, when I was standing on the ROH stage in *Ondine* that season, I wasn't (yet) imagining the day when I might perform there for real. I guess that being dressed in a wig in a ballet with music which wasn't easy on the ears didn't exactly inspire me, although I do remember watching Ondine and Palemon dancing together and thinking about the huge responsibility which dancers in leading roles like that carry, especially on that stage. RBS students also watch Royal Ballet rehearsals and I particularly remember sitting in the auditorium when Alina Cojocaru and Johan Kobborg were dancing *Manon* and wanting to be the one 'in' the story.

That year, Mr. Norman prepared me to dance the male variation from *Paquita* for the Solos Evening. But I think that most people present will remember the occasion more because the piano music went missing than for my, or anyone else's, performance.

Also after the Easter break, rehearsals began for Sir Frederick Ashton's *The Dream,* which was to be coached by Sir Anthony Dowell – what an honour for students to be able to work with him. But that was not to be for me. I had a recurrence of my ankle/foot problems and, this time, with my professional career about to begin, I had to be sensible. Not that I really had any option as the bottom of my leg was like an elephant's and, for a time, I had to wear a boot and be on crutches. My coordination was so terrible that I always seemed to putting weight on my bad side!

So, there I was in my last term at the RBS sitting in my room, using a keyboard to make music or my phone to play games, and stuffing myself with pizzas. That wasn't good but I *felt* good and, as I had a contract by then, I was reassuring myself with

"All you have to do now to be a professional dancer is just heal your foot."

Ben was due to dance Oberon instead of me but, unfortunately, he injured himself during the first of the performances in The Linbury. Nevertheless, our time at the RBS ended as it had begun – together, but looking like a very odd double act with him on crutches and me limping as we were presented with our prizes for being joint Outstanding Graduate of the Year. But our ways then parted as, while Ben went straight into The Royal Ballet, my first contract was with English National Ballet.

Although I left on a high, I knew, of course, that my schooling would not be the end of my training. Throughout my future career, there would always be something else to learn and something more to improve on.

In Retrospect

Re-living my experience at The Royal Ballet School has brought me face to face with the realisation that I didn't make the best use of my years there. Thinking about that now, I can see three possible reasons why that was.

Firstly, when I chose to come to London, I made a faulty assumption that the training methods would be the same as in Russia (minus the shouting) and, as I have already mentioned, I could become negative because I was missing the kind of teaching I was used to. Secondly, I had totally underestimated what the impact of my inability to speak English would be. I would go so far as to say that, for at least half of the time, I wasn't fully aware of what was going on and the whole period of my being with the RBS could, and probably would, have felt very different had I been in less of a 'daze'. Thirdly, and much heightened for me by the language issue, was my ever-present sense of loneliness and separation from my family.

I am sorry that I wasn't the easiest of students and that, back then, I wasn't sufficiently respectful or appreciative of what Ms. Stock and the other staff were doing for me, not just in terms of my ballet training but as far as caring in a more personal way as well.

With Ms. Gailene Stock
Photo: Patrick Baldwin Photography

It must be incredibly difficult to prepare students to take their place not just in The Royal Ballet and Birmingham Royal Ballet but in a range of companies in the UK and abroad, each with a Director who will have his/her own preferences. Things are not as complicated in Russia in terms of students' progression to employment and, as far as their training is concerned, the Vaganova tradition lives through teachers who themselves have been taught by the same method and stay with a group for many years. I have heard people speak of dancers 'showing their Royal Ballet training' but, and perhaps this was just my lack of awareness, there didn't seem to be one defining style when I was at the RBS. My teachers drew on their different roots and therefore introduced some individual nuances. I'm not sure that I altogether managed to adapt to all the technical changes at the time, but I hope that I have been able, nevertheless, to do some justice to what each of them was giving me.

Am I glad that I made the leap to London? I love the city and I have so much to be grateful to the RBS for. I was able to train in a superb physical environment where discipline and high expectations were combined with support; I was given an introduction to, and into, English ballet; my horizons were hugely expanded by the opportunities the school gave me to perform abroad and discover new, and to me unbelievable, places; and, although I was still shy and not entirely 'grown up' when I left, I was better able to take responsibility, to make independent decisions and to face the outside world as a professional dancer.

PART TWO

FROM FIRST ARTIST TO
LEAD PRINCIPAL [2009–2014]

REPERTOIRE WITH ENGLISH
NATIONAL BALLET 2009–2014

[Debuts in bold typeface]

2009/2010 [FIRST ARTIST]: Les Sylphides (man); Scheherazade (Corps roles: Slave and Soldier); The Snow Queen (Wolf and Corps roles: Gypsy Boy and Villager); Men Y Men (featured and ensemble roles); Giselle (Albrecht and Corps role: Wine Gatherer); Nutcracker (Prince; Russian Dance; Arabian Dance and Corps role: Nutcracker Soldier – Hampson production); Cinderella (Prince and Prince's Friend); Swan Lake in the Round (Siegfried)

2010/2011 [FIRST SOLOIST]: Romeo and Juliet (Romeo); The Nutcracker – (Prince/Nephew, Nutcracker and Lead Flower – Eagling Production); Emerging Dancer; Black and White (featured roles in Men Y Men, **Vue de L'Autre and Suite en Blanc**); **Swan Lake (proscenium version – Siegfried);** Cinderella (Prince and Prince's Friend); **Strictly Gershwin in the Round (Rhapsody in Blue, Who Cares and I Got Rhythm)**

2011/2012 [PRINCIPAL]: Strictly Gershwin – proscenium version (Rhapsody in Blue, Who Cares, I Got Rhythm, Summertime and The Man I Love); The Nutcracker (Prince/Nephew and Nutcracker); **Beyond Ballet Russes Programme 2 (Apollo, Le Train Bleu solo** and leading male role in Suite en Blanc); **St Paul's Cathedral (featured in The Four Seasons, Of a Rose** and Suite en Blanc)

2012/2013 [PRINCIPAL/LEAD PRINCIPAL]: Sleeping Beauty **(Prince Désiré);** The Nutcracker (Prince/Nephew); **Ecstasy and Death (featured roles in Etudes and Petite Mort);** Swan Lake in the Round (Siegfried); **A Tribute to Rudolf Nureyev (Jean de Brienne in Raymonda and Song of a Wayfarer)**

2013/14 [LEAD PRINCIPAL]: Le Corsaire (Conrad/Ali); The Nutcracker (Prince/Nephew); **Romeo and Juliet in the Round (Romeo)**

CHAPTER 5

IN AT THE DEEP END

A Surprise Contract

Although I had been very clear about choosing London as the place to continue my schooling, I had no plan as to what might happen subsequently. Indeed, during my First and Second Years at The Royal Ballet School, there were more than a few times when I was asking myself, "What am I doing in the UK?". Other graduate year students were eyeing The Royal Ballet and its repertoire but I was more preoccupied with achieving my dream lifestyle while simultaneously imagining that I would return to Russia to dance. I know I wasn't being logical as that particular living/dancing combination wasn't, and probably still isn't, achievable.

During the first term of the Graduate year, there was indirect talk of auditions. I hadn't thought that process through and preferred to put it out of my mind because it scared me. Then, as I said previously, the RBS had a preview evening just before we set off for Salt Lake City. All the students who had performed came back at the end of the show to take a collective bow and we filed out through the adjacent studio, heading for the changing rooms. I was suddenly stopped by a smiling man and woman who introduced themselves (I didn't catch the names at first) and mentioned English National Ballet (ENB). Prior to that day, a group of us had been to the Coliseum (the Coli) to take class on stage with ENB and Thomas Edur, one of the top male dancers at that time, had spoken enthusiastically to me about the sort of things the Company did. Therefore, although I hadn't consciously considered working with them, I was aware of ENB, albeit (then) without fully appreciating its significant status in UK ballet and the fact that it had been founded in 1950 as the London Festival

Ballet by two luminaries of British dance, Alicia Markova and Anton Dolin.

It was difficult to take everything in standing in the RBS corridor but I remember that Maina (Gielgud) did most of the talking, that I was offered a contract as a First Artist, and that Wayne (Eagling), ENB's Director, emphasised, "I will give you Albrecht at the Coliseum". I'm sure that I looked a bit dumbstruck but Wayne and Maina didn't push me. Instead, they said, "Why don't you have a think about it and let Ms. Stock know what you want to do". This led to Ms Stock talking the offer through with me.

I wasn't sufficiently mature or knowledgeable to think the ENB approach through in terms of comparison with other companies or what the implications might be for my career, but the headline promise that I would dance Albrecht really 'hit the spot'! I suppose, deep down, I knew that spending some years in the corps wasn't really what I was aiming for. So, in what now seems like undue haste, I told my parents that I was going to accept the offer and, just as quickly, ENB took things from there.

At that stage in the year, some students knew that they would be joining The Royal Ballet or Birmingham Royal Ballet, but weren't allowed to reveal that. Others were travelling to auditions elsewhere. So there was no 'I've made it' celebration, just a feeling of liberation and great excitement that I would soon be a professional dancer – with a salary.

As news about graduates' contracts began to seep out, I had many people congratulate me, "A First Artist? WOW?" and as many, if not more, enquire as to whether I would have preferred to go to the RB along with Ruth (Bailey), Ben (Ella), Leticia (Stock) and Tristan (Dyer). My answer was, "No!" In later interviews, I have been asked, often, why I thought the RB didn't want me and all I can say is, "I don't really know". But I have always felt that the people around me at the time had my best interests in mind.

Settling In

There were only three weeks between the RBS performance on the main stage and my starting at Markova House (then the HQ of ENB). Ms Stock had helped me find temporary accommodation before I moved into a flat in Shaftesbury Avenue with Ben and Douwe Dekkers. The injury which had prevented me performing Oberon with the RBS was gradually feeling less sore – and that was just as well as, the minute I walked into ENB, I was into class and a full day of rehearsals. That is, after being pointed in the direction of the changing room. Shiori (Kase) was on a parallel path – also joining ENB from the RBS, with no other contemporaries from school and very reserved, like me. But, in the short space between School and Company life, I had tried to put my head together in terms of taking responsibility for my approach to work and my personal wellbeing.

The ENB schedule was very full because the Company had returned from its summer break and was preparing to go on tour to Barcelona with **Scheherazade** and **Les Sylphides**. As a newcomer, it was helpful for me to be so active. Another major plus was that I was in the corps changing room and that ensured that I was 'in the thick of it' with my new colleagues and joking with them pretty much immediately. ENB is renowned for its friendly, family ethos and I felt 'looked after' by my peers. There is nothing like a shared laugh to make one feel included.

Although I was naïve in so many ways, I knew that there could be jealousy in ballet but I didn't notice any of that coming my way. Everyone was just 'nice' and I guess that ENB has so many shows of each of its productions that there is more than enough for everyone (and, unlike in Russia, the leads are not paid extra!). I suspect, however, that I was a bit of an object of curiosity because I had a slight feeling of being 'watched'. How quickly would I connect with the combinations? How was I responding to corrections? How well did I 'compete' with the other men during the 'fun' 15 minutes between the end of class and the start of rehearsals?

The reason my days were so packed right from the 'off' was that I had calls (rehearsal slots) which included coaching for upcoming roles as well as all the necessary corps sessions. There could not have been a greater contrast between being prepared for the male role in Les Sylphides, with Anaïs Chalendard as my partner, and acting as a Slave or a Soldier in Scheherazade. Every single bit of everything was completely new for me, but it was an enjoyable mix of precise classical purity and roles which could be more ad lib. There was a fair bit of murmuring among my colleagues about how a shy me would cope with the erotic sexual romping that is required of a Slave. But I was ahead of them. I said to myself, "It's a ballet; if you have to, you have to" and, much to everyone's surprise, I went into it full blast. That was probably the first time ever that I had let my head come out of my turtle-like shell and reveal what was inside.

I didn't do so well when Daria Klimentová asked me if I would "try a few things" from the Les Sylphides pas de deux with her while she was waiting for her partner to arrive. It was in Barcelona and Anaïs and I had just finished our session in the theatre studio. When I had looked up ENB online before joining, one of clips I had watched was an interview with Daria about her role as the Snow Queen and I had been completely overawed. It was such a shock, therefore, when this Senior Principal, as they were called then, someone who seemed on an entirely different planet, was actually approaching me, that I initially said, "No – I'm OK". However, Daria, who wasn't going to take my rebuff, pulled rank and insisted – although I was able to make my escape quite quickly, and with huge relief, when her proper partner arrived.

My main memory of preparing Les Sylphides was the meticulous coaching I received. Antony Dowson would give close attention to my partnering and be generally very supportive while Maina, who was concentrating more on other couples, would illustrate what she was needing to see from me and also give me detailed feedback, not just on how I was executing the steps but also how my acting was coming across to her.

Despite the inexperience I was feeling all too keenly, the press in Barcelona asked me for an interview on the basis of my being a "young, rising star" and, in this case, "the new Baryshnikov". Ouch – the only 'new' which applied to me at the time was having been dancing professionally for a mere couple of weeks.

That time in Spain was my first experience of touring with ENB, but there was much more to follow that autumn. While ENB now has a purpose-built HQ with a full-scale production studio, it isn't based in a 'home theatre' and its funding from The Arts Council is dependent, in part, on its touring. During my time with the Company, the 'stops', which included Southampton, Manchester, Liverpool, Oxford, Bristol, Milton Keynes and Woking, reflected the importance of bringing the art to the various parts of England but always made a loss. I'll return to touring arrangements later but, especially in my first year with ENB, the fact that the company was away from home together provided me with another, helpful way of integrating with my fellow dancers.

Men Y Men with Anton Lukovkin
Photography by ASH

Once *Les Sylphides* and *Scheherazade* had been safely navigated, I had even more learning to do and my days were regularly 10.00am to 6.30pm non-stop with corps, soloist and principal roles one after the other. Normally, ENB tends to prepare intensively for one production while keeping one or more 'oven ready'. However, that autumn, Wayne decided to make a piece for seven of us, **Men Y Men**, to precede performances of *Giselle* on tour and in London – and new work doesn't happen overnight. He chose beautiful music by Rachmaninov and built on the individual strengths of his cast as well as using us as an ensemble. The choreographic process was really enjoyable for me, the more so because there was no pressure in being one of the group – except when I had to jump on Anton Lukovkin's shoulders.

It was a little different when I was one of the Vine Gatherers in *Giselle*. I had to enter first, with Laurretta Summerscales, who was also new to the Company, and turn to beckon the others on. Simple enough, you would think but, for the Ballet Mistress (the former Royal Ballet First Soloist, Rosalyn Whitten), I was giving my entrance a bit too much 'oomph' and she would call out the moment I appeared with an order to 'take it easy'. This was not the only moment I felt sheepish as a member of the corps. Blending with everyone else, even breathing as one, is a very special skill – one which I was needing to learn and adjust to quickly.

Albrecht

From a very early stage, my main focus was, of course, on Albrecht and I began by working on his solos and other passages with Maina and Antony, overseen at times by Irmgard Berry who is the guardian of the Mary Skeaping version of *Giselle*. Together, they made me think about the kind of man Albrecht was and gave me amazing detail about both the characterisation and issues of technique. I needed to absorb a lot and to adjust to what they were wanting from me but I benefited from even more individual attention than usual, firstly because my intended partner, Anaïs, had become injured and, later, when I was left behind while most of the Company was on tour to Greece.

One day, without warning, Daria came into the studio and I believe it was explained that she would be my partner until Anaïs recovered. I had no idea that, behind the scenes, Daria had been very reluctant to step in, not least because of the implications for her of dancing with someone as inexperienced as me. Much later on, I was to learn that she had agreed to help out "with the boy" (me) on the basis that she would be in the studio only when the pas de deux were being rehearsed – after all, she was also preparing her role with Esteban Berlanga and Fabian Reimair. I was glad that Daria wasn't going to be around all that much because, initially, I found her presence intimidating. With her (then) dark hair scraped back, she was every inch the prima ballerina and I was no one. In the book she wrote in 2013, she talked about how, in an attempt to break the ice with me, she asked me, "Do you have a girlfriend?". I replied, "Yes" and "No" within the space of two seconds and then wished that a hole would open up and swallow me. But, especially given who Daria was, it was a conversation starter which caught me completely off guard and I guess that, typical young man, I was trying to appear 'cool' rather than alone and a 'loser'. I failed!

To say that I felt awkward in the pas de deux rehearsals to begin with would be an understatement. Some of my unease was about adding partnering into the complex mix of being Albrecht. I had, of course, worked with Anaïs for *Les Sylphides,* but a full length ballet is a very different matter. Besides, it takes time to know how best to 'handle' a particular ballerina and I needed to be sufficiently uninhibited to take physical hold of my Giselle and support her properly in the pas de deux. At the same time, I had to stay in the story, acting the mature cad at first (very much against type) and, then, the grieving man stricken with guilt. My dancing and life experience up to that point was such that I needed a lot of help in pulling all that together – and with a ballerina with whom even making eye contact was hard for me to begin with.

There wasn't time for many joint rehearsals before our first show in Southampton and I would say that, while the atmosphere in the studio was cordial, it was very matter of fact. I was therefore a rather diffident Albrecht at the beginning of my debut show but, when I walked on in the cape, holding the lilies, something snapped. I forgot my nerves and that I was 'only Vadim' and somehow became more Albrecht. The members of the Company, including Daria, hadn't seen this from me before and, even though my partnering had been tentative, even clumsy, I think my Act 2 that day helped her perception of me change. For my part, I was riding on a very happy cloud thinking, "This is what I have been training for and longing for".

Even so, I have a feeling that Daria thought (hoped?) that she would be finished with me after the two shows in Southampton because Anaïs would have returned – but not so. Therefore, rehearsals continued with Daria, but the mood in the studio was noticeably more relaxed. Of course, Daria was everyone's dream partner in terms of her technique, always on her leg, being light as a feather and giving me tips based on her accumulated experience. Then there was her artistry and the way she began to help me to respond to her. She would say, "Just love me – don't be shy"; "Live the story". But, perhaps more than anything in terms of building my confidence, she would make a joke if things went wrong (humour is a great leveller), give me encouragement, "Oooh, that was good", pay me an occasional compliment, "So strong", and speak to me in Russian. This helped me to ask her for advice as to how to make my support better for her. It was almost as if I had been a tight bud which Daria had sprinkled with water and made it open into a flower. Gradually, I began to feel 'normal' around her and, as the weeks went by, our trust in one another grew and my partnering improved by leaps and bounds to the point where, when I was dancing with Daria, I had no fear.

Albrecht
Photography by ASH

While I was growing into Albrecht, the Company was continuing to rehearse *Men Y Men,* which had been very well received, the

94

The Snow Queen, where I had two corps slots – as a Gypsy Boy (which was fun because I could be scruffy) and a Villager (unrecognisable in a heavy coat, boots and a moustache) and a soloist role as a Wolf alongside Zhanat Atymtayev, Esteban Berlanga or James Forbat.

Nutcracker Pas de Deux (Hampson)
with Daria Klimentová
Photography by ASH

As a Wolf in the
Snow Queen
Photography by ASH

Russian Dance
Photo: Daria Klimentová

Then it was time for *The Nutcracker* and I was cast with Daria. This gave me a boost because I knew that she would not have let that happen if she didn't want to dance with me. However, Christopher Hampson's choreography includes some very complicated partnering which really stretched me and must have tested Daria's

95

patience. I actually had three other roles in that production: I parachuted in as a Nutcracker soldier, I was in the Arabian Dance, and I performed the Russian Variation in a pair of very hairy blue trousers, which turned that solo into a jolly piece for the audience.

Then, in January 2010, Wayne delivered on his promise and I danced Albrecht at the Coliseum aged 19. Being given the opportunity to tell the story of *Giselle* on that vast stage was so unbelievable that I don't have the words to express adequately how it felt for me (except that, at times, it was if I was flying like a bird). My gratitude to Wayne, my coaches and Daria for making it possible knows no bounds, even all these years later. Dreams can come true.

After the heavy Christmas Season, where I was in the theatre all day every day, keeping myself going on maltesers, lucozade and chunks of Cheddar cheese (I have to smile now at the juxtaposition of that basic existence and diet with my 'big moment' on stage in *Giselle)*, we were back to touring *Giselle* and preparing for **Cinderella**, where I was either The Prince or one of his friends. It was a hectic period, including getting ready for another tour to Spain (Valencia) but, despite that, Daria and I gradually felt more connected dancing together and ENB's artistic management was clearly regarding us as a regular partnership.

Then, just in case there was any risk of my becoming too comfortable, an unexpected ingredient was put into the mix.

Agony and Ecstasy

The first I knew about a proposed television programme was when cameras arrived in the studio. The idea was that they would follow a year in the life of a ballet company but, of course, like all good film-makers, they were looking for any hint of natural drama. And the preparations for Derek Deane's **Swan Lake in**

96

the Round provided them with a ready-made group of characters – the baddie (Derek); the put-upon star (Daria) and an ingénu (me) - to weave their story around.

The introduction for the first programme says of ballet that "behind the scenes it is a different story". However, when one is part of the action at the time, it's amusing to watch these films and see the extent to which the editing of footage can paint a picture which, itself, is some considerable distance from the reality.

I wasn't in the least bit fazed by the filming in the studio and it was easy to carry on as normal. However, the crew also wanted to interview me, follow me home and catch me in unguarded moments. What they showed me saying: "I should be more confident, but it's coming"; "I think that I'm not interesting... (that)... I'm saying something wrong"; "They want from me more and more" was a very true reflection of my immaturity and how I was feeling. But my eating breakfast was completely fake: I had nothing in the cupboard so I had to borrow some cereal and sit on the sofa in order to keep out of the way of my flatmates in the kitchen. Then there was my 'late arrival' which was presented as indiscipline but had resulted from a misunderstanding on my part as to when the Prince's Friends in *Cinderella*, who do not appear until Act 2, needed to be at the theatre. Antony's interaction with me was sensitive and ended with laughter but, unsurprisingly in the context of the TV programme, the accompanying smiles didn't make the cut.

Derek Deane's *Swan Lake* requires a lot of preparation, especially of the augmented corps of Swans and, from about two months ahead of the shows, I was being coached by Maina and Antony. Daria was cast as Odette/Odile. Although she had apparently said that she wasn't keen to dance the dual role again at The Royal Albert Hall, she was down to do two shows with me later in the run after I had opened it with Polina Semionova, the Russian-born Prima Ballerina in Berlin, who was to be the guest star. Having Daria to practise with in the early rehearsal period was very helpful for me.

Then, according to the film, the equivalent of Carabosse arrived in the person of Derek. He did indeed 'up the ante' in the studio but, even though I felt uncomfortable at times, I completely 'got' the fact that he wanted to get the best out of me – as much for my sake as for any other reason. He said to camera that I was, "Very raw, very young: an incredible physical package and I wanted to test him" and goes on to talk (in no uncertain terms) about getting maximum commitment from the dancers. Prior to his arrival, I had been feeling that I was working *really* hard but he pushed me much more and I needed that from him. He says of me, "I must scare the shit out of him" but he didn't know what my teachers had been like in Perm.

Swan Lake Rehearsal with
Derek Deane
Photography by ASH

Swan Lake with Daria
Klimentová
Photography by ASH

All Derek's pulling the story out of me and trying to get meaning in my every step and gesture was invaluable, and just what I needed and wanted to soak up. Adding artistry to technique was something which Maina had been guiding me towards and Derek added different perspectives and layers to that.

Siegfried at The Royal Albert Hall
Photography by ASH

Once the rehearsals moved to the studios at Three Mills, where the arena could be fully marked out on the floor, Derek's emphasis was not just on expressiveness but also on the need to communicate with the distant, higher parts of The Royal Albert Hall. At this point, stress levels were rising and rising again and several dancers were frequently in Derek's line of fire, including me. He is shown on film saying, "He's so immature, that's what I'm worried about"; "He's looking like a boy because he doesn't know how to walk (I agree), stand (I agree); or say good morning (I was just afraid of appearing over-familiar towards him)". It was all very intense and I was leaving the studio completely drained but, in the much bigger space, I could really feel myself making progress, not least in terms of my strength and speed.

Hanging over everyone was the increasing panic about Polina's visa and the ever-diminishing amount of time for rehearsal. I was relieved when it was accepted that she wasn't going to make it because I could see from videos that Polina was of a very different build from Daria and I knew that I would need time to make the partnering transition. Of course, the thrust of the film then shifted towards Daria and her stoicism in the face of Derek's cutting observations about her. She mentions in her book that she didn't know about some of what was being said. I knew only too well what Derek thought about my efforts because his often harsh comments were directed straight at me rather than to camera, but it didn't suit the film-makers' narrative to include those. That is all the more the pity because Derek's corrections were 'spot on' and still reverberate inside my head whenever I am being Siegfried.

I hadn't been inside the The Royal Albert Hall until we went there to rehearse ahead of the whole company. And, Wow! I had never seen a theatre like that before and it took my breath away. There were many new factors to take on board: the energy-sapping entrances and exits up and down the stairs, the disorientating spotlights, the audience all around the dancers, and the distances needing to be covered. Although the floor space had been replicated at Three Mills, any studio is contained compared with the 'real thing' and there were many adjustments to be made. Derek wasn't best pleased because what I was showing him wasn't 'carrying' and I was getting: "I want to see everything I've taught you"; "I've told you a thousand times"; "Just do it" called out to me a lot. Yet I was to discover from the film that, at the same time as he was giving me a hard time, he was explaining, "You have to look at it psychologically because you can damage the person, not build them". In this context, I must also quote what he said to me before I went on: "I've travelled the world to find you. Really enjoy it. Be calm. Think of all the other things except the dancing". He then patted my shoulder and added, "You'll be very good".

And the performance itself? Being completely alone in that arena during Siegfried's soliloquy is unique for a dancer as, usually, there are people close by in the wings. At The Royal Albert Hall, Siegfried is entirely wrapped by the audience and truly 'giving it out' for them. It is so liberating in that vast space, especially when one is young and almost fearless. And, thanks to the support Daria gave me, I was able to enjoy myself and, more or less, to follow Derek's last minute advice. There are surprises in every performance and, that night, the main one was being clapped at length when I ran on searching for Odette in Act IV. This somewhat undermined the tragedy of the ballet but it also made me sense that the audience was rooting for me. That's a good feeling which comes across in a very special way 'in the round'.

It was equally special afterwards to go down to the dressing room and be met by generous congratulations from company members. In the programme, Ros Whitten was shown saying, "He was fabulous. Twenty years old, just out of School – bloody amazing!" With a microphone pushed in front of me, I managed to say, "It was alright, yes. It was really hard work but the second time will be easier". I was told the reviews were really good (I didn't read them); but Episode One of Agony and Ecstasy ends with the voice over saying, "Since *Swan Lake* Daria and Vadim have become ENB's number one couple with their performances winning rave reviews comparing them to Nureyev and Fonteyn". Mmmh – that was being said quite a lot and it was obviously a huge compliment although, in our own minds, we were Klimentová and Muntagirov, Daria and Vadim, and very much our own 'brand' of ballet partnership. But more about that later.........

With her visa finally issued, Polina Semionova did arrive eventually and we danced two shows together. She is taller than Daria but she has an upper body carriage which made lifting her feel as if her body was made of air. Surprisingly, the arabesque presage was easier with Polina because I didn't have to bend down so far to mirror her plié. In addition, by the time we performed together, I had the opening night behind me: the arena itself no longer felt so daunting, I was less preoccupied with my own uncertainties, and I was therefore in better position to be the host partner to a famous guest.

The run ended, fittingly, with Daria and I re-united for two further performances.

All in all, it was a satisfying season at The Royal Albert Hall and I shall always be grateful to Derek for being brave enough to give me the opportunity to perform in that incredible environment so early in my career and for giving me so much help in doing so.

CHAPTER 6

ONWARDS AND UPWARDS

Romeo and Juliet

The second part of the TV series was preoccupied with a number of challenges facing ENB both financially (the extent of the Arts Council cuts and whether or not there would be a pay rise) and artistically (whether there were enough men to populate Rudolf Nureyev's version of *Romeo and Juliet)*. The latter dilemma affected me directly and this meant that, initially, I had to learn the corps roles of Acrobat and Flags, both of which involved testing choreography and closely knit teamwork. Max Westwell and I were both new to Romeo and he was the one on whom the cameras lingered. He was also 'my' Benvolio, so he was exceptionally busy during a packed rehearsal period of no more than five weeks. I was lucky as, on the male side, 'team Vadim'

Flag Flying

also included Fabian Reimair as Tybalt and, variously, Yat-Sen Chang, Juan Rodriguez and Anton Lukovkin as Mercutio. Throughout the previous year, I had had to share Daria with other partners, or vice versa but, this time, we were cast 'exclusively' and were therefore able to build our interpretation together from the outset.

Staging the production were Patricia Ruanne, the original Juliet (the ballet had been made on ENB 34 years previously) and her husband Fréderic Jahn, the original Tybalt. Understandably, both of them were very concerned to ensure that the ENB of 2010 did full justice to a 'masterwork'. I share that view. It is impossible to imagine any ballet which could make greater demands on the main man – and, actually, Mercutio is amplified too because Nureyev also envisaged himself in that role.

The personal investment that the two stagers had in the work resulted in extra tough rehearsals for all of us and Patricia would sometimes show her frustration by walking out of the studio with a gesture of despair. I really tried to take on board every piece of advice and execute all the instructions I was given and generally managed to stay out of her line of fire. However, in an early show, I got the timing wrong with Friar Lawrence (Michael Coleman) in the wedding scene and felt the full force of her annoyance. It was entirely my fault and I heard afterwards that, as Patricia calmed down, she turned to the Ballet Staff and said, "He's only a young boy; he'll be a good Romeo one day". I think that that's what's called damning with faint praise!

My preparation began as one of a group of Romeos being talked through the role and I identified with him immediately. Romeo was aged 16 to 20, full of energy and very much in love. Vadim too was young, had plenty of bounce and had recently discovered the wonder of falling in love. Living the story was so real and beautiful for me that I could (almost!) forget all the technical hurdles.

Romeo and Juliet
Fight Rehearsal
Photography by ASH

Romeo and Juliet Pas de Deux
Rehearsal with Daria Klimentová
Photography by ASH

I was so elated that, one night, I climbed over the fence into Hyde Park and danced one of the solos under the floodlit statue of Prince Albert – only to discover that I was being watched by some passers-by who applauded and called out to me for my name because they wanted to Google me! Spell duly broken!

Balcony Pas De Deux Joy
Photography by ASH

Romeo needs an unbelievable amount of stamina to get through every scene he is in – and he is in a lot! The famous finale to Act 1 comes after several earlier solos and, while Juliet stands almost still, Romeo runs impetuously across the stage and performs a sequence of cabrioles and doubles assemblés followed by a manège – all before the pas de deux proper begins. Even more vigour is then required of Romeo to the extent that one's legs can either become tight or turn to jelly and, by the time the kiss comes, it is almost impossible to breathe. It's not the most romantic of moments because pausing for that kiss actually provides a much-needed opportunity to draw in air before it's 'all go' again. Towards the end, exhaustion transports you to a point where there is no world beyond the two of you. When Romeo mimes to Juliet, "I love you to the moon and back", the ecstasy within me was something that I had never felt before.

Of course, it's vital to run the whole six minutes many times over in rehearsal because, unless you keep pushing through, there is no way of knowing whether or not you have enough strength to 'make it'. And let's not forget that it's not the end of the ballet and those same legs have to be ready for Act 2 after only a short interval. Being invited by Paris Opera Ballet to dance the role more than 10 years later would, if it had not been impeded by the Covid-19 pandemic, have been a test to see whether I could still rise to that challenge.

Romeo and Juliet Pas de Deux
Photography by ASH

Romeo and Juliet Act 3
Photography by ASH

As the weeks passed, my partnership with Daria grew stronger and our trust in one another enabled us to become more natural in the way we portrayed the roles. On one occasion too much so, because, when I dashed on in Act 3 frantically looking for Juliet, I collided with her pillows, causing them to slip and her nose to hit the floor. In that performance both of us met an unintended bloody end.

Of all the ballets I have danced, including other versions of *Romeo and Juliet,* being able to run on stage as Romeo in this season of shows is what I shall remember for ever as giving me the best imaginable feeling.

Wayne Eagling's Nutcracker

The autumn of 2010 could hardly have made more demands on the Company as *Romeo and Juliet* had stretched every dancer to the full in rehearsal and on tour. Nevertheless, it had been decided previously that Wayne would create a new *Nutcracker* for the December/January season at the Coliseum. It was to be ENB's 10th version and a lot was riding on its success because around a third of the Company's income came from 'Christmas treat' ticket sales.

There were only six weeks between us all arriving back in London and the opening night, within which Wayne was needing to re-choreograph most of the ballet he had made for the Dutch National company when he was Director there. The adjustments were necessary so that ENB's version would be suitable for touring but it was obvious from the outset that time was not on Wayne's side and that he was under an intolerable amount of pressure. While the atmosphere in the studio had often been tense when we were rehearsing *Romeo and Juliet,* the development of the new *Nutcracker* was on an altogether different level because 'everything' needed to be done and the clock was ticking relentlessly.

I was first cast Nephew/Prince with Daria (Junor Souza was the Nutcracker and Fabian Reimair was Herr Drosselmeyer). I was also preparing to be Anaïs's Nutcracker and dance a Lead Flower alongside Jenna Lee (at ENB, everyone below Principal level can be cast wherever they are needed) – I believe the Dance of the Flowers was the only segment of his original ballet which Wayne left untouched. Just listing what I was down to dance gives an indication of the scale of the task for Wayne and the Ballet Staff with multiple casts needing to be taught and rehearsed after the choreography had been set. Having two leads (the Nephew/Prince and the Nutcracker) was an additional complication, not least because several of ENB's men were cast as both and therefore had calls with more than one Clara/Sugar Plum Fairy. Interestingly, when Wayne mounted the production in Japan, he combined the two roles and, having danced it there, I think that that made the ballet more satisfying for the leading male dancer and easier to understand for the audience.

As the days and weeks went by in the studio, it became obvious that Wayne was trying, and not altogether succeeding, to divide his time between some complex ensemble scenes and the need to choreograph the solos and pas de deux. Therefore, by the time we travelled to ENB's warehouse in Marden, Kent for an intended run-through, some sections of what I was meant to dance, on my own or with my partners, were still missing. The BBC film reveals that we were not alone: some corps members were trying to memorise their steps and formations from videos on their phones and Ksenia Ovsyanick was despairing about her Mirlitons sequence being "far from ready". Despite the overall situation, Wayne couldn't resist stopping the action to make adjustments, much to the consternation of staff and dancers alike.

The weight on his shoulders must have felt like an elephant to Wayne especially, as he said, because, "Any failure will be my failure, not anyone else's". But we really were very much behind him and wanting to make it all work. The last-minute final touches to the choreography for the Grand Pas, with technical rehearsals going on all around us, may not have been ideal but it didn't really worry me. I think that I would still have been OK if Wayne had wanted to change the steps one minute before curtain up. I suppose that it was no wonder that we fluffed the 'bum lift' at the General Rehearsal, at which there was a large paying audience eager for a preview of the new production. However, we had no option but to shake off that mishap, try to get our heads around the very demanding choreography the next day, and give it everything we had on our debuts. In spite of all that had gone before, the whole Company really rose to the occasion, the reviews were largely positive and Wayne could heave a sigh of relief. So could we all, except that I was on again, fully masked up as the Nutcracker, in less than 48 hours.

The Nutcracker Pas de Deux
'Bum lift' with Daria Klimentová
Photography by ASH

Nutcracker Prince
Photography by ASH

I was to dance in that *Nutcracker* production countless times but there was not to be another performance with quite the frisson of that particular opening night.

Snippets from 2011

The ***Emerging Dancer*** event came about a month after the run of *Romeo and Juliet* at the Coliseum. The competition was in its second year, having been initiated in 2010 by the then ENB Chairman and sponsored by his company. Everyone employed by ENB, whatever their role, had the opportunity to nominate one dancer and the six with the most votes became the finalists. In 2011, I was chosen alongside Shiori Kase, Ksenia Ovsyanick, Laurretta Summerscales, James Streeter and Max Westwell. Quite a line up as the three ballerinas were all to become Principals with ENB and/or abroad, James has become a very prominent interpreter of Akram Khan's ballets and, among other roles elsewhere, Max has starred as Matthew Bourne's iconic Swan/Stranger.

Although the structure has changed over the years, back then each of us had to perform two solos. I chose, for contrast, those of Albrecht from Act 2 of *Giselle* and Phillipe from *The Flames of Paris*, a rather 'blink and you've missed it' kind of solo. I felt honoured to have been selected but, in the wake of what I had experienced over the previous 18 months, I didn't have quite the heart for competitions that I once had. I think that, in the introductory films we all made, I spoke of my ambition "to be a nice person" rather than mentioning what I hoped to be able to achieve in ballet. I suppose, in a way, that I had already 'emerged'! The absolutely right dancer – Shiori dancing Giselle's Act 1 solo and the Black Swan – was the winner and I was very content to be rewarded with a comment from Carlos Acosta, who was a judge, to the effect that I was a 'Rolls Royce' kind of dancer.

Vue de L'Autre with Daria Klimentová
Photography by ASH

That spring, Wayne realised his ambition of having an additional Coliseum season and, for me, this brought in its wake the opportunity to work with the Company dancer Van Le Ngoc on his new work **Vue de L'Autre** set to music by Ludovico Einaudi. This was classically based and is actually one of the very few pieces that has been made on me. I enjoyed the whole process which carried with it the extra treat of travelling to Vietnam to perform the ballet in Van's home country. The second week at the Coli was a return to 'the lake' but with much less ground to cover behind the proscenium arch and more energy left for the dancing. Then, it was back to touring *Cinderella* again at home and abroad.

I have contrasting memories of that period. I was feeling much better blended with the Company and very supported but there was talk that Wayne's contract might be reviewed and that was, of course, unsettling for the dancers. I recall being in a meeting where the Principals and First Soloists were invited to share their experiences of working with him. We liked and respected Wayne – for example, for the way he related to us, his choice of repertoire and his willingness to let us take up invitations to perform elsewhere – and we all said so. If there had been a problem, there was no sign of it that summer when we were back at The Royal Albert Hall (hurrah!). This time, it was for **Strictly Gershwin** where, instead of being exposed as I had been with Siegfried, I could have fun with some featured roles within group numbers such as *Rhapsody in Blue, Who Cares and I Got Rhythm.* The music creates a distinctive vibe and I could let myself go and experiment with different styles. The opening manège, with a lot of dancers in the arena, made a fantastic start to the show and really got the audience going. That venue must be the best place in the world to execute a manège: not only is the shape of the arena perfect but, instead of moving upstage, a dancer is sharing his leaps and turns with each section of the audience and the ripple of applause seems to follow one round.

In fact, it felt as if we were all caught up in the mood, even Derek. He had created the work in response to the popularity of *Strictly Come Dancing* and, for the most part, we saw a softer side of him than he had revealed to us with *Swan Lake.* For the run at the RAH, Derek had invited a number of guests, including Tamara Rojo (who was then a leading ballerina at The Royal Ballet), Guillaume Côté (from the National Ballet of Canada) and Friedemann Vögel (from Stuttgart Ballet) and they combined with ENB Principals in the most starry numbers. However, when the show went on tour to no less than eight venues the following season, my roles were extended to include *Summertime* and

111

The Man I Love from Strictly
Gershwin with Daria Klimentová
Photography by ASH

The Man I Love. This meant that I was switching happily between the neo-classical and the jazzy for many weeks. I think opinion was divided about that show, with a section of the audience preferring ENB's more traditional repertoire, but I had a 'ball'.

I was promoted to Principal at the end of the 2010/11 season. I don't recall thinking, "Phew, I've arrived!" or "All my dreams have come true," because the need to work hard remained the same; but it did make me feel valued and that meant a lot.

Snapshots from the 2011/12 Season

I have already mentioned the extensive tour of *Strictly Gershwin,* but the autumn of 2011 was not untypical for ENB whose dancers live much of their lives 'on the move'. In my first year, I had been fortunate because Shevelle (Shev) Dynott and Grant Rae, both experienced 'travellers', invited me to share an apartment they were renting. Most dancers prefer to flat-share in order to make the weekly allowance go further. However, there were also 'special hotel offers' to take advantage of and I tended to do that from my second year onwards. Once I was a Principal, I could also travel independently if I wished and, in the case of Milton Keynes, drove there and back on a daily basis. In contrast, it was also convenient at times to join the Company's bus, especially the ones which carried us all back to London after the Saturday evening shows further afield. Did I get to know the cities we performed in? Unfortunately not really as there wasn't time: we all tended to know more about the local markets and where we could pick up a quick, cheap meal than any of the real 'sights'.

The Company's March 2012 appearance at the Coliseum, **Beyond Ballet Russes**, consisted of two programmes and I was cast in three of the four works in the second of these. I was reprising my roles in **Suite en Blanc** and also performing the short solo from **Le Train Bleu**, for which I was coached, together with Nathan Young, by Antony Dowson. There could hardly have been a greater contrast between the acrobatic cheeky swagger in that role and dancing Apollo.

Le Train Bleu
Photography by ASH

Suite en Blanc Pas de Deux
with Daria Klimentová
Photography by ASH

There were three casts for **Apollo**, with Zdenek Konvalina, Dmitri Gruzdyev and myself cast in the title role. 'My' muses were Erina Takahashi, Anaïs Chalendard and Senri Kou. The 12 of us together were a mix of those who were very familiar with the ballet and others, like me, who were coming to it for the first time. Rehearsals began with all the casts being taught together by Maina. Such an arrangement can result in the second and third casts marking their roles at the back of the studio while the focus is on the first cast. However, in this instance, from my point of view as the third cast, it was really well-managed to help me and other newcomers put down the basics before Nanette Glushak, from The Balanchine Trust, arrived to give individual attention to each group of us.

My experience with Apollo is a good example of how difficult it is for dancers to judge how best to approach a role for the first time. I like to arrive in the studio having done some preparation but it's all too easy to learn something one way, or think about an interpretation, only to find that one has to start all over again because the 'stager's' memory is of different movements and characterisation – and even the specialists approved by the trustees of various works tend to

Apollo
Photography by ASH

bring their individual ideas. But my main memory of my first Apollo remains that of a lovely coach (Nanette) who was very straightforward about what she wanted from me, honest in her feedback, and generous with praise alongside corrections.

ENB dancers were often called upon to perform in 'pop up' locations, the most prestigious of which was, of course, Buckingham Palace. The first time I went there, it was to dance a pas de deux which George Williamson had choreographed on Daria and me. The security was such that, having performed for the Queen on an outside stage in the first half of the programme, we were shepherded away to change and sent on our way. Only the dancers appearing in the second half were introduced to Her Majesty. On the subsequent occasion with ENB, in front of Prince Andrew, Daria and I performed the Cave

114

pas de deux from *Le Corsaire* on a specially erected indoor stage. Of course, this was even more exciting because we were inside amongst all the grandeur. I have been to the Palace with groups from The Royal Ballet too (to dance the pas de deux from *Winter Dreams* and, then, *Don Quixote*) and being able to go there remains an enormous privilege.

In 2012, ENB's other 'small group' venues included Tate Britain, St Paul's Cathedral and a Dance GB tent in connection with the 2012 Olympics. All involved dancing on temporary stages but the Tate was unusual, firstly because the audience could stand all around us, or even just walk by and barely pause, and secondly because the performance was shown 'on repeat' three times during the day. I was Apollo and, probably because everything we did was being watched in such close up, my face became the object of much unexpected scrutiny.

I'm one of those very unhairy people who can get by for a month with a 'single use' razor, apparently to the envy of some of my fellow dancers who struggle to mask their five o'clock shadow and wonder what to do when their chests are exposed. However, after the first show, I was told that I needed to get rid of my moustache which, of course, I did. But my second attempt was judged as not having applied enough make-up. So, on the third try, I plastered more on, especially around my eyes, which seemed far too much to me to be viewed in close up but which, apparently, was regarded as being 'just fine'.

At the end of the 2011/12 season, we had holidays before returning for another run of *Swan Lake* at the Coli. – except that I didn't get back. As a result of a misunderstanding with the ENB Office, my visa and those of a couple of other dancers had not been sorted out before we went away. The only option for me was to try to apply for a British Visa in Ekaterinburg but, unfortunately, it was to be a long process.

Timing was crucial, not only in terms of my performances but, also, my eligibility to apply for British Citizenship. If I had had more than 28 days without a visa, the years I had accumulated in the UK would have been struck out and I would have had to start counting again. That fate befell at least one other dancer, but I scraped through with 24 hours to spare. Unfortunately, it wasn't in time for me to be able to dance Siegfried again – well, not under Wayne's Directorship because, sadly, that was coming to an end.

CHAPTER 7

ALL CHANGE

Tamara Rojo's First Season as Director

The announcement that Tamara Rojo, then a star Principal dancer with The Royal Ballet, was taking over as Artistic Director (AD) came, quite suddenly, in March 2012. At the time, many ENB dancers had already served under more than one AD and therefore found the news quite worrying. Having not experienced such a major change before, I was very sorry that Wayne would be leaving but I knew Tamara slightly from having danced the *Le Corsaire* pas de deux with her in an *Ave Maya Gala* and I was optimistic for the future.

In late September, there was a hotel reception to introduce Tamara and her new artistic team where she also announced her plans for the 2012/13 season beyond what Wayne had scheduled. The Principals were asked to mingle with the guests and we had the opportunity to hear Tamara set out her vision for the Company and her immediate plans.

By then, we were well into preparations for **The Sleeping Beauty** and Tamara had cast me to partner her, while Daria, at her own request, became 'our' Lilac Fairy. I first had to learn the role – my third Tchaikovsky Ballet – before being coached alongside Tamara by the legendary Loipa Araujo, who had become Associate Director. During a pas de deux call, it's all about your partner and you, nothing else, and, in this case, there was no hint of Tamara also being my boss. She was just a very focused and helpful ballerina, one who really danced *with* me and from whom I could learn. Our sessions together were extremely pleasant but, of course, all about putting in the hard work to ensure, by correction and repetition, that everything was precise and that we both had the required stamina. And there was an inbuilt bonus! Because of her other responsibilities, Tamara's calls were always immediately after daily class so, usually, we would be finished by around 1.30pm. I could gladly have made a habit of that kind of working day!

Rehearsals for *The Nutcracker* with Daria began alongside work on *The Sleeping Beauty* with Tamara and this required

Sleeping Beauty with Tamara Rojo
Photography by ASH

adjustments from me as they differed from one another as dance partners in every possible way. On the opening night of the Christmas Season in December 2012, I was on stage with Daria when Tamara suddenly appeared to announce my promotion to Lead Principal and present me with a large bouquet. The official line was that it was spontaneous but (spoiler alert) Tamara had promoted me a couple of months previously and my salary had been at the higher level for several weeks. However, what happened was *indeed* a lovely surprise for me because I had not expected the on-stage 'ceremony'. It was quite strange afterwards because I found myself thinking that I would never again have a meeting with the AD along the lines of, "How's it going?" .....(discussion) "And I'm promoting you to ....". Those three occasions with ENB were moments to savour.

The March season at the Coli introduced Jiří Kiliàn's poetic *Petite Mort* to the rep. Its six men, six women and six fencing foils symbolise, respectively I believe, energy, silence, sexuality and, when the foils become dancing partners, they represent the brutality in everyday life. It was a very different work in

Petite Mort with Marize Fumero
Photography by ASH

terms of its concept and choreographic language from what I had encountered before and this took some getting used to. My partners were Marize Fumero, a Cuban dancer, and a fencing foil! There were, however, passages in the work where the dancers needed to mingle as they ran around on stage and I had to keep reminding myself not to 'home in' on Daria out of sheer habit as she, too, was paired with someone else.

It was good to experience the contrast, on the same *Ecstasy and Death* bill, with *Etudes* which celebrates the journey dancers make from daily ballet class moves and simple stretching at the barre to the classical virtuosity and bravura of a performance. The fact that my debut, alongside Erina Takahashi, James Forbat and Esteban Berlanga, was at the Company's 747th performance goes to show how essential a part of ENB's repertoire *Etudes* has been. On this occasion, the link with the choreographer, Harald Lander, was maintained not only by having a fellow Dane, Jonny Eliasen, staging the work but also by the presence of Lise Lander, Harald's widow, as Artistic Adviser. This is another superb example of how ballet benefits from the handing down of expertise from one era to the next, and being able to be on the receiving end of all that accumulated knowledge is worth more than its weight in gold for a dancer.

It's very tempting, when you've had all that valuable input, to try to go on and perform, even if you are in such agony that you know you have more than just a twinge or a spasm. But, unfortunately, I could only manage the opening night of *Etudes* before consulting the Company Doctor and Physiotherapists and being advised to rest.

Almost constant pain goes with the territory for a dancer and, as time has gone on, I've grown to accept that there will always be 'something', however much I try to look after my body. When I was with ENB, I tended to keep pushing when that was decidedly unwise because I didn't want to be the cause of any problem but, as time has gone on, I've become more prepared to admit it to myself if a 'fix' is needed. I've been fortunate not to suffer any serious injury but I have given myself a scare or two. Some years ago, having landed awkwardly while rehearsing for a gala, I found myself limping at the airport and googled my symptoms while waiting for my flight. Not a good idea because the online diagnosis pointed to something badly wrong with my knee. I consulted the organisers, got a scan and flew back to London without performing. Luckily, further scans gave reason for optimism and, as it was at the start of the season, I was able to miss class for a month and work with the physio team on strengthening exercises to build up my muscles and reduce pressure on my knee. That episode taught me to listen when my body says to me, "Be careful" and, with The Royal Ballet, I wouldn't hesitate to say (very reluctantly) if it wasn't safe for me to go on.

But, back to Spring 2013 with ENB.......Much to my surprise, I was informed in March that I had been nominated for a Benois de la Danse Award for my performance in *The Sleeping Beauty.* The Jury for this was led by the renowned choreographer and former Bolshoi Ballet Director Yuri Grigorovich and the ceremony was held at the Bolshoi Theatre. The first part of the evening was sort of 'red carpet', with everyone dressed for the occasion, when the winners were celebrated. Then, the dancers involved had to do a quick change and warm up before performing a relevant extract. This gave me a longed-for opportunity to dance on the Bolshoi stage and I felt doubly honoured to be the youngest ever winner of the main prize (jointly with Alban Lendorf) because the award was based in my home country.

After June at 'the 'lake', again in the RAH, it was time for *A Tribute to Rudolf Nureyev* back at the Coli. I was fortunate to have two roles which really resonated with me personally. Nureyev recreated *Raymonda Act 3* from memory for The Royal Ballet in 1969 and it is a real celebration of dance with some spectacular choreography that I have come to understand typifies Nureyev. The steps for Jean de Brienne are almost like a class combination – cabrioles; doubles assemblés; pirouette en dedans; pirouette en dehors; manège - all without the breathing space of linking movements and a real test for the male dancer, as, of course, is the pas de quatre which is performed by four soloists. Daria and I danced one show – the opening night – but little did I realise then that I would be revisiting Jean in other locations in the years to come.

Maurice Béjart's *Song of a Wayfarer*, set to Mahler's first song cycle, has to be one of the most beautiful ballets ever made for male dancers and it was the first emotional neo-classical work which I had tackled. I must quote from an ENB note of the time: *"The story follows a romantic wayfarer who wanders from town to town looking for freedom but condemned by destiny to a life of eternal unhappiness and loneliness. Béjart created this piece especially for Nureyev, believing that it expresses the errant life of the dancer........"* The poignancy of this was emphasised for me when, together with Esteban Berlanga (my partner and a kind of 'fate' figure) and Fabian Reimair and Francisco Bosch (the other cast couple), I spent a week in Lausanne working with the Béjart company under the guidance of Gil Roman. It was very inspiring to be amongst dancers who were not really moving classically but had a wonderful way of presenting themselves with joy and showing their hearts. I hope that I was able to carry something of that back into my performances and convey real yearning in the beautiful, sensitive duet.

Song of a Wayfarer
with Esteban Berlanga
Photography by ASH

Song of a Wayfarer
Photography by ASH

My Last ENB Season

The air was full of anticipation when the dancers returned to prepare for the 2013/14 season as Tamara had asked Anna Marie Holmes to stage her version of **Le Corsaire** for the Company. Originally purchased from the Bolshoi and then re-worked for American Ballet Theatre (ABT) with Ethan Stefel and Julie Kent in the leading roles, the production was lavish, with great opportunities for dancers at all levels. It was almost as if it was 'made' for ENB. The fact that the development of new costumes, sets and lighting design was well under way by that August only added to the excitement.

We began by learning as much as we could from the ABT DVD before Anna Marie Holmes herself arrived to guide the preparations. I was originally cast with Alina Cojocaru, who had just joined ENB from The Royal Ballet and, because I was the 'main man', Conrad, I was involved in calls all day and every day.

Studio Rehearsal for Le Corsaire

Of course, I was happy to be so busy but, by the time I was scheduled to rehearse with Daria, who was the third cast or, indeed, with Tamara, Fernanda Oliviera or Ksenia Ovsyanick who also danced Medora, I was a rather 'spent force'. That meant that I wasn't able to give Daria the kind of support in rehearsals to which she was accustomed from me and I knew that that was hard for her, especially as she often spent many hours in Markova House waiting for our late afternoon call.

I suppose, as well, that, after more than two years of everyone linking us together and making us feel more 'special' because of that, it was also very strange to hear 'Alina and Vadim' being headlined instead. I know that this happens all the time in ballet but I couldn't help feeling wounded on Daria's behalf because, while my career had momentum, it seemed as if she would no longer be the first in line for leading roles and I was sensing that our partnership was at risk of disappearing within ENB.

Compared with Daria and Tamara, dancing with Alina was a very different kind of experience for me. I suppose this was mainly because of the fine detail in which she approaches every movement, slowly seeking to get everything exactly how she feels she needs it in order, in performance, to interpret a role in her uniquely spontaneous way. I very much respect Alina's need to work like that and, of course, how wonderful she is on stage. However, the process was hard for me because we rarely got to the point of being able to run it so as to enable me, also, to play with it, be inside the story and find my character's connection with hers. I suppose that I was probably more Alina's supporter than I was her partner – which is fine insofar as that is what the man should be there to do. So my preoccupation, of course, was with giving her what she needed within each show (sometimes in unexpected ways).

Conrad
Photography by ASH

Conrad in Flight
Photography by ASH

Although it has lovely roles for ballerinas (two leads – Medora and Gulnare and three Odalisques), Le Corsaire is also about the rivalries between the male characters and there is tremendous physicality in the dancing. Conrad might be the leading man but what he is given to dance is less exciting for the audience than the choreography for Birbanto and, especially, that for the slave, Ali. I think I did manage to give Conrad a piratical swagger and to brandish my sword fearsomely. However, while Conrad has danced a lot and Ali has basically been subservient to him, once it comes to the famous pas de deux (a pas de trois in ENB's and many other versions), all the plaudits from the audience are directed at Ali for his one big solo. At times, the applause and cheers for ENB's Alis almost brought the roof down, including when he took his curtain call at the end and it was sometimes a case of Conrad? Conrad who? I should add that I did dance Ali just twice, so I was able to 'get my own back'! Of course, all of that competitiveness was very good natured.

The show opened in Milton Keynes on the 17th October 2013 to critical acclaim – who could not thrill to that production – but that was only the beginning for me of what can only be described as a Corsaire-fest with four weeks of touring in the autumn, two weeks at the Coli followed by another in Manchester, five different ballerinas and the role of Ali in my repertoire as well. It might be difficult for others to believe this but, for the first time, after four months of continuous rehearsals and around a dozen shows, I began to feel as if the repetition was making me a bit stale and that I needed to shake myself up with something different.

I had asked Tamara some months back if it would be possible for me to guest elsewhere and she had been cautious about agreeing. I had been allowed to dance abroad quite a lot by Wayne, although that was something which I held back from saying to Tamara. However, during the run of *Le Corsaire,* and very unusually for me, I did go back to her and mention that it could be a plus for ENB to have Company dancers appearing abroad. She had then kindly said that she would try to release me.

Nutcracker Pas de Deux
with Daria Klimentová
Photography by ASH

By then, preparations for **The Nutcracker** had begun to run alongside the ongoing rehearsals and shows of *Le Corsaire* and that meant a part-time reversal to the Daria and Vadim partnership. Only it wasn't quite as it had been because, whereas previously I had held Daria in a way which made her relaxed and comfortable and had been able to bring off some complicated lifts almost with my eyes closed, Daria could feel that I had adapted to other partners. We laughed about my having 'cheated on her' but the sharing did need to continue as I was down to dance five Nephew/Princes with her but also seven with Alina.

Resignations

The fact that we were dancing less together and that while I had, in effect, become ENB's 'leading man', the light was shining less brightly on Daria than it had previously was, of course, causing to us to talk about what the future might hold. We wished that we could dance together for ever (and, perhaps, a bit more exclusively) but, at the same time, we knew that the moment would come when Daria, who had had several surgeries, would need to retire. That painful prospect gradually led to our thinking that, maybe, when she felt she needed to stop dancing full-time, my career might also take a new direction. I was feeling an urge, as well, to experience what lay outside the ENB cycle of productions. So there was a partially formed plan in our minds, although we hadn't expected events to unfold quite as soon as they did and in the way that they did.

Following my conversation with Tamara about guesting, I had been holding onto the hope of being able to dance in a gala in early 2014. However, as the date drew nearer, Tamara explained that she was unable to let me go because I was needed in London when Alina was available to rehearse, adding that ENB would recompense me for my fee. I could see Tamara's point of view. But it's no use pretending: I was crushed by the decision at a personal as well as professional level.

My opportunity to guest in *Swan Lake* and *La Bayadere* in early February with St. Petersburg Ballet Theatre looked safe, however. But there was a complication: the prima ballerina, Irina Kolesnikova, was unable to dance and I was informed that Daria would be a very welcome guest if she was available. She thought that she would be but found, when she asked permission, that she couldn't be spared because she was needed in the studio to begin work with Russell Maliphant on *Second Breath* for the *Lest We Forget* programme at The Barbican that spring (I was provisionally listed for Akram Khan's *Dust)*. Of course, the rational side of me could understand such decisions from the point of view of an Artistic Director but I was very upset for Daria and that was somehow worse than my own, earlier disappointment about the gala.

So, there we were, during the second week of *Le Corsaire* at the Coli, preparing to dance Medora and Conrad together but feeling rather 'down'. All of a sudden, I found myself using the word 'resign' in our conversation and, although Daria didn't think I was serious and tried to dissuade me, the more we talked, the more the idea crystallised in my mind. So I went upstairs to the 'office' area of the Coli to seek advice as to what I needed to do and find someone to give me a piece of paper on which to write my resignation – which I did right there.

It just so happened that David Makhateli, a former Royal Ballet Principal turned entrepreneur who had also acted as a kind of mentor and agent to me, was doing class on stage. I sidled up to him and said, "I've just resigned". "WHAT?" said David, "NOW?" No sooner had I whispered an explanation than David went into overdrive and called Kevin O'Hare, the Director of The Royal Ballet (RB) to arrange a meeting. This involved my dashing out of the Coli, bumping into fans who must have wondered what was happening but, fortunately, didn't ask and panicking as I failed, initially, to find the club venue in Soho which had been agreed for the meeting. I had to stop rushing and say to myself, "For goodness sake, Vadim, calm down!".

I should add here that, quite a while previously, Derek Deane had invited me to join him for a coffee and, as a former Royal

Ballet dancer himself, he had talked enthusiastically about the repertoire there. I listened with interest to what he was saying but the possibility of moving to the RB didn't really lodge in my mind, especially as I had heard that, having been asked about me in an interview, Kevin had said that he was not someone who would ever poach dancers from another company: the approach would need to come from them. But, on the 18th January 2014, I was about to meet him within hours of resigning from ENB.

When I walked in, David was already with Kevin who said that the RB would be happy to have me at any time but that it was important for me not to feel rushed into a decision and to take as long as I needed. As part of my 'thinking process', David took me into the ROH to show me round. I remember we bumped into Christopher Carr who looked at me quizzically with a, "What are YOU doing here?" It wasn't long before he was able to say, "Aaah! Now I know".

All this was going on when the whole of ENB was at the Coli and Loipa waylaid me, seeking reassurance that I was fully aware of what I was doing. That conversation was very uncomfortable because I thought the absolute world of her and didn't want to disappoint her but, at the same time, my mind was pretty much made up.

Harder still was relating to Daria in the midst of the commotion. After all, we had agreed a joint plan for when she retired, a decision which would be *hers* to make, and I had just upended that. I think that Daria was in a state of shock and her first thought was to consider resigning immediately too. Better sense prevailed, however, and she felt that, if she was going to leave at the same time, as we had previously envisaged, it would be preferable all round to do so after Romeo and Juliet at the Royal Albert Hall where, with the RB's cooperation, I might be able to partner her. Although I had been headstrong, the very last thing I wanted to do was to let Daria or ENB down, so I was hugely relieved, and very grateful, when Tamara and Kevin facilitated that June finale.

The *Le Corsaire* performances at the Coli ended with Daria and me dancing together and an amazing flower shower for her – which, although nothing had been said, seemed to suggest that Daria's fans had a feeling that it might be her last ENB show there. My own 'mini Corsaire send off' came at the end of the Saturday performance in Manchester where I was tossed in the air by the boys and cheered loudly as I boarded the double-decker bus which was taking us back to London. I knew that I would miss that camaraderie.

I was glad to be able, subsequently, to be released by the RB to guest with ENB, partnering Tamara and Fernanda Oliviera in Madrid. Being with the Company abroad was a sort of healing experience - maybe not just for me. I very much enjoyed being prepared by Loipa and dancing with Tamara. Both of them generously offered me support, with Loipa telling me, "Remember, you will always have this Cuban mother," and Tamara saying that ENB's doors would always be open. Of course she, too, had moved from ENB to the RB around 14 years previously.

Daria's Farewell Performance

Because The Royal Ballet was preparing to go on tour and I would not have been able to make any debuts, Kevin said to me, "Why don't you go and finish things off?". Therefore, from the end of April to the 22nd June, although I occasionally took class with the RB, it was almost as if I had never left ENB. There was plenty of time to learn and rehearse Derek Deane's in-the-round production of *Romeo and Juliet* in the familiar surroundings of Markova House and Three Mills under the supervision of Derek's associate, Ivan Gil-Ortega.

I was immediately struck by the difference between that version and Nureyev's. Rudolf's Romeo 'owns the stage' and the audience lives the story very much through his eyes. Derek, and I mean no criticism here, devised a show where the overall look of the arena production is of equal, if not more, importance. Consequently, while Romeo dances a lot, there are always other people running around him. That time, as well, all the spotlight was fortunately on Carlos Acosta (guesting with his former Company), Tamara (with whom he had forged a famous partnership at The Royal Ballet), and Yonah Acosta (Carlos's nephew) as Mercutio.

It was a very happy time for me. Daria had, by then, been appointed as a teacher at The Royal Ballet School, to start the following September, and I was simply delighted to be at The Royal Albert Hall for her and with her. Our final performance was, of course, very emotional. Daria had danced with ENB for 18 years and that chapter of her performing life was closing. The only thing which was important for me was that everything should go well and I think it could be said that it did. Daria had rave reviews and I must quote from one (from Emma Kauldhar of Dance Europe): *"Klimentová, as lovely as ever, gave the performance of her life. Certainly, this was no last show by a fading ballerina about to turn 43 the very next day, but an exhilarating performance by a reckless Juliet of some tender young age. How gratifying to see a dancer retire so eloquently – and still at the top of her game".*

The 'send-off' for Daria was spectacular. As we took our bows, the whole arena was on its feet cheering, numerous dancers were throwing flowers, others were presenting Daria with individual bouquets and, then, 'Juliet's Friends' carried in two enormous yellow baskets full of flowers to lay at her feet. It felt like a pop festival but with a real feeling of love in the air. It must have been one of the very best farewells to a dancer in ballet history – exactly what Daria deserved.

Daria's Farewell
Photography by ASH

CHAPTER 8

AN ENB CODA

I have saved reflections on my time with English National Ballet for a separate Chapter because they cover the whole spectrum of my 4/5 years with the Company.

My 'Influencers'

I have referred throughout this section of the book to the Directors, Teachers. Coaches and Stagers with whom I had the privilege of working, but I want to say more by way of special appreciation about ENB's 'home team'.

I owe the deepest possible gratitude to Wayne Eagling who thought I had potential, employed me, took risks in giving me leading roles, persevered with me and thus gave me the most amazing, speedy start to my professional career. But, on top of that, he created a nurturing environment which fostered my self-belief, enabled me to absorb all the guidance I received, and helped me to flourish.

The two members of Wayne's Ballet Staff with whom I had most contact were Maina Gielgud and Antony Dowson and what both of them gave me whilst I was with ENB was invaluable, the more so because they complimented one another so well. Antony was especially helpful with technique, including partnering. If dancers were having difficulty, he would de-construct a sequence and help build it back up again so that it would work better. And, of course, although I have mentioned earlier that the incident was misrepresented in the documentary, Antony's "if you want to be great, you can't be late" warning was a timely one. Maina gave attention to style and, importantly, to the motivation underlying each step. Her explanations as to 'why' a character needed to move or behave in a particular way and the detailed feedback she gave me fundamentally influenced the way I danced and expressed myself and have continued to help me unlock, and show, my passion and soul when I perform.

Later, there was Loipa Araujo who was kind enough to encourage and share her expertise with me in Russian. Her particular focus was on strength and this meant that the classes she gave often pushed me to my limits, which they needed to if my technique was to be 'up to speed'. In rehearsal, Loipa would tend to run a solo or pas de deux, to ensure dancers got the 'feel' and had the necessary stamina, and then offer corrections, fixes and advice at the end. In doing so, she would sometimes convey how leading dancers she had seen all over the world had approached a role or a particular technical issue. That kind of knowledge was very precious – as was the whole experience of working with her.

ENB Overall

There was so much about ENB which was the right fit for me and I have recognised that even more as I have been reliving my years with the ENB 'family'. Being part of a touring company with significant London seasons offered the best of both worlds, especially in terms of leading roles. I was fortunate to be cast to perform them multiple times and was thus able to experiment, get to know my characters better and grow my interpretation. The pace was often relentless but that was another plus as no amount of rehearsal can replicate stage experience. I was given the priceless opportunity to develop my stagecraft from the outset, for the most part in venues where there was little external pressure. In fact, for my first two years. I felt a sense of freedom when I performed which I will probably never recapture. It isn't possible to convey adequately how unbelievable it all was and, even though I still had so much to learn, to be able to feel that all the years of training had been worthwhile.

At the beginning, I also benefited from being part of the corps team where adapting to others, keeping in line, and feeling the movement in unison are essential requirements. Although it necessitated my being exceptionally busy, time spent on stage as one of a group was a welcome counterbalance to my more prominent roles and it was important for me to learn that being in the corps carries not only the heaviest workload, but also a huge responsibility. That appreciation remains very much with me, as does the knowledge of the repertoire I acquired from a different perspective.

I kick myself that I didn't begin to make a note of my performances until 2012, but even a quick scan of the list I have made gives a feel for how broad and plentiful my ENB repertoire was, as does the tabulation below, which is drawn largely from memory. And to think that, for every one of my debuts in principal roles, I was presented with a bottle of champagne – but I don't drink it!

Year	Number of productions danced in	'Leading Man' Roles	Soloist or Featured Roles	Corps de Ballet Roles
2009/10	8	5	6	5
2010/11	5	5	10	2
2011/12	2	2	6	-
2012/13	4	3	1	-
2013/14	3	4	-	-
TOTALS	22	19	23	7

I doubt that there is any other company in the world where that range of opportunity would have been possible for someone as young as I was – and I am thinking here of the way both Wayne and Tamara were constantly extending the repertoire as well as their casting selections.

I must not forget, either, what each of my dozen different partners contributed to my development. Of course, in that connection, there was one particular factor to which I have alluded already – rather a lot..........

Daria

As everyone will know, Daria Klimentová had been a Principal with ENB since 1996 and, in the eyes of many, the Company's Prima Ballerina. She tells her own story in her 2013 biography *Agony and Ectasy: My Life in Dance,* where she says of me, "He makes me a better dancer". That is a compliment I would return with interest and add, "She made me a better partner".

Yes, in the beginning, things were awkward but, as fellow 'Eastern Europeans', with Daria speaking my language, a shared sense of humour, and a willingness to give and receive one another's corrections, we gradually achieved the kind of instinctive communication and emotional rapport which any kind of partnership needs and which, in the case of ballet, the audience is able to connect with. We seemed to share the kind of musicality and 'feel' which enabled us to move as one. Those who described us as the 'new Fonteyn and Nureyev' did so largely because of the age difference between us but neither of us was aware of that: we just saw the character when we were dancing and, in everyday life, the person we clicked with.

The ups and downs of our dancing together with ENB cemented our relationship as did sharing 'adventures' more widely. Every dancer needs a range of life experiences to draw on in order to develop as an artist and, by inviting me to teach at her Masterclasses and to partner her when she was guesting abroad, Daria widened my horizons literally, but also insofar as I was able to watch and learn from many international artists. In terms of my own dancing, she spread me round the world – and not only with her as she also negotiated for me to dance elsewhere, with the Mikhailovsky and Mariinsky companies in St. Petersburg, for example.

I felt very proud to be invited to Prague in the spring of 2010 to celebrate Daria's 1,000th performance and, even more so, to appear with her in May 2014 for her farewell there. The way Czechia acknowledges Daria's achievements is phenomenal and both those occasions can never be forgotten.

Daria didn't stop dancing immediately she left ENB as we continued to perform in galas and she kept herself so 'ballerina fit' that she was able to help me prepare for my roles, especially those abroad, for many years. As I write this, she is still teaching at The Royal Ballet School and acting as Artistic Director for her summer International Masterclasses in Prague. In 2022 she was on the Jury for The Prix de Lausanne and one of the teachers at the Youth America Grand Prix Finals. So, although it takes a different form now, her ballet career remains a highly active one.

Would I have progressed as much as a dancer if I had not been paired by chance with Daria at ENB? There is no way of knowing for sure but maybe the answer lies in the fact that I have written about her here in the way that I have. What I do know is that she opened doors which helped to 'launch' me, she bolstered my self-confidence and she helped to unlock a lot of what was hiding inside me sooner than might otherwise have been the case.

During her performing career, Daria was truly among the ballet elite and I am honoured to have been able to partner such a special dancer. She mentions in her book that dancing with me extended her career by several years but I know that, when she left ENB, she was feeling, indeed grieving, the loss of her full time ballerina life. And, although (or perhaps because) I had most of my career ahead of me, I couldn't be entirely happy dancing without her. We were even more interdependent as a dance partnership than I had realised. My career opened up with, and because of, Daria and it will take a lot to better the years of discovery I had dancing with her. It makes me very happy to know that Daria wrote about her time working with me as being "the very best part".

PART THREE

ROYAL BALLET MOMENTUM
[2014–2022]

REPERTOIRE WITH THE
ROYAL BALLET 2014–2022

[Debuts in bold typeface]

<u>2013/14</u> – The Sleeping Beauty (Prince Florimund); The Winter's Tale (Florizel)

<u>2014/15</u> – Manon (Des Grieux); Symphonic Variations (central couple); Alice's Adventures in Wonderland (Jack/Knave of Hearts – 2 casts); Don Quixote (Basilio); Onegin (Lensky); Swan Lake (Siegfried – Dowell Production); The Four Temperaments (Melancholic); La Fille Mal Gardée (Colas – 2 casts); Afternoon of a Faun (Robbins); Le Train Bleu (on tour in the USA); Don Quixote (Basilio) – on tour in the USA

<u>2015/16</u> – **Romeo and Juliet (Romeo);** Afternoon of a Faun; **Tchaikovsky Pas De Deux; Carmen (Don José); The Two Pigeons (Young Man); The Nutcracker (Prince); Within the Golden Hour ('Tango Couple'); Giselle (Albrecht);** The Winter's Tale (Florizel); **The Invitation (The Boy);** Romeo and Juliet (Romeo) – on tour in Japan; Giselle (Albrecht) – on tour in Japan

<u>2016/17</u> – La Fille Mal Gardée (Colas – 2 casts); The Nutcracker (Prince – 2 casts); The Sleeping Beauty (Prince Florimund); **Human Seasons; Jewels (Diamonds); The Vertiginous Thrill of Exactitude;** Symphonic Variations; The Winter's Tale (Florizel) – on tour in Australia

<u>2017/18</u> – Alice in Wonderland (Jack/Knave of Hearts); **Jeux (Boy); Sylvia (Aminta – 2 casts);** The Nutcracker (Prince); Giselle (Albrecht); The Winter's Tale (Florizel – 2 casts); Manon (Des Grieux); **Marguerite and Armand (Armand); Swan Lake (Siegfried – Scarlett Production);** Swan Lake (Siegfried – Scarlett Production) – on tour in Madrid

<u>2018/19</u> – **La Bayadère (Solor – 2 casts); Symphony in C (1st Movement);** The Nutcracker (Prince); **Winter Dreams (Lt. Col. Vershinin);** The Two Pigeons (Young Man); Don Quixote (Basilio – 2 casts); Romeo and Juliet (Romeo); Within the Golden Hour ('Tango' Couple); **Le Corsaire pas de dex – Fonteyn Gala; A Month in the Country (Beliaev);** Don Quixote (Basilio) – on tour in Japan; Winter Dreams (Lt. Col. Vershinin) – on tour in Japan

<u>2019/20</u> – Manon (Des Grieux); **Raymonda Act 3 (Jean de Brienne – 3 casts);** The Sleeping Beauty (Prince Florimund); **Coppélia (Franz);** Swan Lake (Siegfried); **Dance of The Blessed Spirits**

<u>2020/21</u> – Don Quixote Pas De Deux; Tchaikovsky Pas De Deux; Le Corsaire Pas De Deux; The Nutcracker (Prince); Within the Golden Hour ('Tango' Couple); **Apollo (title role);** Tchaikovsky Pas De Deux; Winter Dreams Pas De Deux; The Sleeping Beauty Act 3 (Prince Florimund)

<u>2021/22</u> – Romeo and Juliet (Romeo); Giselle (Albrecht); The Nutcracker (Prince – 2 casts); **Don Quixote (Basilio – with Birmingham Royal Ballet);** Swan Lake (Siegfried); **Scènes de ballet (principal couple);** A Month in the Country (Beliaev); Swan Lake (Siegfried in Act 3)

<u>2022/23</u> – **Mayerling (Crown Prince Rudolf)**

CHAPTER 9

MORE THAN ANOTHER POSTCODE

On the 19th February 2014, a month and a day after resigning from English National Ballet in WC2E 4ES, I became a Principal of The Royal Ballet (RB) in WC2E 9DD. Someone joked about my 'only changing postcodes' between the Coliseum and The Royal Opera House but, although it is just half a mile in actual distance, it was much further in terms of the world that I was leaving and the one I was joining.

Settling In

I was very fortunate in having David (Makhateli) on hand to help with salary negotiations (I started with a small increase on what I had been earning with ENB) and other contractual and practical arrangements, including the crucial understanding that I would be able to guest elsewhere. Then it was, "Take a deep breath; here I go" on day one, eager for new experiences.

I had walked into many theatres before, but going in through the Stage Door of The Royal Opera House (ROH) felt completely unique because it was to be my new home. Initially, space was at a premium, so I joined well-established Principals in their two-person dressing room, with my base being a sofa rather than an area with the normal work surface, mirror and drawer. 'Sofa camping' wasn't a problem as I knew that I wasn't going to be at the ROH all that much in the coming months and there was the dancers' rest area to relax in if things felt crowded. My companions were very friendly but, when one moves in with existing residents, each with their own habits, and is surrounded by their 'stuff', it's impossible not to feel like an intruder. It was the same when I transferred to Room 16 at the start of the following season. It took time to settle, make it my place too, and be able to be myself in the way I was with 'the lads' at ENB. [Perhaps I should add here that, since 2016, when he was promoted to Principal, I have been very lucky to share with Alexander Campbell. Not only does he put up with my untidiness but we do seem to be 'in tune'. We can joke, be ridiculously competitive at basketball (a great distraction), laugh at ourselves, and speak honestly to one another about our dancing without causing hurt. I remember, when we were both cast as Jack in *Alice in Wonderland* and there was a bit of a hiccup with the double cabrioles, we took to filming each other's stage calls from the changing room monitor and messaging one another with the clips, not always in a

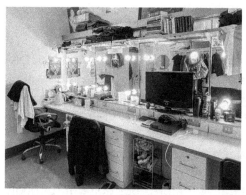

My Royal Ballet Home

complimentary way. I guess that we might make it difficult for other RB dancers to cope with our constant banter (Marcelino Sambé came and went and Cesar Corrales risked joining us when he was promoted to Principal), so it is probably just as well that our dressing room is the one which normally accommodates guest artists for relatively brief periods of time. For me, it has become a place where I can let go and try to be in the right frame of mind prior to a performance.]

I was not all that familiar with the composition of the Company in 2014 as compared with 2009, when I had left The Royal Ballet School. I had been to a few shows and had appeared in galas alongside RB stars, but a dancer's life is necessarily focused and I was living mine mainly within a Vadim/ENB cocoon. The longest conversation I had had with an RB Principal was a year or so previously when I was visiting an orthopaedic clinic. RB dancer looking up, "Hello, Vadim. How are you?" Me, "OK, but I need my arm looked at. How about you?" Other dancer, "I'm totally fine – nothing the matter at all." Me, "I'm not 'off', but….." Other dancer, "No, I'm not 'off' either. I'm fine, absolutely fine……(pause). But please don't say you've seen me here." As I smiled I thought, "Hmm …..right….." and digested the message.

Dancers generally arrive into The Royal Ballet at the beginning of a season within school friendship groups and at the apprentice or corps de ballet level. Being promoted through the Company was, and remains, something of an RB trademark as far as its Principals and Soloists are concerned. I came half way through the year on my own and as a Principal. There were other Principals there at the time who had joined after first appearing as a guest but, at that point, I think that I was one of only three (the others being Federico Bonelli and Nehemiah Kish) who had come 'straight in' as unknown quantities, as it were. So I was a bit apprehensive about what the interpersonal relationships at the RB might be like, especially as I found myself, the youngest Principal at that time, in the midst of huge 'names', including Carlos Acosta whom I had long admired from afar. But, contrary to my fears, I felt included and everyone was really welcoming and generous towards me.

As was my new Director…….. From the outset, Kevin O'Hare seemed very accessible: he made me feel comfortable about approaching him and, although I was very much the newcomer, treated me with real consideration. For example, very early on, in March 2014, when Thiago Soares got injured and was unable to dance Prince Florimund to Marianela Nuñez's Aurora, Kevin asked me how I would feel about standing in for him, especially in view of the fact that it would be only three days after my second show with Akane Takada. "A whole 72 hours," I thought, "With ENB I could have been going on again within less than a day. Of course I will do it." It was almost a shock to

141

be asked and to have the option of refusing as well as accepting. That was a real boost to my confidence

There was an early discussion as to whether I would be involved in new works and I was cautious. On the one hand, I wanted to grow as an artist – I *want* to grow as an artist – but I was concerned that my classical technique might suffer as a result of the strain which some modern choreography exerts on necks, hips and knees. I also felt that I was probably too classical a dancer to do such new ballets justice. And yet, on reflection, there have been additions to the RB repertoire with movement so grounded in classical technique that, by declining at that stage, I probably missed a trick.

Nowadays, I am more aware that Directors have to find a balance between using dancers as they think best for the Company and giving them a 'say' in casting. I think that there might be others who are more assertive than me, but I continue to appreciate how 'open' Kevin is and his willingness to consult and to listen. I also rather admire the way he manages to make me feel content with the outcome of a conversation even though I might not always have got all my own way.

As I had learned when I was with ENB, a change of Director can make a fundamental impact on a dancer but, compared with what I was accustomed to, there were very many other differences at the RB which shaped my working life. The plusses with the facilities were obvious immediately - for example, the RB was resident in its own magnificent theatre shared with The Royal Opera, an arrangement which was evocative of my childhood. I love it that, with Principals' dressing rooms on the same level, I can walk across the stage every day with Rudolf Nureyev's portrait presiding over it. I love it how the sound of singing reverberates throughout the building. The onsite purpose-built studios and a fitness/treatment suite with a range of specialist practitioners felt like luxury. It was even possible to find an empty studio in which I could rehearse on my own out of hours and sometimes even during the day – a real boon. And, whereas at ENB, we had a kitchen area where we could heat and eat our own food, the ROH had both a snack bar and a proper canteen providing a full breakfast, lunch and dinner menu. In addition to the sense of all the celebrated artists, including Nureyev, who had used the very same studios and facilities in ENB's Markova House, the squashed accommodation there had the advantage of bringing the dancers together physically, enhancing the 'close family feel'. So the RB's ethos seemed, on first acquaintance, more like an 'extended family'. I think this is because the dancers are much more dispersed during their working day, several productions are in rehearsal at once, and the various segments of a ballet and ranks of dancers often don't combine until quite near to a production going on stage. Consequently, it took me ages to recognise who everyone was, let alone learn their names. I remember talking about all these first impressions with Papa - and his reaction? "Well, I'm glad to hear that you can get some proper food!"

Daily Class

My recollection of my first day is a little hazy but I know that I went straight into class and found a gap at the barre, trying to be careful not to occupy anyone's favourite spot. The RB's daily classes are of 75 minutes (shorter than ENB's), Principals can choose which of those on offer they attend (another difference), and there are many world-renowned guest teachers on the roster. So there's plenty of scope for variety.

Whatever its duration, wherever it is and whoever is taking it, class is an essential part of a dancer's regime. It's so ingrained in me that it's like brushing my teeth, except that it takes far longer. If I skip doing it for more than two or three days, my body starts complaining, as if my muscles are saying, "Move me". If I ignore that message, I know that I will pay the penalty of losing 'tone' and having to make extra effort to get back into condition.

143

But, more than that, class is about maintaining the 'vocabulary' a dancer needs in order to do his/her job. For example, it's not possible for a male dancer to perform manèges or for a ballerina to achieve multiple fouettés unless they are integral to their daily routine. Some dancers augment class with an exercise regime whereas, until recently when, given enough time, I have tried Pilates, I have preferred to build my strength through constant repetition of the movement, sequences and lifts I will need in performance.

To explain.....I was brought up to believe that a dancer needed a particular aesthetic, "You are not an athlete, so you must not look like a cupboard." In other words, I needed to be slim and strong and avoid any hint of a beefy body-builder image. Sixty nine to seventy kilograms is my natural weight and I can put on muscle up to around 75 kilograms. But, although that might make me a better 'lifter', it also has the effect of restricting my movement. Jumping and bending then become more laboured and I feel more pressure on my knees and ankles. There have been occasions when I have built myself up but my metabolism is such that it can all go in a matter of hours, just like a balloon losing its air. So I have learned to judge what is the optimum dancing body for me and how best to maintain it in 'performance fit' condition.

I should probably mention here as well that people tend to claim that I 'make it look easy'. Believe me, dancing really isn't. I have a good base and an understanding, from what I was taught as a child, that the engine inside me should be not be seen on the outside; but, as far as execution is concerned, 'practice makes perfect'. Well – never quite in my case but 'repeat, repeat, repeat' and 'repeat, repeat, repeat' is the only way I can come anywhere achieving that goal. And the daily class plays a big part in that.

Ballet class tends to follow a traditional format and does not necessarily reflect a company's repertoire at any one juncture. It begins at the barre with pliés, the knee bends which are the foundation of everything, and other stretching exercises which get the feet, legs, back and arms up and running, Even if there's been a show the night before, twelve hours later a dancer's body is sleeping and needs to be woken up, warmed and manipulated so that it can do its work later. Irrespective of any 'fashion', I like to wear a close-fitting tee shirt and tights so that I can see, judge and adjust my movement better, with a warm top and trousers layered over them to start with. At first, everything and everywhere which can hurt does hurt but the pain eases as I heat up and my blood begins to flow. If a dancer isn't warm there is a real risk of 'body shock' or injury when pushing hard in rehearsal.

What each dancer needs from class is a very personal thing and the content set on any one day is unlikely to be a perfect fit for everyone. For example, a long barre and, perhaps, very quick petit allegro centre work suit me less well than having more or less equal time for barre, centre and grand allegro. I also prefer it when the pace of a class is sustained in such a way as to give me a sense of building, building, building rather than an approach with long pauses.

While there is an amount of variation in how dancers apply themselves in class, the environment is normally very disciplined with little interaction as we are all focused on ourselves and the areas of our technique which we feel the need to work on. Everyone is following the exercises as directed but there might be subtle differences in execution and emphasis. Whereas, early in my career, I would use class in order to practise jumping ever higher, in my thirties I need to work on coordination, building stamina, and constant 'cleaning'. I suppose that it's true to say that the better dancer one becomes, the more one needs to push oneself and self-correct to maintain a technical level on which a role can be built.

In this respect, two elements of class are especially valuable for me. The slow combinations away from the barre are important for balance and control; but I don't feel that I'm set up to rehearse unless I've done my daily quota of jumping – and here I mean grand allegro combinations (large, expansive movements including tours en l'air, manèges, grand jetés and cabrioles). These are like a drug for me. So, on my very first day at the ROH, it was thrilling to be able to stretch out instead of always reining myself in and I continue to draw inspiration from watching my fellow dancers eat up the studio space. Teachers can really push us out of our comfort zones by the way they use their voices and I remember a particular class at the Mariinsky with the RBS student group where the encouragement was so loud in the grand allegro that I had the sensation of flying. Then there's the music to provide an extra 'lift'. And, by the end of such a class, even if a touch of fatigue washes over me, I end up feeling stronger, invigorated and better prepared to face the day ahead.

I have to admit that, in the first few RB classes, I had a slight sense of being watched. After all, who *was* this person who had suddenly landed a Principal contract? But there was no time to dwell on what anyone else might be thinking as I needed to gather myself to dance *The Sleeping Beauty* exactly a month after I joined the RB and to occupy the TBA slot in the second cast of Christopher Wheeldon's *The Winter's Tale*.

The Sleeping Beauty

The Prince Florimund vacancy had arisen because Dawid Trzensimiech, an RB Soloist who had been announced to make his debut, had accepted Johan Kobborg's invitation to become a Principal with the Romanian National Ballet in Bucharest. This change somehow made it doubly important for me to able to support Akane (Takada) when she performed Aurora for the very first time.

It was once pointed out to me in an interview that I had swapped being at the 'top' of ENB for appearing at an RB Schools

Matinée. But I went into the RB as 'me'. I didn't (don't) think about my standing relative to others, my position in the casting, or what other dancers are doing. I just want to be on stage, keep on trying to improve, and give the best that I can.

Akane had been preparing with Lesley Collier, herself a much lauded Aurora, so Lesley coached me too. She made me feel very comfortable in the studio as all her corrections were offered with a smile. I also discovered, in the Ashton Studio, that ROH tour parties would stop to watch. But, to this day, the guides always seem to pull them away just as I am about to start my solo, leaving me calling out silently, "Please stay. I like you being there. It helps me!" That's how much I need an audience!

I was familiar with most of the choreography, except the RB's hunting scene, so I tried not to analyse anything too much but, instead, allowed my own dancing to flow freely enough to see me through and to concentrate mainly on partnering Akane. As the run of the production had begun several weeks earlier we didn't get a proper stage rehearsal, but we did have a studio full call. This meant that I needed, and received, help from the Lilac Fairy (Beatriz Stix Brunell) in negotiating the forest scenery on foot and mounting the electric float, which can be hazardous.

On that first afternoon, I waited alone in the dressing room, looking in the mirror at a very different 'professional' hairstyle from the slicked back and heavily gelled one I had used on myself with ENB. I felt very unsure about how the performance would go and, despite all my 'be calm' intentions, my mind was racing to the extent that I even imagined that I might get booed for deserting ENB. However, once I got into the wings, it was obvious that the audience of schoolchildren was super-excited to be there. So, to my surprise, my entrance was greeted with some applause and a few squeals. Being clapped on, even a little bit, was almost unheard of with ENB because audiences tend not to 'know' individual dancers, but it happens regularly with the RB and I like that because it comes across the footlights as if people are saying, "Hello. We're pleased to see you" and "Come on; we're ready for you; we're on your side and waiting to travel with you...." And, in turn, whatever the role, I want to welcome them to join me.

Of course, by the time the Prince strides on in Act 2 of *The Sleeping Beauty,* the audience has been wowed by Aurora's Rose Adagio and tends to think that it must be an easy show for the man. He's had his feet up in the dressing room for two acts – right? Not quite! Also, what he dances is technically very demanding and the Act 2 solo, which comes soon after his entrance, is very exposed. It has to be done cleanly with complete control: there is nowhere to hide on an empty stage and no way of covering up if something goes wrong. It's also weird because the music seems to end in a way which leaves the audience unsure about whether the soliloquy has actually finished. The vision scene soon follows and, when partnering Aurora, it's important to make her look like a weightless apparition not (yet) in the same world as that of the Prince. Then there is there is the

Act 3 wedding solo. There are male variations where, if something goes awry, you can put in an extra flourish to disguise it, but that option is not available to Florimund. Therefore, the rehearsal process also enables one to be ready to make any mistake look as if nothing has happened. It is also essential to me to try to emulate the way in which Nureyev was always able to show the difference between the first and second rounds

Fish Diving with Akane Takada
Photo: Tristram Kenton

148

of coupé manèges. The same degree of preparation obviously goes for the hazardous fish dives where the tempo of the music can so easily disrupt one's practised timing! But there *is* a happy ending to *The Sleeping Beaity* (for a change) and I do love the RB's 2006 production.

After the matinée, Kevin congratulated me with some words which I think were about my being an asset to the Company but, once a performance is over, it is difficult to take in what is being said because one is swamped by one's own emotions and exhaustion. My second show was in the evening and there was more riding on it because it was Akane's and my official debut. I knew that some of my supporters from my time at ENB would be there but it transpired that some critics attended too. I think that both Akane and I felt that the performance went quite well and it was a relief to hear that the reviews and online comments were positive. So, first RB hurdle negotiated – except for the red-run curtain calls....... With ENB, the usual practice is for the whole cast to line up and walk forward together a couple of times before the curtain finally comes down. In galas, dancers normally come on stage in performance order, take a quick bow and join the whole group for a lot of running backwards and forwards and clapping one another. So coming out in front of the curtain at the ROH was a new experience which I must have rushed because, at the Stage Door, some people I knew were saying: "Whatever were you doing?" "If we'd blinked we would have missed you!" "We tried to cheer you but you'd gone!" Accepting applause takes practice too!

The following day, I was rehearsing with Marianela, coached by Alexander Agadzhanov whom I had bumped into about two years previously when he had made an encouraging comment about the possibility of my joining the RB. He greeted me with, "Nice to have you here", which made me feel at ease. I soon learned that his approach to coaching was to consider every move in fine detail – so much so that, the first time I prepared to

149

start my solo, he called out, "Stop!" I thought, "What? I haven't done anything yet". But the 'crash course' he gave me was really helpful in preparing me to partner Marianela within a very short time frame. Little did I realise then that she and I would dance together a lot in the future.

The Winter's Tale

The concurrent preparations for Christopher Wheeldon's new ballet were still at the creative stage in a cavernous space which was geographically set apart from what was otherwise going on in the Company. So much so that I really needed SatNav to locate the rehearsals! The studio had been fitted out with almost the full set which, for Act 2, features the enormous tree which my character hides inside. It looked even more impressive than it does on stage but lurking on it isn't quite the fun it might appear. That's because Florizel has to make his first entrance across the trunk and one needs to tread very, very carefully while also being 'in role'.

Florizel and Perdita
Photo: Johan Persson

Because *The Winters Tale* rehearsals were leading up to the April opening night, the hours were very long – 12.00 noon to 6.30pm with a one hour break. That was no different from an ENB day but Beatriz (Perdita) and I found ourselves needing to concentrate even harder than usual. This was because our roles were being created on Sarah Lamb and Steven McRae with innovative moves which suited their style and preferences – in Steven's case, very quick and busy steps, some of them almost like tap-dancing, and all with right turns (I'm a left turner). Being second cast meant that we had less attention but had to be sure that we were mastering all the intricacies as it went along. Whereas Christopher used his first cast to help develop the solos, where the pas de deux were concerned, he came into the studio with the structure of what he wanted to achieve already in his mind. As this choreography unfolded, it introduced me to holds, flips and other supported moves which were new to me, but Beatriz was a 'Wheeldon veteran' and we were fortunate to have the bonus of an exclusive rehearsal as part of an Insight evening. That helped a lot, not least because we were able to run the long and non-stop pas de deux.

Florizel also dances with the corps and I was glad to be in that mix in a crowded studio, with dancers sitting round the sides (very much as they did at ENB). At the same time, I couldn't help feeling like the 'new boy' and therefore a bit exposed. So my acting was rather restrained. However, once we were into stage calls, my inhibitions disappeared and I think our four shows went well. Certainly, the new ballet as a whole was very well-received and I was privileged to have been included. It was my first neo-classical RB story ballet.

My four Florizels and four Prince Florimunds provided me with an almost ideal introduction to my new Company and I was able to start thinking of myself as being a Royal Ballet Principal. In fact, substituting for another dancer and having three different partners in the space of six weeks proved to be a taste of what was to come in the following seasons.

CHAPTER 10

DIVERSE DEBUTS

I couldn't wait to begin my Royal Ballet career properly at the start of the 2014/15 season. Every dancer is hungry for new roles and I was aware that the RB's heritage repertoire is regarded with envy across the globe. In the years that I have been with the Company, just over 50% of the ballets I have appeared in have involved my dancing in productions new to me and I have been fortunate to experience the work of more than 20 different choreographers.

In fact, although such opportunities inevitably reduce over time, until the Covid-19 pandemic got in the way, I had been extraordinarily privileged to be introduced to several amazing works every year. This gave me a constant sense of discovery and source of inspiration - plus the joy of having a lot to do. I have sometimes drawn a laugh in interviews when I say, "A busy dancer is a happy dancer." But that's so true for me: the, initially novel, experience of rehearsing up to three different ballets in one day is how I would like my schedule to be all the time.

Season	Ballets/Extracts Danced	Debuts with the RB	No. of Choreographers
2013/14	2	2	2/3
2014/15	10	10	9
2015/16	10	8	7
2016/17	8	3	3
2017/18	9	4	5
2018/19	11	5	6
2019/20	6	3	3
2020/21	7	1	4
2021/22	7 (incl. Don Quixote, BRB)	2 (incl. Don Quixote, BRB)	5 (incl. Acosta)

[The dates included in brackets below refer to when I made my debuts.]

Starting Points

Having joined The Royal Ballet Upper School, I don't necessarily have my eye on future roles in the same way as many of my contemporaries who were at the Lower School in White Lodge. But of course, once I'm cast – and Principals are consulted/informed before any public announcement – I am immediately eager to learn more and sometimes tense with anticipation.

My usual first points of reference are videos. These give me an idea of the shape of the work, help me to become familiar with the music, and enable me to begin thinking about my role. What other dancers do with a character is illuminating, of course, but I'm not them and it's essential for me to grow my own interpretation from the inside out, not copy someone else. Therefore, gathering information from other sources – books; old programmes; films, if available - is important too, as is to keep asking myself, "How would I feel if this happened to me?"

I might also begin to commit the choreography to memory as I can then arrive better prepared for the early rehearsals. However, this can be risky as, while that approach is often welcomed, self-taught steps can easily be slightly 'wrong' in the eyes of the stagers/teachers/coaches leading a production. They might also prefer dancers to count whereas I don't usually do that because it makes me feel a bit like an automaton – unless, of course, the movement and the music are not obviously 'in sync'. [While on the subject of 'getting the steps right', it seems to be becoming more OK than it once was for dancers to 'adjust' some of the classical choreography. I'm not thinking of the iconic moments or the addition of 'tricks' to ramp up the excitement but more about allowing for individual technique or preferences. It will be interesting to see where that flexibility leads.......]

A lot of the 'buzz' for me within The Royal Ballet has been becoming acquainted with so many choreographers who were not part of my upbringing where the 'old masters' were the ones to be revered. Nor have I had the benefit of the insights which starting in the RB corps can bring. So the Ashton and MacMillan heritage has been like opening up a 'treasure chest' – particularly that of expressing emotions through movement. I must admit that I have sometimes come fresh to one of their ballets with a bit of trepidation, but it takes no time at all to become completely absorbed, dancing through the stories they weave. Although Ashton and MacMillan are very different choreographers, their narrative works are very naturalistic, with each of them using the movement itself to define their characters and express emotion in way which also gives each dancer scope for interpretation. Not exclusively, of course, but it is through learning and performing their ballets in particular that I feel that I have been able to grow as an artist.

And the days, weeks, or even months of preparation which ensue are all about trying to do justice to their and other choreographers' intentions and reinvent the worlds they have created.

Rehearsals

The rehearsal period is about so many things, both physical and mental. It's a bit like putting a puzzle together. Of course, there is the need to assimilate the steps (from a notator or coach and by oneself) and mould them into one's body (muscle memory is very different from knowing something in one's head), repeating, analysing, correcting, refining and building technical stamina. Everything needs to be done with consideration for one's partner but it's important for me to push in rehearsal because, without my 'machine' turning over as smoothly as possible, I can't feel free to be the character.

All the while I'm going through the steps, I'm thinking about how they make sense for me in terms of the drama – as an obvious example, the way one's arms move into a particular position can differ greatly according to the intention at that moment – and how I envisage the role on me. It's important to immerse oneself in the role in rehearsal and to weight, shade and phrase the dancing to express a real person whose journey the audience can connect with. I even weave a kind of story in my head for abstract ballets, drawing from the spirit of the music.

There've been times in rehearsal when I've needed to learn that less is more or, conversely, that the only way is to go completely over the top. Either way, for me, it's only possible to be instinctively 'in role' if I have a secure foundation as a result of practice. But it's hard to get the balance right because too much rehearsal time, overthinking things especially for a new role, and too many corrections can kill spontaneity and I do have shows where all the steps to go well but I end up feeling dissatisfied with my performance artistically.

Of course, rehearsals are about so much more than the part I play in a particular ballet as there is much to work on with my partner and in terms of partnering itself (which I'll come to in Chapter 13). 'Getting to know' the other characters in the story usually comes later but building the interaction within the 'team' is an essential part of the process even if there are no intricate Romeo and Juliet style fights involved. If mime is part of the interaction, the words behind the gestures are in my head but there are situations on stage, between Siegfried and Benno in Act 1 of *Swan Lake* for example, where we end up almost talking.

Photo: Bill Cooper   Photo: Andrej Uspenski

Contrasting Studio Rehearsals

When I am about to make a debut I find myself wishing that the costumes or a mock up of them could be available for studio rehearsals. Yes, we have fittings and I can break in new shoes, especially if they are dyed, but the cut and feel of a jacket can so fundamentally affect one's movement - for example making it difficult to bend, pulling one's shoulders down or rising up under one's chin - that it really can impact on an interpretation if one isn't used to wearing it.

Once the studio runs are under way it's even more important to go full out to get as realistic as possible a feel for pacing oneself. But the studio is the studio and it's only when stage calls begin that I fully come up against the reality of how a role will pan out for me as that sets me free to express myself. For one thing, there is no option other than to keep going whatever the new hazards, especially lights shining in from the wings which can completely blind dancers if they're not used to it. Moreover, in some ballets, there is 'mood lighting' which can make for all kinds of difficulties. A case in point is the soliloquy which bridges

Acts 1 and 2 in Liam Scarlett's *Swan Lake* where there is always the risk of Siegfried being unable to see the floor sufficiently well to execute his jumps with the necessary sense of abandon and despair.

The scenery may create the mood wonderfully in both abstract and story ballets but it can take a bit of getting used to as well. When dancing Colas's 'bottle sequence' in *La Fille Mal Gardée,* my legs didn't have much room in front of the painted front cloth to bring off the pirouettes en attitude before the split jumps, and moving any further forward would have risked a tumble into the orchestra pit.

Trying Not to 'Bottle It'!
Photo: Tristram Kenton

There is no way of preparing for when things do go wrong – but that does happen occasionally. Such as when my Nutcracker Prince jacket came undone and the hook caught on the Sugar Plum Fairy's tutu in such a way that my face was stuck between Marianela's legs. It was for no more than 20 seconds but it felt like for ever. Similarly, we once became snagged up together in

Act 2 of *Swan Lake* and missed a lift – which absolutely *everyone* noticed (of course they did!).

I like General Rehearsals very much because they not only represent additional stage time but they are a sort of 'preview' with the added dimension which only a live audience can bring. Also, very importantly, I can hear the music fully in a way which can help the characterisation. A good example of this is Solor's first warrior entrance in *La Bayadère* where the full-blown sound makes me feel like a fighter as I leap on – and helps me to 'own' the stage from the 'get go'. 'Generals' can also provide an indication of the tempi the Conductor will adopt, which can sometimes come across very differently from how things sound to me in the studio.

Rehearsals do, of course, continue until one's shows in a run are over but they are taken in the light of how the previous performance has gone and the work and talk is about building on that base.

First Time Flashbacks

I was familiar with the kind of quick steps which **Frederick Ashton** employs (a lot) in ***La Fille Mal Gardée*** (2015) from my second year at The Royal Ballet School, but not with the need to use twice as much upper body movement than I was used to. Neither had I come across his 'half way' lifts which need to be locked into position and can reduce the circulation in one's arms. What I love about this ballet, though, is the naturalness of it all, the 'hey, I'm here' entrances, the casual way that Colas walks, the opportunity to make the audience laugh and the fun one can have performing it. But..........there are difficult jumps and pirouettes which have to be executed with a smile on one's face and a stick in one's hand, not to mention the infamous ribbons.

For my debut, I was paired with Laura Morera, a truly great artist who was just the kind of relaxed Lise that a new Colas

A 'Fille' Pas de Deux
Photo: Tristram Kenton

needs. Asked about dancing with me by *Dance Europe* in 2016, Laura said, "*… It wasn't until a few days beforehand that it all came together. Donald MacLeary rehearsed Vadim and was fantastic for him because it was all about knocking out that prince, that natural presence that he has, and making it more earthy, peasant-like. And he just took it like a sponge. He's an amazing partner, a hard worker and we just got on. I only saw this in performance because we rehearsed so little, but he has such honesty on stage. He's this long, tall, super-elegant man and I'm this short fireball, but it worked…….."* Laura helped me to feel as happy as my character despite all the concentration the role requires. And we achieved the bum lifts, which are much harder than the ones I had done before because Colas holds Lise's hand rather than her leg, all without showing any effort.

I didn't encounter the 'pony poo' hazard in *Fille* until a later run but being able to manage animals is integral to the role of the Young Man in **The Two Pigeons** (2016). The birds arrive with their trainers about a week before opening night for everyone involved to learn the basics – for example, no grabbing them from behind but letting them see your hand go over their head before you hold them. Near the end of the ballet, the Young Man has a pigeon on his shoulder as he comes down the staircase but, as he turns midway, the pigeon can get disorientated and then has to be extricated from the back of one's neck before being presented to the

Young Girl to caress and then settled (hopefully) on the back of the chair.

For me, though, this ballet was memorable for a reason quite apart from the birds or even the welcome 'normal' clothes – and that was Christopher Carr. I am going to say more about stagers later but, after Christopher had admonished me on the basis that the Young Man wasn't Spartacus (!), I really felt that, in his hands, I was 'growing up' as a dancer. It was nice, too, that the ballet is the Young Man's story and, maybe in consequence, less classical than **Sylvia** (2017) which is all about the heroine and leaves Aminta trying to appear manly despite his 'skirt'!

My first Ashton ballet was actually **Symphonic Variations** (2014) and what a place to start! I mistakenly thought from watching recordings that the choreography was quite simple. But everyone was saying, "Just you wait; you'll find out!" And I sure did. The greatest test is that of maintaining one's stamina throughout – not just because the man doesn't leave the stage but because there's no story to bury oneself in. I know that, for many people, it is the most sublime dance work ever; but all that ballerina floating can only happen because of the man underneath her!

'Symphonic' with (L to R)
Yasmine Naghdi, Marianela
Nuñez and Yuhui Choe
Photo: Tristram Kenton

'Scènes' with Sarah Lamb
Photo: Helen Maybanks

Scènes de ballet (2022) is from the post-war era as well and was created on the same male Principal (Michael Somes). However, the sophisticated staccato style is unusual for Ashton, noticeably different from that of today and harder in terms of technical precision. Some jumps need to be made without a preparatory plié and the double tours do not provide for switching legs in the air. It is not unusual to find that choreography which suited a particular dancer needs some very slight adjustment for a subsequent interpreter. In Scènes, because the male role was tuned to the strengths of its originator, the turns are to the right. I could have tried to stay with the original but a small step forward was added in order to put me in a position to do my more natural left turns. The nature of the music and the way the steps relate to it also meant that, very unusually for me, I needed to concentrate on counting in this ballet when it is not something I usually do.

My very favourite Ashton ballet has to be ***A Month in the Country*** (2019), for which I had the treat of being coached by Beliaev's creator, Sir Anthony Dowell. It placed me back in my own childhood – the dacha, the surrounding scenery, the family games and the dancing. I haven't the words to express how it felt

Rehearsing 'Month' with Anna
Rose O'Sullivan as Vera
Photo: Tristram Kenton

'Month' on Stage with Lauren
Cuthbertson as Natalia
Photo: Tristram Kenton

161

to debut as Beliaev, and indeed Armand (in *Marguerite and Armand* 2018), except to say that that both scenarios seemed so real that, once on stage, I didn't really feel like a dancer and even forgot that anyone was watching.

I was cast as Lt. Col. Vershinin in **Kenneth MacMillan**'s *Winter Dreams* (2018) half a year before 'Month' so that was the first time I had 'returned' to a house in my homeland and, as I danced, found my mind firmly in the Urals countryside, not on the ROH stage at all. But Vershinin couldn't be more different from Beliaev. According to the play *(The Three Sisters)* he is married with daughters and knew Masha, who married Kulygin in her teens, since her childhood. Kenneth MacMillan had created the role, the Commander of the local garrison in the ballet, on Irek Mukhamedov with the kind of speciality jumps and full-on passion which reflected his talent and charisma. And Irek came back to the RB to coach the new Vershinins!

Marguerite and
Armand with
Marianela Nuñez
Photo: Tristram Kenton

Winter Dreams with Sarah Lamb
Photo: Alice Pennefather

Realising that I would need to give it my all to come anywhere near the choreographer's intentions, I was striving to do that in rehearsal – or so I imagined. But I was clearly not conveying anything much to Irek who wanted more contrast between the stiffness of Vershinin as a soldier and his ardour as a lover. We talked about the many different things which could be going through his mind at the point when his command has to move on and he is leaving Masha – for example: "Parting is tough right now but, hey, there'll always be another girl at my next posting"; or "I really do care for Masha but I'm a soldier (stiff upper lip) and I mustn't let having to leave her get to me too much, especially as she is so distraught"; or "This has been a genuine, passionate relationship, leaving is heartbreaking for both of us and I can't bear to tear myself away".

Irek also told me that, in order to walk and jump as the character, "You need to 'go over the top', even if you fall over." So I 'went for it' and ended up on the floor. "Much better," said Irek, adding with a concerned frown, "Are you OK?" "OK, but exhausted," I gasped. "Good," added Irek. I think that I might have got somewhere near to portraying Vershinin at my second attempt and, although I had a third performance in Japan, I can't wait to take him further.

That was more than four years after my first MacMillan ballet, **Manon** (2014), which opened my initial full season with the RB. I had joined ENB shortly after they had toured the work and people had kept saying, "What a pity you missed *Manon!*" But there I was preparing to dance Des Grieux and I really couldn't ask for more, including being able to work with both Lauren Cuthbertson, who unfortunately got injured, and Sarah Lamb, both of them experienced in the title role. Looking back now, I know that my debut performances were only a first draft of Des Grieux. I was being the character in my head and was able to bring off the fiendishly difficult throws in the bedroom and swamp pas de deux, but I was aware that it was one of those roles which needs to be developed over time. Even so, I remember being so overwhelmed after my first performance that I said to myself, "I can retire happy now.....!"

In the Act 3 Swamp with Sarah Lamb
Photo: Alice Pennefather

Since my arrival into the RB in 2014 had coincided with preparations for **Christopher Wheeldon**'s *The Winter's Tale,* it was great to find myself cast as Jack, the Knave of Hearts in *Alice's Adventures in Wonderland* (2014) the following Christmas. He was my first young, silly boy character (which I probably was myself back then). The role was full of enjoyment but, with Alice's journey as the focus, Jack's involvement in the ballet is patchy. Also, in Act 3, he has to stand for 10 minutes in the courtroom 'witness box' getting cold before his pleading solo. Although due to debut later in the run, with Francesca Hayward as Alice, my first show was actually on opening night with Sarah Lamb. In another Wheeldon ballet, *Within the Golden Hour* (2016), back with Beatriz Stix Brunell, each principal couple has also to dance as part of an ensemble and that brings its own challenges for dancers who are no longer accustomed to timing and aligning with others.

George Balanchine couldn't be more different in terms of movement but each of his ballets requires extraordinary stamina. It will come as no surprise that the **Tchaikovsky Pas de Deux (TchaiPas),** in which I debuted with the RB in 2015, is the one where both dancers become most exhausted while smiling throughout. But **Symphony in C** (2018) isn't far behind in terms of needing to hide increasing tiredness, although the First Movement man does not have to sustain his spark for as long. Diamonds in **Jewels** (2017), a homage to Imperial Russia, has an altogether different energy. It doesn't follow the usual structure of a classical pas de deux but the challenge is to come on stage and dance 'expensively' to reflect the most costly of the jewels. All of these ballets are simply wonderful to dance.

Debuts with a Difference

I think that my mind went first to the neo-classical works in the RB's repertoire because it was through them that I was experiencing the adventure of the unfamiliar. Many of my classical RB debuts, along with *Romeo and Juliet* (2015) and *Apollo* (2021) were more about acquainting myself with different productions of some dozen works I had performed before.

That said, although I grew up dancing a heritage edition of Basilio's solo from **Don Quixote** and I had performed the whole ballet with Alina Cojocaru in Tokyo, working on Carlos Acosta's version (2014) was more like approaching something completely new. Much of the difference is to do with the musical arrangement. The most spectacular element of the Act 3 variation is more usually accompanied by the brass section of the orchestra whereas, with the RB, the music goes faster and has castanets playing.

It was hugely gratifying to work with Carlos (alongside Akane Takada for my debut) and, despite what I have just said, the role of Basilio contains a lot of his preferred movements and is therefore very physically demanding. But Carlos wanted to push me further. "You are too young for the easy version," he said – I was 24 at the time – "You have to include more tricks." So I took the opportunity to test myself and my fitness by including some jumps of my own. The good thing about Don Q, when dancing the whole ballet, is that one can play to the comedy and have fun adding Spanish flourishes.

Don Quixote
Photo: Andrej Uspenski

'He's Behind Me': Coppélia
Act 2 with Gary Avis
Photo: Bill Cooper

Another classical ballet with which I was familiar was **Coppélia** (2019) as it was regularly performed by my school in Perm and therefore held a mix of memories. Nevertheless, the RB's version felt very fresh and was pure enjoyment to be cast in because it has both comedy and pathos. There is, however, a choreographic quirk: all the accents in the music are on the down beat and that makes it harder for the man – well, for me at least – to execute the jumps. It's a very real reminder of just how symbiotic the music and movement usually are in ballet.

My Third Romeo
Photo: Alice Pennefather

I came to Kenneth MacMillan's ***Romeo and Juliet*** (2015) not much more than a year after partnering Daria Klimentová for her farewell performance in Derek Deane's 'in the round' production for ENB. I have also written earlier about my first outing as Romeo in the Nureyev version and the reasons why that was, and remains, very special to me. As was the case with *Manon* a year earlier, there was a mid-rehearsal change of partner, with Sarah Lamb coming to my rescue again. MacMillan's Romeo is a 'killer' of a role because he's so busy running around, with a lot of interaction with other characters, but I find Nureyev's choreography much harder technically. MacMillan's fighting is in league of its own and, for every Romeo, getting the spacing and rhythm right with 'his' Tybalt is an art in itself. I have danced a fourth Romeo more recently (Veronica Paeper's *Romeo and Juliet* for Cape Town City Ballet) – a version where, for me, the very different choreography makes both Romeo and Juliet feel very young indeed, as does Nureyev's in my view.

Albrecht in ***Giselle*** (2016) was another re-visit debut but, although Sir Peter Wright's production is very different from the one by Mary Skeaping, in which I had had my very first leading role, the classical choreography is largely retained. This meant that I was able to come into the studio feeling more confident than is usual for me and with many of the recurring ENB corrections still in my mind. With the RB, I think I was more aware of the different sides of Albrecht than I had been when I was only 19: the Count of Act 1 who doesn't understand love and plays with Giselle's feelings and, then, once she dies, the man who suddenly grows up knowing what it is to lose the woman he has come to adore. The story may be set well in the past but the overwhelming emotion of love, the anguish of loss, the manipulation by adverse forces, and the despair of not being able to make reparation are so resonant today that they almost don't need to be

Giselle Act 2 with Marianela Nuñez
Photo: Tristram Kenton

acted. Neither does the exhaustion which is very real even if the version being danced does not include the famous 32 entrechats six – and neither ENB's nor the RB's does, although the RB production has some. However, their presence or absence doesn't change the feeling I always have at the end of *Giselle* - that of having danced a masterpiece.

Of course, the RB's production of **The Nutcracker** (2015) is also by Sir Peter Wright and I came to that in my second full season. The role of the Prince varies from version to version and, with the RB, it is relatively minor in terms of stage time to the extent that dancing it can almost feel like being in a gala. For the famous pas de deux, at the end of Act 2, both the Sugar Plum Fairy and the Prince usually wear blonde wigs and the pins and glue involved in making sure that they don't fall off are rather painful. So my early performance memories are of trying to smile (perhaps grimace?) through a certain amount of discomfort.

The one debut which was virtually a repeat for me was as Jean de Brienne in Nureyev's **Raymonda Act 3** (2019) which I had danced with ENB, not only in the same version but also in a costume and against scenery borrowed from The Royal Ballet for whom Nureyev made the work.

It's astonishing to think that Balanchine's **Apollo** (2021) dates from 1928 because it seems so modern. The title role is one to 'die for' and its choreographic demands are considerable, especially as quite a lot of the movement is in a squat position and involves the use of muscles which aren't familiar with that kind of exertion. But what an honour to have that challenge as the RB emerged from the Covid 19 pandemic.

I had been a 'baby Apollo' with ENB and, when I began to think about being him over nine years later with the RB, I was aware of bringing a more mature perspective to the role. I hadn't initially bargained for the fact that Patricia Neary (who was staging the work) would also have her own, distinct ideas about the character. We had scarcely begun on the steps when she pounced on me, "Oooh, naaah. Who taaaught you?" I replied, "Mumble, mumble", trying to dodge the question because everyone is aware that there is a bit of 'competition' among the various stagers of The Balanchine Trust. But Pat pushed me to give a name and her reaction was exactly as I had anticipated! Yet I know from working with her – which is great, of course - that even Pat's 'true version' of Balanchine ballets can change as the years go by.

The main difference in interpretation between the two coaches was that Nanette Glushak's Apollo becomes playful as he matures whereas Pat's grown up God is angry with the world. This fairly fundamental mood change was easier to accommodate than some more subtle adjustments, for example to arm positions. Even years later, my body tried to insist on moving as it did on the previous occasion and it took real mental application to perform in the 'new correct' way immediately I was expected to do so.

When some ballets or sections are 'run' in the studio, it's possible to pace oneself or even mark the steps but, with Apollo, I found that the only way for me to rehearse was to dance 'full out'. It just wasn't possible to find a 'half measure'. Perhaps, in part, my approach reflects how fulfilling it is to inhabit Apollo. One can completely 'disappear' into the role and identify completely with the character's development from birth to full manhood, discovering so much about life and himself along the way with the help of the three muses (thank you Yasmine Naghdi, Mayara Magri and Anna Rose O'Sullivan). I was really 'into' that journey, especially at that moment in time.

Apollo Rehearsal with the Three Muses
Photo: Andrej Uspenski

Apollo
Photo: Helen Maybanks

New Work, New Choreography

Having missed out on dancing Don José in Roland Petit's version with ENB, I was thrilled to be chosen for Carlos Acosta's new *Carmen* (2015) with Tierney Heap. From my experience of being second cast in *The Winter's Tale* I was familiar with the need to learn from the back as the concentration is inevitably on the dancers who will create the roles. Therefore, in *Carmen,* while Carlos built his ballet on himself

As Don José
Photo: Tristram Kenton

170

and Marianela, Tierney and I settled into doing just that, trying as we went along to enact the drama and to think also about how we would master the various scenic devices and props. But I had a lucky break as Carlos needed to be able to watch what he was making as well as feel the movement on himself. So he would sometimes put me into the role, including some of the stage business, and then adjust his intentions in the light of what he saw. As a result, I felt very much part of the creative process in a rather unusual, and very special, way.

Where personal debuts in new productions are concerned, it doesn't really come much bigger than *Swan Lake.* Sir Anthony Dowell's production, in which I debuted in 2015, doesn't include much dancing for Siegfried in Act 1, but it had appeared at first that the new version (premièred in 2018) would give him more to do. Liam Scarlett saying that he wanted to focus on the Prince's journey had led me to think, erroneously, that the outcome might be similar to Nureyev's version where Siegfried is 'on the go' throughout the first act, including within a pas de six. In the event, Benno gets the lion's share of Liam's Act 1, with the Prince standing around at the side of the stage. It's no wonder Siegfried is dispirited!

Because Liam arrived with what he wanted to achieve firmly in his mind, for the most part all the principal casts were in the studio together trying to help him realise his vision. The additional preparation for me was mainly concentrated on the interaction with the international Princesses in Act 3, on a new pas de deux in Act 4 and on the heartfelt soliloquy which leads into Act 2. In the last case, the movement needed to be adapted to provide for the wonderful scenery to transform from outside the palace gates to the forest/lake in a way which wasn't overly obvious to the audience. Speaking of adjustments, it was interesting for me to see/hear how some of the new choreography required the music to be played rather differently from how it was originally written.

White Act in Rehearsal; Black Act on Stage
Photos: Bill Cooper

It was an unbelievable privilege to be involved in the development of a new production as the first cast and to dance the opening night with Marianela Nuñez. I will never forget the audience reception because it reverberated as if the ROH was staging a rock concert rather than a classical ballet. Speaking of which, I am honoured that a solo is being created on me by the ground-breaking choreographer Michael Clark, who famously melded punk and pop with ballet.

CHAPTER 11

ON THE DAY OF A SHOW

The Lead In

The extent to which a dancer feels 'ready' to perform 'on the day' can be affected by so many things in addition to the rehearsal process: how familiar one is with a particular ballet and its style; whether it is the first, second or last show in a run; how one's body is feeling generally; specific physical 'niggles'; how a range of conflicting emotions (excitement, insecurity etc.) plays on one's mind ; how much sleep one has been getting. All of that 'baggage', and sometimes more, comes with me when I go into a kind of 'Vadim zone' up to a couple of days beforehand.

That happens almost subconsciously as my mental preparation intensifies, my sense of anticipation builds and my need to conserve my energy is amplified. I think that people around me can feel that I am somehow 'different' and my somewhat reduced messaging will signal to my family that I have gone into 'pre-show hibernation'. The night before a performance I can find myself fighting with my mind – on the one hand, looking forward (a lot) to sharing my dancing and my character's story with the audience but, on the other, trying not to stress about particular aspects of a role or to think about the responsibility, especially if it is an opening night – (there are no previews in ballet like there are for other forms of theatre). I don't think that I ever manage to banish negative thoughts entirely, but I find that I can weaken them if I lose myself playing the piano or a TV game. Sleep never comes easily and the Heathrow flight path directly over my home is not on my side.

The early part of a show day is the same as any other: get up; have breakfast (that can be porridge and/or toast/ham/cheese

173

so as to feel full); catch the usual train; arrive in time for class. Class is essential for me if I am to be able to dance full out later. If the evening performance is a triple bill, a rehearsal session might follow but, generally, I am able to go home, enjoy the quiet (the ROH and any dressing room are not the most peaceful of places) and even have a nap. About six hours before I am due on stage I will have some lunch, followed by a protein-rich snack some four hours later.

Then, three hours plus beforehand, I'll travel back to the ROH – at which point my battle with myself not to overthink everything goes into overdrive. When I dance a role many times in quick(ish) succession or a work has returned to the repertoire after a relatively short period, my mind can feel more free. But, when one has two or, at most, three shows after a gap of many years, there is much more space for doubts to creep into one's head – especially about executing the choreography well enough to really inhabit the character or feeling under extra pressure because there is insufficient opportunity to work one's way (back) into a role and then develop it further from performance to performance. I can find myself focusing negatively on something if it's not always worked in the studio but, equally and illogically, I can dwell on an aspect which has been going well and begin to ask myself whether I will fail in that respect in the performance. Almost anything and everything - unwieldy props, an uncomfortable costume, the tempo taken by the orchestra etc. – can be a cause of worry.

It is only on rare occasions that I feel what I call 'special'. I don't mean that in the usual sense of the word but, rather, that everything seems aligned: my thoughts in the right place; my body ready; my stamina assured; and my mind free of stress. The more it can be like that, the better the artistic outcome.

But, either way, there comes the point in the day when I have to put myself together........

Getting Ready

I usually go to the Principals' hair and make-up room around two hours beforehand. The process there can be long and complex – I have already mentioned the Nutcracker Prince's wig having to be glued as well as pinned in place – but, even for 'ordinary hair', there is powder to be rubbed in and oceans of spray to be applied. The RB tends towards a 'natural look' for men's make-up, with even less when there is filming, whereas my personal preference is for more, especially around the eyes.

The RB's Principals have their own Dressers who deliver the costumes to our rooms a couple of hours before curtain up and, if required, help us to put them on and take them off. Once my tights are on, my track suit bottoms go over them immediately and then, about an hour beforehand, I'm off to the studio to warm up, with the amount of barre and centre work varying according to how my body is feeling as well as the requirements of the performance. Maybe I'll practise some of the steps, visualise the narrative, remind myself of recent corrections, or envisage how I will remain in character if the music and my dancing part company at any point. Partners may see one another during warm-up and it can be helpful for me to lift the ballerina a little bit so that my body can be reminded of what lies ahead. But, although we do interact, we are probably too self-absorbed to have much of a meaningful conversation.

If I'm not on in earlier Acts (e.g. *The Sleeping Beauty*) or the first/second work in a Triple Bill, I can be in my dressing room with the stage video on the screen and the music playing. About 20 minutes ahead of the start (or my entrance), I like to be on stage moving around to keep warm. As I am shaking my legs, I am also feeling more 'hyped-up', maybe with my 'performance face' on. Company members are very supportive but, especially at the last minute, verbal encouragement from them, any expressions of anxiety in my vicinity and reminders from my coach can make me feel more nervous – and extra nerves can drain one's energy. For the same reason, I would rather not know if 'important people' are in the audience, although it's rather nice to discover afterwards that a member of the Royal Family or someone from the dance world whom I admire has been watching.

And I'm 'On'.......

I'm sure that some dancers are already 'in role' while waiting in the wings but it's not until I'm in my entrance position and hearing 'my' music that my head switches Vadim off and my character on. The energy and presence of an audience ready and waiting to go on a journey confirms that 'transformation: I can feel them paying attention and their warmth induces confidence even when a 'clapping on' is inappropriate. I've heard it said that what a dancer shows on stage is a magnified version of who they are as a person. That might be true but, in every performance, my colleagues play an absolutely essential part in what the audience sees. RB artists are always so fully involved in the action that they make it feel like 'the real thing' and help my character unfold. Curiously, the scenery, which does so much to create the environment I am lost in, doesn't

usually impact on me, at least not initially – except for *Winter Dreams* with its family dining table at the back which cannot fail to take me straight 'home'.

In some cases, the principal man is dancing almost as soon as he enters (occasionally with big leaps) but, especially in story ballets, it's preferable to have time to settle into the scene

Manon Act 1 Solo
Photo: Alice Pennefather

before the first solo. For example, Romeo can hang around with his mates in the square in Verona and at the Capulets' house before he has to dance properly, whereas Des Grieux is expressing his feelings for Manon comparatively soon after he wanders into unfamiliar surroundings for a young student. Conversely, having an early solo can help me leave technical issues on one side and push me deeper into the character.

The feeling of being so 'totally in it' that the only world which exists is the one on stage can be enhanced for me by being tired and sweaty, as in the balcony pas de deux in *Romeo and Juliet,* even though that is by no means the end of the ballet. It's strange that, the more weary I am, the more I can let go because my mind just allows the dancing to happen. [Actually, that well-known balcony sequence is preceded by one of the most fiendish of costume changes. Romeo exits the Capulet residence behind a man who is sick centre stage and every second he takes to vomit and walk off shortens the time available for Romeo to change his top (in a suitably screened off corner of the stage).] Which leads me naturally to..........

What Happens in my Interval

Although it would sometimes be preferable to be able to stay on the stage and 'in the moment' during an interval, this is not allowed because of scenery changes. A red light indicates that everyone apart from the technicians must leave and not return until it goes off – and waiting for that moment can feel as if it's for ever when one needs to get back there, even to simply walk around.

However busy an interval might be with a costume change or having hair and make-up refreshed, I don't go back to being Vadim. My character is still there but he is on a pause button. I mainly stay on my feet and on the move so as to keep all my muscles warm and mobile and I try not to brood over anything which might not have gone so well or issues over which I have

177

no control myself. However, I do receive notes in the interval – not so much corrections about what has passed but reminders about what is to come, not only for me but for my partner as well. Sometimes, also, people try to draw me into conversation about completely different, unconnected things (problems on the Piccadilly Line even!) which I really need to keep switched off until the show is over. I think that I ought to create a "Please Keep Away" sign because interaction of any kind has the effect of pulling me out of where (and who) I want and need to be at that moment.

When My Character is Off Stage

It's easier to maintain focus when one's character isn't on stage for part of an act or scene. In a narrative ballet, I usually stand in the wings, often in darkness, full of the story and perhaps visualising what is still to come.

That can sometimes have quite an emotional impact, but in different ways. For example, in *Manon,* one's horror at what the Gaoler is doing with and to Manon transfers naturally into the way Des Grieux reacts as the scene proceeds. However, in *The Invitation,* where two young cousins are preyed on by a married couple, I was in the wings while the girl was being raped but, as the young boy I was playing, I had to return to the stage looking innocent and unaware of the terrible crime.

Occasionally, in the darkness, one bumps into another character from the ballet, maybe one's adversary on stage: I remember passing Tybalt (Thomas Whitehead) after I had killed him during a performance of *Romeo and Juliet* and him casually remarking, "But I like you, by the way.....!"

Being off stage during a classical pas de deux is a different matter entirely. Each of the adagios has its own challenges, with lifts which can easily sap the energy of the man but, with luck, the applause provides a moment in which to regain composure and position oneself for the solo. That done, I retreat into the wings, bend double to recover my breath, hit my muscles, and shake my legs. In fact, while the ballerina is dancing her solo, I'm a bit like a boxer withdrawing to his corner: I grab a tissue; mop my sweat, sip a drink, reapply rosin and then compose my face, mind and body ready to maintain the essential sparkle in the coda.

After the Curtain Finally Closes.........

No matter which ballet I have been in, I feel 'spent' – perhaps more so emotionally than physically – as the curtain comes down. It is a unique and usually fleeting moment before I become Vadim again but the effect of the story stays with me for longer, maybe more in my heart than in my head. I suspect my adrenalin level must be abnormally high as there are times, standing there, when I'm not certain who I am or it doesn't seem as if I am the person who has just been dancing. I suppose it's a mixture of being overwhelmed and a sense of fulfilment.

The curtain calls are directed by the Stage Manager and one goes with the standard flow for a particular production: the two leads on their own; the whole company moving forwards and back again on cue; the flowers for the ballerina and now, sometimes, for the men; the 'thank you' to the Conductor and the orchestra. The order of the 'red runs' which follow is also pre-determined and, yes, it is rewarding to hear a roar for individual or combined bows in front of the curtain even if it feels surreal (especially if I know I could have done better). Everyone is free to acknowledge the

Curtain Call
Photo: Rob Sallnow

audience in their own way and partners usually try to gesture towards various areas of the audience as a way of saying, "Thank you; hope you enjoyed it." Sometimes, I think according to the level of applause, it is suggested for the final 'appearance' that we include more of the auditorium by walking to each side of the stage in turn.

I believe that there have been standing ovations at some of my RB performances, such as at a new production (*Swan Lake* in 2018) or for a ballet which hasn't been seen for a while (*Don Quixote* and *Coppelia* 2019), when the audience reception is for everyone concerned. Foot stamping can definitely be heard from the stage but, at the ROH, we can't really see well enough to know whether people are on their feet to applaud or are just wanting to hurry away!

Afterwards, there is scarcely a moment to thank my partner and no time to 'be with myself'. Once the applause has died down, the stage is quickly filled with ballet staff offering comments and/or corrections, with me sometimes adding my own critique. Then there are guests of management to meet and photos to be taken. Moreover, if the show has been a debut or the first for me of a revival, my mind rapidly moves on to how I might do better at my next attempt. [I think that, even if I have enjoyed the performance, it is a legacy from my training that I am pre-set to think about continuous improvement.] If the show has been the last in the run for me, I can be mourning the fact that I will not have a further opportunity to dance the role for some considerable time.

Sooner or later I am back in my dressing room, with a much-needed chance to breathe and get changed and showered as quickly as possible. In some cases, though, the process is a lengthy one – especially after dancing the Prince in *The Nutcracker* where one has to wait patiently while the wig is unglued from one's hair. It is either in Hair and Make Up or in my dressing room that I eventually sit down – often for the first time in well over four hours. It's only then, mostly alone, that I can relax, stretching my thighs and hamstring, applying some cream and downing some recovery drinks.

Occasionally, after a show, the dancers who have taken the lead roles are invited to join a drinks reception or a dinner for Royal Opera House supporters. I am happy to represent the Company but I have to admit that a 'drinks only' event is not altogether easy when one is longing to rest one's legs. Dinners are more to my taste (!) and it's good to be able to have conversations with the guests. I like to be able to hear about the lives and thoughts of others outside ballet although, if I ask questions, they do tend to be deflected back to me. I don't think that I will ever be able to see myself as a Principal Dancer who is the centre of attention at a table. And yet .....In November 2020, there was a completely unexpected surprise which brought a big smile to my face. A picture of a horse pinged onto my phone and, when I looked further, it turned out that *Vadream,* owned by a Royal Ballet benefactor whom I have had the pleasure of sitting next to at some after show events, had won the Maiden Fillies Stakes at Newmarket at odds of 6:1. If I'd known I could have backed her!

More usually, I wrap myself up to help my body 'come down' from performing as slowly and safely as possible and then head to and out of the Stage Door. Some RB dancers, including me, refer to what happens then as 'Act IV'! The Stage Door is an historic meeting place for the audience and artists and many people are kind enough to have made the choice to wait, sometimes for an hour or more, often in the cold (even if they are allowed inside) when they could be having supper or be home already. Besides which, there is the opportunity to chat with people who have been at the show and care about what they have seen. It is especially rewarding to meet and hopefully encourage young people who are training to be dancers or who are the audiences of the future. Some of the people waiting have travelled internationally to

I'm In There Somewhere

see my performances and I appreciate that very much; others have been following my career for years and have seen me grow.

They will have noticed that, as time has gone on, I have got slightly better at accepting compliments. But, deep inside, I remain uncomfortable when someone praises my performance: even saying, "Thank you" can feel conceited. However, when someone tells me, for example, that they have become a ballet fan as a result of seeing me dance, it feels more OK because it's a win for everyone concerned in the art.

All in all, even if it is late, being there signing programmes or posing for selfies is always enjoyable, sometimes real fun and I can find myself going home with several gifts (often of food!).

If the RB is performing abroad, 'Act IV' can be rather different and last much longer, with tables for dancers to sit at and security guards lining people up to file past for autographs (e.g. in Japan) or so many ballet fans waiting that dancers can become completely buried by them in the street or square outside (e.g. in Madrid). The presents given me overseas are more 'exotic', often more numerous and, of course, equally appreciated.

Home Time

The London Underground is a bit of a contrast to the ROH stage but it gets me home in about 40 minutes – by which time it will usually be 6 to 7 hours since my pre-performance snack. At that point in the night, I'm really hungry and a ready-made meal or soup is ideal. I usually eat while catching up with my parents, reading personal messages on various apps. and scanning social media posts.

I suppose that this 'normal' activity should help me to 'wind down', but it doesn't and, however tired I might be, I find it almost impossible to relax into sleep. Even if I'm not completely happy with my performance – and I rarely, if ever, am – the exhilaration of being on stage produces a 'high' which takes ages to subside. Added to which there is a certain elation at having completed my time in one role or anticipating what is on the schedule for the following day.

I might have climbed one kind of mountain on the day of my show, but the job is not done: there are always more challenges to come.........including ones which cannot be predicted.

CHAPTER 12

A CAREER ON HOLD

As much of this book was being written during the Covid-19 pandemic, what was unfolding inevitably loomed large and I made a number of diary entries as well as thinking chronologically about my life.

There was no way I could have anticipated that what had been a relatively smooth career trajectory was shortly to be 'put on pause' and life was to change fundamentally for the whole world. It was possible to see from the many social media posts, online blogs, articles written for magazines, and podcasts that dancers' reactions to the ever-changing situation throughout all those months were very individual.

This journal, which is less than half of what was written originally (!), is just me sharing my perceptions and personal ups and downs during a period like no other.

A Broken Rhythm

March 2020

I suppose the question that was hanging in the air for everyone on the night of Swan Lake on the 12th March was whether everything might have to stop. There was definitely a different vibe and the company seemed to be dancing as if it might be for the last time, for a while at least.

The performance itself was very special and the audience was on fire. At the end, they cheered us for ages as if they didn't want to ever let the curtain close. The Company didn't either. Unexpectedly, Marianela suddenly stepped sideways and turned to salute the Swans, so I quickly followed suit. I learned later that many dancers had taken that as a sort of goodbye signal. Everyone in the theatre sensed deep down that that night was a turning point. I was lucky. I'd had my first two shows; but there were many other casts who had been working so hard and hadn't got on stage.

[14ᵗʰ March: message advising the dancers to take a long weekend; update about our collecting anything we really needed; 19ᵗʰ March: ROH closed; 23ʳᵈ March: UK in 'lockdown'.]

The dancers who could return to their families abroad were allowed to do so, but that wasn't really an option for me as I was worried that I might give the virus to my parents. So, like so many people, I was on my own in my flat hearing daily from The Royal Ballet about what might be offered via Zoom, listening in on Company meetings, and being told that everyone's salary would be cut by 20%. This reduction was not good news for us because, just like anyone else, dancers' various financial commitments are related to their earnings. Yet, at the same time, I knew, we all knew, that we were among the very lucky ones: there were so many people in a far worse situation than us, including freelance dancers and other performers and creatives. We also understood that this was going to help The Royal Opera House to manage its finances without any ticket sales and therefore, perhaps, secure our future - again, we were fortunate as there were smaller companies fearing for their survival. It was also explained to us that, under the furlough arrangements, the dancers could not be required to do anything; but the Company would provide virtual classes, in which we could participate on a voluntary basis, dance mats and regular updates via e-mails or Zoom meetings.

April 2020

Initially, things seemed relatively busy; then five of my guest dates wobbled before the CANCELLED messages came thick and fast. But I actually felt quite happy - it was a sort of release from the relentless routine of a very active life and a chance to recuperate physically. Maybe, I thought, I could find out what it was like to be a 'normal person', at least for a while. But I soon realised that I needed to come up with a survival plan to keep in condition and, also, to be sure to challenge

 myself every day. I was very grateful for what The Royal Ballet was providing, and it was nice to see familiar faces on screen, but I felt I needed variety. So I searched and found a number of different classes on YouTube which I hoped would help me keep in shape even though I only had the space to jump up and down.

Keeping Going in my Flat

I had reached a 'special number' on my birthday which made me realise even more that I was losing precious moments of a fleeting career which I could never get back. Everyone's routine had changed, of course, but dancers have a very particular way of life, a time-limited one, which, as I turned 30, was completely upended.

By this stage of the lockdown, images were appearing across the internet of dancers finding imaginative ways of keeping themselves in condition and people looking to dance for exercise. Various companies were mounting 'digital seasons' and streaming videos from their back catalogues. All this activity had the effect not only of bringing the dance community together but also of raising the profile of dance in a way which could be of benefit in the future.

May 2020

By the second week in May, the restrictions were eased to allow people who couldn't work from home to begin to go back. I thought, "That's me!" My flat was feeling more and more like a cage and going shopping wasn't providing enough of an escape. However, Elena Glurjidze, whom I knew from when she was a Lead Principal with ENB, said that I could use her Masters of Ballet Academy Studios on a confidential basis. This was amazing; it was freedom! At last, I could stretch out and flex parts of my body which had been parked for weeks. Just as importantly, I had a structure to my day. No more staying in bed and doing class when I got round to it. Instead, disciplined once more, I was "off to work" at 9.30am with my mix of recorded classes.

Having a studio gave me a renewed sense of purpose and I usually did class for about two hours followed by various sequences and solos. This was a period without any immediate goals. But I had an overwhelming feeling that it was time which I would never have again and that I needed to use it well. The best way of dealing with the uncertainty was to limit my exposure to the daily news and to try not over-think things. And I did nothing on Instagram for several weeks. I wanted to share my elation in moving freely again but, when others were still doing class in their kitchens, it would have felt wrong to show how very lucky I was to have a studio to work in.

June 2020

The cancellations of several Roberto Bolle and Friends Galas was especially upsetting because these were affecting my ability to give money to my family. This was a really low point for me: it almost felt as if everything I had been working for and aiming for had been taken away. Could I really call myself a dancer if I couldn't perform any more?

Then, out of the blue, Kevin rang to explain about the three concerts the Royal Opera House was going to put on for live streaming and to ask whether I would perform Dance of the Blessed Spirits at the second one on the 20th June. It felt as if I had been thrown a life-line: I had something to aim for again. We talked about how the rehearsal process might work and agreed that I would prepare myself in the studio with the help of the recording made when Sir Anthony Dowell coached me at an Ashton Re-Discovered event in 2016.

It was really strange going back into the Royal Opera House after 3 months. When I arrived for a run-through the day before, I had to go to the audience door. The people there asked my name, searched a list for ages, took my temperature and directed me to go up via the stairs and escalator, along the terrace (where I disturbed all the pigeons which had settled there during lockdown) and in through the secret door to the Blue Core. It felt as if I was going to a hospital appointment!

My changing room still had the feel of the day after the show and I was completely alone there as I got into costume and did my make-up. Then, onto the stage which felt huge and dark, although only about 70% was available because of the way they arranged the musicians down the side, and the steps I had to walk down were very narrow and difficult to see in the dim light. I wanted to give Kevin a hug, but all I could do was to wave him a distant 'hello' through the blackness.

On the day of the streaming, I was very nervous and very happy at the same time. It was amazing to feel the stage - that particular stage - even though there was no atmosphere - just empty seats where normally there would be an audience sending me their energy.

During the build up to the performance and on the day itself, I couldn't help but think of how much all dancers, whatever stage of their career or training they were at, were missing performing and about how so many families had been artificially separated by the lockdown. So, I felt that loss and sadness very much as I danced. But, in my mind, I also wanted to give hope to everyone everywhere that we would all be performing again and we would all be seeing one another soon. I was very touched that so many people wrote about it afterwards, saying what their feelings had been.

Their words were more beautiful than I could have expressed myself, but we all seemed to be needing our spirits lifting somehow and it was a privilege to have been the one to represent that through dance.

Dance of the Blessed Spirits
Photo: Tristram Kenton

After a couple of days, however, it all went quiet and I felt very flat and negative. There wasn't anything to work for and it was more difficult to motivate myself to do class. My brain was a whirl of valuing my career more because it wasn't there and wanting it more because I couldn't have it. It was almost as if I no longer had the only identity I had ever really known.

July 2020

[Updated Government regulations: dancers able to train and work part-time (flexi-furlough).]

In early July, it was permissible under the guidelines for other people to be with me in the studio.

So Alex (Alexander Campbell) and Claire (Calvert) came along. We took turns to give class along with some from YouTube and (keeping our distance!) we would talk between exercises, push ourselves to work harder, and play mini ball games.

In the Masters of Ballet Academy Studio

The brief period when we were together made me realise how very strenuous a regular Royal Ballet day really is and how important it is to share the process with other people.

Then Daria returned from Prague ready for the Royal Ballet School's Summer Intensive and, after she had quarantined for two weeks, I timed my class sessions in the studio to fit around her teaching. This really gave me a filip because, finally, I could practise pas de deux and try to get myself back into shape as a partner. On some days we almost killed ourselves, but those studio sessions were great fun.

Many more dancing dates were then either cancelled or plunged into uncertainty. In fact, when I left to teach at the Masterclasses in Prague (which somewhat miraculously did take place) and take a short break in Turkey, I hardly knew what clothes and kit I might need over the coming weeks.

A Stop/Start Autumn

September 2020

Early in the month, there were positive signs of ballet coming back throughout Europe and I was glancing enviously at the social media posts of friends whose companies were already rehearsing full length, adapted shows. I managed two performances in Latvia but my time in Slovenia was cut short at the final rehearsal by the sudden implementation of 'red zone' regulations for returning travellers to England.

At the ROH, the atmosphere was subdued in the midst of all the Covid-19 safety regulations. Half the Company had class in three studios in the morning and the other half was scheduled for 1.00pm. Perhaps it was my imagination, but it seemed as if were we all a bit inhibited in our interactions with one another. There was a lot of eye and eyebrow movement and some looking sideways as if to see who would be the first to say, "Hello".

For the first two weeks I was back, Marianela and I were timetabled for very short rehearsals and, although I soaked up every moment, I was always left wanting more - much more. We were one of the 'couples-who-don't-live-together' bubbles whereby we would only dance with one another. The protocol for us both was to be

Masked Up in Rehearsal
Photo: Rachel Hollings

tested for Covid-19 twice a week to ensure that we were virus negative and for neither of us to have any physical contact with anyone else in the Company. This meant that we generally didn't have to wear masks when we rehearsed together. That was a relief, because when we did have them on, I realised immediately that I couldn't see Marianela's legs to partner her properly or judge my own jumps because my view of the floor was distorted. Besides, it is very different to find one's 'performance face' when covered up and gasping for air.

During an Equity Meeting, we were informed that our salaries would, at some point, be set at 90% rather than at the 80% level we had been paid for several months. Good news for us but, again, in the world outside, so many people were suffering terrible hardship and there was worrying talk of massive job losses. In the midst of so much uncertainty for the performing arts the RB was protecting us from the worst levels of anxiety.

However, and I appreciate that it might sound selfish to say this, many dancers were continuing to feel very keenly that there was no end in sight and were experiencing the very different kind of stress which comes with not having enough to do.

In addition, because of the work I had put in abroad, my body was saying to me it was ready to go and it wasn't easy to tell my brain that it still needed to wait. Whatever stage of their training or career dancers were at, it seemed, after 6 months, as if enough time had been stolen already.

October 2020

During the week before The Royal Ballet: Back on Stage performance there was, once again, a welcome quickening of pace and a feeling of momentum building. I'd like to say that it was as it is for a normal show but, of course, the circumstances were very different with a whole raft of social distancing rules.

In fact, we were so separated out that, when Marianela and I were asked by the BBC what the arrangements were for everyone else, we couldn't really answer. Although I don't think it was broadcast, Marianela told the reporter about my joking that there were so many instructions I was forgetting the choreography! I only found out later that most of the Company hadn't seen one another without masks until the full stage run-through. Being able to reconnect was therefore doubly special.

The Thursday Stage Call was filmed, I suppose as a back-up, and I was uneasy about my dancing being recorded after more than half a year away from performing that kind of classical piece. Nerves and insecurity were blotting everything else out and there's nothing like doubting oneself to undermine enjoyment, even around an event as significant as that one.

So to the 9th October itself.....The orchestra occupied the Stalls area and there was a far away, socially distanced audience of VIPs, health care workers and Upper School students from The Royal Ballet School.

Don Quixote Pas de Deux
Photo: Rachel Hollings

We had all had to see to our own hair and make-up and then, in our case, wait until nearly 9.00pm before going on. During the wait, we were set apart from the buzz which was building within the Company. So we came on almost in a vacuum, in an eerie silence and, of course, without the set or the dancers who usually create such a great atmosphere in Carlos Acosta's production of Don Quixote. The applause actually sounded surprisingly loud and Marianela and I were lucky to get a red run curtain call, not so much for us but so that the conductor and orchestra could be properly acknowledged.

We were, of course, so grateful to be able to perform again. But I felt numb and disappointed with myself. I wanted to be positive but my mind wasn't where I wanted it to be. I suppose it's like that sometimes. You want something so much - too much - that you end up spoiling it for yourself.

At the end, there was euphoria and celebration all around me and I was so happy for the RB. After all, having been pulled away from our stage, we had overcome many obstacles and were back on our feet as a Company. What's not to like? But I was conscious of being rather quiet while others, including Kevin who could not contain himself, were bouncing around celebrating.

I believe that about 20,000 people purchased the streaming and, in the days that followed, I heard about some of the comments which were being made. Apparently, I had returned from lockdown 'more mature' than before. The irony was that, in contrast to what was being said about me, I wasn't feeling at all like someone who had been on stage for over 10 years and it was clear that any come-back wasn't going to be as straightforward as I had been hoping for.

Anyway, older-looking or not, at the end of that week, I was glad of the chance to relax, just in little ways like being able to go home and not need, immediately, to have to reply to e-mails, apply recovery cream, or clean my flat. And I didn't have any urge or need to teach, be interviewed or be a funny man on Instagram which, in combination, had seemed at times to be my alternative career. Just slouching in front of the TV became very attractive.

It was a short-lived respite, of course, because, while there was good news about the two Royal Ballet Live programmes being made available for public booking and confirmation that an adapted version of The Nutcracker would be performed through December into early January, no further mainstream shows were being planned until the end of March at the earliest.

So, once again, we were on the roller-coaster of not knowing quite what the future would bring. This added to my longing to find a way of feeling more like a proper full-time professional again. But there was no prospect of guesting abroad to fill the gap.

[15th October: news that London would be moving into Tier 2, with more restrictions; 22nd October, the Royal Opera House sold its Damien Hurst painting of Sir David Webster for £11m.]

I was gradually becoming less sore with myself over my Don Q performance and somehow more content. I suppose that, over the whole period since the previous March, my mindset had been like a barometer with my mood as changeable as the weather but, before the two November shows, the needle had moved into a more sunny zone. I went to work, got on with it, and lived with things how they were rather than dwelling on what might have been.

World Ballet Day (WBD) went ahead on the 29th October, billed by the ROH as a "global celebration to unite the ballet community as it faces the challenges brought about by the Covid-19 pandemic". It was the 7th year for WBD which, since 2014, has seen collaboration between major ballet companies, each streaming 'behind the scenes' videos according to their time zones. Marianela and I were among those shown rehearsing and, when we walked into the Clore Studio before our session with Christopher Saunders, the studio lights and the cameras almost made it feel as if we were going on stage. So we both 'went for it'

TchaiPas Rehearsal
Photo: Rachel Hollings

with the Tchaikovsky Pas De Deux as much as we would in a performance. We were quite pleased with the way it had gone that day and were looking forward to the following Wednesday - except that, 24 hours later, and just when the Company was geared up ready to perform again, news started to break about the likelihood of another lockdown.

[31st October: announcement that England would go into lockdown from 00.01am on the 5th November until the 2nd December with all theatres closed.]

November 2020

Kevin was very supportive in the way he communicated with us and provided 'signposts' when he could. So it wasn't long before he explained that the show on the 4th November would be expanded to include items from the planned second programme in order that more dancers could perform in front of a live audience. Soon after that, it emerged that professional dancers and choreographers could continue to train and rehearse in a Covid-secure studio environment and were permitted to use theatres to prepare and perform behind closed doors for streaming or recording purposes. Classifying dancers as being among those unable to work from home was a real improvement on the first lockdown, when the difference between office workers who could carry on from home with relative ease and those such as ballet dancers who would need to fundamentally reinvent their daily lives had not really been understood. It was also a huge relief for everyone.

The good thing about TchaiPas is that it doesn't have any really tricky steps to worry about, so it's possible to go on stage and 'just dance and enjoy it'. For the 4th November Royal Ballet Live, I was able to put all the parts of myself together, I went on eagerly but without tension, I could really feel the music, and I was so happy to perform for, and feel a connection with, a real audience whose presence ramped up the excitement.

On this exhilarating night, the uplifting response from the auditorium reminded us that the fourth wall, as they say, is absolutely essential to us as performers. It wasn't just about the applause: everyone there seemed to be living every moment with us all, even though the medley of works contained little actual drama.

The way I felt afterwards was completely different from my reaction in October. I was reignited with the joy of dancing - chatty, happy, feeling alive again, not really tired at all. I even got home unusually early because the dancers involved in the divertissements did not have curtains calls at the end of the evening. As I snatched something to eat in my flat, I felt the glow of having had some very precious time on stage 'doing what I do' once more.

[9th November: wonderful news that a vaccine (created by Biontech and manufactured by Pfizer) had been proved to be 90% effective in trials; the Job Retention Scheme extended to end of March]

We were straight back into rehearsals for Le Corsaire as part of The Royal Ballet Live Streaming

- *in the studio for five days, then a stage call, a day filming, and, finally, the performance itself on the 13th.*

It was a terrific programme with the classics, RB heritage works, modern pieces and new choreography all represented and I wanted everyone who was watching the streaming to be thinking to themselves that the whole RB was wonderful. The filming definitely brought with it some pressure which hadn't been there the previous week and I was conscious of being apprehensive again.

Le Corsaire Pas de Deux
Photo: Emma Kauldhar

There were probably no more than 30-40 RB Company members and ROH staff watching but they were in the stalls and they were obviously cheering as loudly as they possibly could. And there was one other important difference from the performance on the 4th........Because the man in the Le Corsaire pas de deux goes off stage left where no one was looking, I was able to take a couple of sips of water at the key moment before going 'all guns blazing' into the leaps and jumps. I enjoyed that night. The tempo was spot on for me and I judged myself as having done OK.

I believe that the reviews and other posts online were very positive overall for both the live and the streamed shows and that was great for the company because everyone on and off stage had been pulling together so hard and we had kept the Covid-19 virus away from all of our performing bubbles. Kevin summed up the feeling perfectly when he wrote us all a lovely note to say "thank you", telling us that 10,000 people had already subscribed for that second streaming. That was a big boost to dancers' morale.

I did see some of the comments afterwards, including the perception that I had emerged as a "changed man" (again!) and that Marianela and I provided "the fireworks missed on bonfire night". But these shows were all about the team, including everyone who had been working so hard on the additional measures to make it possible for us to dance. And, in any case, praise from outside doesn't mean that I can say, "Phew - top of my game!" to myself. I have to work just as hard to improve the very next day.

It felt good to have been on stage two weeks running but it left us all even hungrier to tackle a full-length work. However, another four weeks lay ahead of my next performance so it felt like entering another tunnel with very little dancing light coming in. The general talk that theatres wouldn't be able to open at full capacity until April 2021 at the earliest was depressing for all performers everywhere.

But I must divert from ballet for a moment to say how almost magical it was during the second (November/December) national lockdown to be able to walk around Covent Garden and other parts of London with almost no one else about. I noticed things and went along streets I hadn't seen since I arrived to join The Royal Ballet School in 2006. It was possible to pause to admire individual buildings and features without anyone in the way or any surrounding noise. At the same time, it was incredibly sad to see all the theatres closed as well as so many shops boarded up.

[26th November: announcement that London would return out of lockdown to Tier 2 on the 2nd December with theatre audiences capped at 1,000 people or 30% of capacity.]

Christmas Nuts

December 2020

In the first week of December, the rehearsals for The Nutcracker gained pace with each scene taken separately in order and strict "don't touch one another" measures in place on stage. I learned that the two Senior Répétiteurs, Gary Avis and Samantha Raine, had been through every element of the corps activity in great detail to adjust it with social distancing restrictions in mind. Such an achievement!

Although the London Underground had been noticeably more crowded all week, it wasn't until the Saturday after the end of lockdown (5th December) that, following another Stage Call, a nasty shock awaited us as we stepped out into the

Piazza: people - lots of them; too many of them! Not as many as in the photos of the crowds in Regent Street and outside Harrods, but enough to make us worried. RB Soloist Meaghan Grace Hinkis summed it up perfectly when she posted pictures on Instagram with the caption, "Our Covid safe bubble has been burst!"

We were acutely aware that, if someone in the Company caught the virus as a result of how people were behaving outside, the knock-on effect would be really serious. But it proved impossible to hold back the tide.

[London moved into Tier 3; 15th December was the fourth and last performance of The Nutcracker.]

At first, the shows were cancelled only up to Christmas Eve and, only later, were the subsequent performances abandoned as well. For all the dancers who were lucky enough to have got on stage there were others who had been working hard in anticipation of their debuts in one of the four main roles. Some of them were cast in minor roles as well and were therefore enjoying some stage time, but two of the Princes who were due to debut later in the run missed their opportunity altogether.

In my case, it felt good on that Friday afternoon to be part of a complete ballet again. It isn't just about going on stage and dancing but having the experience of all the preparations in the dressing room as well. Interestingly, from far away where I was backstage, it was possible to detect that the audience was much smaller. There was none of the usual hum coming from the auditorium.

So Lucky to Have
My Nutcracker Shows
Photo: Rachel Hollings

The reduced numbers on stage and small changes, such as Drosselmeyer putting the necklace on Clara and giving the badge to the Nutcracker, were almost imperceptible. The audience seemed to be willing everyone on and making as much appreciative noise as they could from behind their masks. I was content in myself and, for the first time since March, I felt that I was back at the level I had reached then - in other words, where I wanted and needed to be. The Sunday matinée was equally enjoyable for me. The adrenaline was flowing again and it was nice to sense that the performances were making people feel happy.

But what next? At that point, what lay ahead was half of December, a Company break through to the 19ᵗʰ January and a space beyond which might or might not include rehearsals for future productions. The contrast with the same time the previous year couldn't be greater.

[19ᵗʰ December, London put into Tier 4; regulations the same as in the recent lockdown, allowing professional dancers to continue to work in the studio and film for streaming.]

An e-mail arrived from Kevin saying that The Nutcracker live stream would not be able to go ahead, there would be no Company classes before Christmas, and that it wasn't expected that any rehearsals could begin until after the January break. My first thought was for those dancers who would have been involved in the live stream. That message must have been especially heartbreaking for them. Everyone was confused as to why the ROH needed to be closed down and a sympathetic Kevin clarified that the decision, taken by the ROH on logistical grounds, had been accepted by him very reluctantly. We could go in and collect any belongings on the Monday or Tuesday and regular updates were promised.

That message had a certain familiarity but it somehow felt more ominous than in the previous March. Then, we had left the building with no idea what was ahead and with the hope that the lay off would be short. Now, we knew only too well that we were going back into a world of uncertainty and, for dancers, a bare life with no obvious goal in sight. It was really difficult to grasp and almost impossible to accept.

Out in the wider world, things seemed even more surreal than they were in ballet. Not only were there bans on travel out for most people in the UK but, one by one, countries in Europe were preventing flights, ferries and trains from entering from the UK so as to protect them from the newly mutated version of the virus. All that alongside the possible effects of Brexit!

But then there was some good news: the RB dancers would not only have the opportunity to attend class at the end of December but, also, if they wished, during the holiday break. This was imparted during an online Company gathering where Kevin made a really generous speech thanking everyone for their efforts and attitude during such a turbulent year. Having that meeting also brought the Company together after the few days when we had felt very shaken up by the suddenness of the ROH closure.

Not surprisingly, soon there were pictures of dancers in their homes popping up on Instagram with "Here we go again!" captions. But Elena Glurjidze came to my rescue, as she had before, and allowed me to use her studio over the Christmas period.

During the holiday weekend itself. BBC4 showed The Royal Ballet All Star Gala comprising extracts from across the RB's streamed shows. Cameras can never quite capture the essence of a live performance but it was great that ballet - we - were on free-to-air TV.

December 2020/January 2021

And so to the turn of the year......... I'm not a great one for looking back because my sights are usually set firmly on what lies ahead and I don't see much point in making New Yew resolutions, especially when so much is outside any individual's control. But it's almost impossible not to compare 2020 with the previous calendar year.......

I appreciate that everything is relative: I was one of the luckier ones as I was able to perform much more than most of my Royal Ballet colleagues. But a 60% reduction for me reflects the plight of the ballet world. Nearly half of my 21 opportunities to be on stage were pas de deux for galas and 15 of the shows *were in the first 10 weeks of the year before Covid-19 took hold.*

When I went to check the logbook where I record all my performances, I found that I hadn't written anything after 12th March 2020. That omission probably said more about how I had been feeling during the previous 10 months than I had been prepared to admit to myself.

Back in Hibernation

January 2021

[4th January: England in full lockdown for the third time; travel restrictions tightened]

Here we were, in limbo once more, with not even a distant performance date to spur us on. But, relief - it was clear that we could use the ballet studios throughout the Company's official mid-season holiday. There were not all that many dancers coming in, but I wanted to go to the ROH to maintain the feeling of being part of something and to have an external teaching input. The lack of people made the atmosphere feel rather downbeat and, behind my mask, I was not only feeling unstable but I was also losing my proper facial expressions.

[News backcloth positive about the development and roll-out of the vaccine (various kinds); but new variants more transmissible and, very sadly, death rates rising]

It was easy to get dragged down by information overload. So I turned off the news, went into Elena's studio and put on some ballet music. The minute

I heard it, I was able to lose myself completely and dance my heart out. The best possible antidote to gloom!

I also recorded some combinations for when my parents were watching on Viber and, despite all the disruption, they were saying, "Whatever has happened, you have not become a worse dancer." It was no bad thing either to have Papa remind me how hard the pandemic was making life for his students and young dancers on the threshold of their careers.

After the mid season break, there was a Company meeting where Kevin confirmed the disappointing news we had been fearing - that, because Covid safety was paramount not only for the dancers but also for the musicians and technicians, it would no longer be feasible to think in terms of a return to performing anything large scale. Christopher Wheeldon would start on his Like Water for Chocolate - working, in the first instance, with real-life couples. Maybe I would be cast in a Triple Bill in the summer but, at that moment, I was out of the frame as far as any focused preparations were concerned.

Answering questions for the Japanese magazine DANCE Shinshokan also gave me a bit of a buzz, not least because it felt good to connect with a country where I love to dance. Then the Wellerman sea shanty climbed to the top of the charts and I decided to 'perform' it on Instagram. If I couldn't be on

stage with 2,000 people watching, I could at least dance for an online audience of many thousands. The bonus, when I 'let go' like that, even though I am on my own in the studio, is that I can forget everything else that is going on. I seem to keep saying that, but it's true.

February 2021

Had it not been for Instagram, I would not have received an unexpected message from Derek Deane. "You are such a fantastic example to all of those coming up behind you and also to your contemporaries!! It's a blessing for me that I was given some time to be able to work with you and help you go forward!!! You should be very proud, as I am, of what you have achieved and for what still lies ahead of you. Bravo, Vadim." It is very special, and very unusual in the ballet world, to have someone say something like that and I felt humbled and elated at the same time - especially as it came from Derek who would himself admit to being a very hard taskmaster.

Derek's mention of "what still lies ahead" was well-timed because, on the 19th February, it was seven years since I had joined the RB and that made me conscious (again!) that my career clock was ticking.

[22nd February: a four-step 'Road Map' announced by the Government to ease restrictions and provide a route back to a more normal way of life; the date for when theatres could re-open set at 17th May]

Kevin then felt able to share some of his plans for summer performances consisting of three Triple Bills. This should have been a eureka moment but, understandably, there were a lot of 'perhapses' and 'not after alls' as permissions were sought and the continuing need for social distancing was worked through. In common with all my colleagues I was longing for the moment when the words, "We're back" meant the usual kind of 'back' - no 'ifs', no 'buts', no 'maybes'.

March 2021

Of course, the only thing was to put on my thick skin and get on with it. But get on with what?

On the one hand, there were a lot of offers coming my way so, in theory, I had a packed few months ahead of me. On the other, the quarantining and testing required at both ends of any guest appearance made it feel like a computer game where things keep getting fired at you along the way and you never reach your goal.

[3rd March: Budget announcement of many more millions to support theatres]

Then Paris Opera Ballet (POB) confirmed the earlier invitation for me to have four performances in Rudolf Nureyev's Romeo and Juliet. To my mind, this ballet is a masterpiece and I have such fond memories of being this Romeo with ENB, so I got started on rehearsals by myself. The leading role is incredibly demanding for the man but starting to dance it again felt liberating and very special. However, my elation - which was verging on bliss - was short-lived as a total of three weeks of quarantine were out of the question for any dancer who needs to be 'ready to go', especially in Nureyev's ballets.

It soon transpired that, had I gone to Paris, I would have missed the second and third Triple Bills at the ROH and, by then, Kevin was talking about George Balanchine's Apollo being included. Yes, please! That was another role that I had really longed to revisit and, of course, I also wanted to be able to reconnect properly with the ROH audience. Completely coincidentally, the day that Kevin mentioned Apollo, I had posted a photograph on Instagram of myself in that very ballet. Almost immediately, I contacted Maina Gielgud, who had been my coach at ENB, for a recording and watching it made me even more eager to get started, but with fingers firmly crossed that it would actually be able to happen.

My telephone conversation with Kevin about Paris and the RB's May to July programme was on the 12th March, a year to the day when the 2020 run of Swan Lake had been dramatically cut short. Referring to that 'moment' in an interview for the online magazine DanceforYou, Kevin said, "It was the first night cast.....and it was just incredible. The atmosphere was beyond electric from the moment the curtain went up........... Obviously Marianela and Vadim were superb but also right across the company. It was a standing ovation ...... it was as if the audience didn't want them to go." Asked about how the dancers were faring, Kevin added, "They've opened their eyes to other things...........(which have).........added layers to them. Someone like Vadim has grown even more - other people have noticed it too. As good as he was, it's as if he's grown up, even greater than before." I hope that it doesn't appear immodest to quote that, but the fact that Kevin

211

chose to mention me was incredibly touching - even if I wasn't sure that I could altogether agree with him.

For much of March, in addition to the Paris conundrum, I was trying to work out how to manage the summer holiday period from early July onwards. It was like a jigsaw puzzle with all the Covid-related pieces missing, except that the World Ballet Festival in August seemed just about do-able and I was keen to be in Tokyo. It's a wonderful tri-ennial event and it would enable me to return to Japan (YESSSSS!) - unless the third wave of the coronavirus in Europe grounded us all or I couldn't get the certification necessary to travel.

That was an added concern because all the talk of vaccine passports was making it appear that they would only be available if one had had both jabs - the first of which, for me, would be in May/ June at the earliest which, with a 12 week gap, would take me well into July, August or even later for my second.

During the week before the official announcement of the RB's 2021/22 Season, I appreciated being able to meet Kevin in person and to hear some very good news about his plans. However, I suppose because everyone was still needing to be cautious, the detail wasn't going to be released until June.

Previously, when I have had this kind of meeting with Kevin, I have been very much the listener, accepting what was coming my way in terms of roles and scheduling and understanding that decisions were made in the overall interests of the Company. This time, I approached it with a newly found resolve to make sure, as well, that I had the opportunity to do what felt right for me and my career. I don't know quite how it came out of my mouth, I hope not discourteously, but, in my head, I was thinking, "I have to catch up". "I need to dance whenever and wherever I can". "I must make things happen". And, perhaps most importantly, "I need to be on stage to recapture the feeling of being an artist." Whatever I ended up actually saying, Kevin's response was very receptive and understanding and I was given freedom to dance elsewhere if the dates fitted in with my RB commitments.

The official announcement of the RB's forthcoming season in outline was on the 23rd March, coinciding with the anniversary of the first lockdown. Strangely, in many ways, it didn't feel as if 12 months had passed, probably because I had spent so much time on 'stand-by'. A schedule packed with rehearsals, performances and travel somehow seems much longer. Inevitably, on such a date, I couldn't help but think (again!) about the world keeping on turning, although I was shouting, "Pleeeease stop!"

I am very conscious that, even when there is no pandemic, ballet operates in quite a closed environment and that one can easily sail along insufficiently aware of life's wider picture. I had tried to remain connected with how really awful the pandemic had made things for so many people, the turbulence it was causing and the various policy developments but to balance that with my personal need to keep focused and therefore sane.

There were actually some plusses: I had more time for myself; instead of being a rushed chore, cleaning was an almost therapeutic pleasure; and, best of all, could go to bed free of thoughts about 'tomorrow'. But the enforced rest, especially during the early part of 2021, made me even hungrier to perform.

My pattern of activity in March was what was becoming a habitual mix. Firstly, I was receiving several invitations to dance in June/July which were either unlikely to come to fruition or I couldn't accept if I was to see my parents. It felt great to be wanted but, alongside feeling grateful, I was saying to myself, "Here we go again"; "Please call me for the autumn or later"; "It's too upsetting now". Meanwhile, I was also juggling different kinds of mainly online teaching: individuals, small mixed ability groups and, in addition, for Danceworks, a series of much larger classes.

After all the levels I had been trying to accommodate in virtual lessons, it was a treat to be asked to coach some Royal Ballet men and to be relating to professional dancers. Occasionally, young Artists approach me for advice, "Erm....can I ask you something?" "Yes, of course." "So I want to be a Principal like you. How can I get the chance to show what I can do?" I talk to them about working hard, taking responsibility for their own progress, and sharing their ambitions with 'management'. But have to remind them that I have no influence whatsoever. I don't think they would believe me if I told them that Principals too are always longing for more in terms of roles, shows and stage time - especially during 2020/21.

The Shows Go On

April 2021

Easter was wrapped by a week of class at the ROH augmented with practice in Elena's studio. Then something very unusual happened! After nearly four months, my name was listed for rehearsals. I stared at it wide-eyed. Could this be for real? For me this was for *Within the Golden Hour* as anticipated, but other dancers were putting the final touches to *Draft Works* for streaming or learning the two pieces by Crystal Pite, also for the 20th Century Choreographers triple bill. In combination, the May to July programmes had been very sensitively planned to ensure that as many of the Company as possible at every level could be on stage as much as practicable.

I had initially thought that, maybe, the 'tango' pas de deux and the ensemble segments in 'Golden Hour' wouldn't feel 'enough'. However, as soon as my partner, Anna Rose O'Sullivan, and I got started, I realised that it was probably going to be an ideal 'easing in'. I had recently been trying out some of Apollo's quite slow moves but, otherwise, I had been concentrating on keeping on top of my classical technique. Christopher Wheeldon's choreography makes very different demands on the body and his lifts are 'puffy' at the best of times. So being in his ballet proved a really good way of way of preparing for a 'full throttle' return to the stage.

When I came to realise that it was in May 2019 that I had last danced in 'Golden Hour', I found myself thinking that it wasn't really all that different from the normal pattern of the repertoire at the ROH. The longer the spacing the harder it is to get the choreography back into one's muscle memory, even if one knows the steps. However, the big plus this time was that I would get four shows. Confirmation of the casting for the Balanchine and Robbins programme soon followed and I was down for Apollo and the Tchaikovsky Pas de Deux with four and three performances respectively. In fact, there were going to be 11 days near the beginning of June when, including the General Rehearsal, I was going to be on stage eight times. I couldn't wait!

Mid April saw a reopening of restaurants outside and that, combined with an unusually bright spell of weather and the most amazing tree blossom everywhere around, lifted everyone's spirits.

If I had thought to hold back the passing years, my second pandemic birthday on the 16th April served as reality check. It was a work day but there was time for lunch and a celebratory game of dressing room basketball. Papa's students had been filmed singing Happy Birthday and holding little cakes with candles on them - lump in my throat time. One card I received carried the message, "Life is not a Rehearsal" and I said back to it, "You're telling me - that's why I'm feeling the need to squash in everything I can once we're let out of the starting blocks again."

Late on my birthday evening, the sad and sobering news came through that Liam Scarlett had died, aged only 35. Over the next few days, the press and social media were filled with reports and no little speculation but, whatever the reasons for Liam's departure from the RB in 2019, his early death was a tragic loss of someone so young and so talented.

May 2021

Early May saw rehearsals continue in anticipation of being able to perform again from the 18th but, also, with a cloud of fear hanging over us that our hopes might be dashed again and, in my case, no little frustration about how I was progressing (or not) towards being performance ready. I think that Mikhail Baryshnikov once said, "I do not try to dance better than anyone else. I only try to dance better than myself" and that sums up exactly how I feel.

Coincidentally, just when Within the Golden Hour required quite a bit of synchronised dancing from all involved, I had reached the part of this book where I was thinking about my time with ENB and how helpful it had been to dance alongside others when I first graduated. Rehearsing Golden Hour became more and more enjoyable and this reinforced my resolution to try to relax and be less hard on myself than I had been during the earlier 'pandemic comebacks'. The ballet also proved to be a really good vehicle for getting on stage and feeling the floor, the space, the environment and the audience again.

Just before the opening night it was announced that several dancers were to be promoted, including two new Principals (Cesar Corrales and Fumi Kaneko) with immediate effect and two more

(Mayara Magri and Anna Rose O'Sullivan) from September. This was a cause for many congratulations and much celebration but there was also some joking around the building that there were now so many Principals and Soloists that, soon, in any future production, everyone would be taking the lead in just one act of one performance!

By the time Within the Golden Hour was on stage, we were also rehearsing Apollo and TchaiPas. At last, the daily schedule was more like it used to be - well, even busier than normal. I had been cast as Apollo with ENB in 2012 when, in terms of my dancing and my life experiences, I was a sort of 'baby God'. I knew that returning to the role as a '30-something man' with nine more years of living and performing behind me was going to make my 2021 character feel very different.

June 2021

I've included most of what I wrote at the time about Apollo in Chapter 10. Inevitably, the reviews went to town on amusing allusions to space exploration. The praise, which came to be described as 'stratospheric' was nice, of course, and it somehow carried extra resonance in my case because it was for a performance, not just for something I had posted on social media. Actually, it was more than enough just to be back on stage with a live audience in an iconic work. The ballet ends with Apollo climbing to the top of a mountain and, as me, Vadim, I felt as if I was up there too.

Apollo and Muses
Photo: Helen Maybanks

The TchaiPas, which followed Apollo after a five minute pause (but featuring a fresh cast, of course), is more of a gala exhibition piece than a 'proper' ballet. It is rumoured that Balanchine was amenable to Principals performing their own versions of the steps but, with Patricia Neary in charge, there was no chance of that. Marianela and I performed on the second night of that triple bill and the warm applause which followed Apollo (Matthew Ball's beautiful cast) really energised us while we were standing waiting in the wings. We looked at one another and agreed, "OK, everyone, if this is what you want, we'll give it to you. Let's go for it."

I've often talked about loving being busy but there were times during the run of the Balanchine and Robbins programme when neither Marianela (who was also in Dances at a Gathering) nor I could fit in rehearsals for the third programme. In fact, my body went on strike for a couple of days after my last Apollo and told me that it needed some breathing space.

Nevertheless, the final bill of the season (entitled Beauty Mixed Programme and designed to mark the 90ᵗʰ anniversary of the founding of what was to become The Royal Ballet) was a matter of days ahead and I needed to focus on Prince Florimund in Act 3 of The Sleeping Beauty and Lieutenant Colonel Vershinin in the pas de deux from Winter Dreams. Those two characters and their style of movement are very different from one another and, as Marianela and I had not danced any Macmillan together before, it took a bit of time to 'feel' one another in the Winter Dreams context.

Prince Florimund is not exactly complex to portray - he is a Prince celebrating his wedding. On the other hand, Vershinin is harder to pitch outside the rest of the work even though MacMillan choreographed the pas de deux for Darcey Bussell and Irek Mukhamedov before he made the whole ballet where character portraits sit alongside the narrative. Actually, without the preceding story, The Sleeping Beauty also felt more like a gala even with the surrounding wedding guests - especially when the run began with fewer of them than usual because of the need for several dancers to self-isolate.

The unwelcome reminder that Covid-19 was far from behind us impacted far more on Valentino Zucchetti's new classically-based work, Anemoi, necessitating adaptations to the choreography and the use of last-minute substitutes to cover for absentees. The ballet, set to music by Rachmaninov and showcasing the Company's younger dancers, was very well received. Bravo Valentino!

July 2021

Outside ballet, I was struggling with what seemed like daily changes in travel regulations. I had bought my air ticket to Chelyabinsk but.......Could I get home? If I could, would I then gain entry into Japan for the World Ballet Festival? Would I have a partner there if I did? Would I be in sufficient shape to perform if the arrangements for visiting dancers were too restrictive? What stipulations might I face on return to the UK? It seemed that, every time I thought I'd got a handle on the situation and made a plan, a possible itinerary was snatched away from me.

But, all in all, the RB's summer revival had given me eight weeks to treasure from - well - nothing at all to a total of 17 shows. No full-length ballets, of course, but plenty of stage time, huge variety and the dream role of Apollo. The final performance on the 11th July included the farewell to Beatriz Stix Brunell whom I had had the pleasure (and fun) of partnering several times. As the final curtain closed, the whole company gathered to say goodbye to this amazing dancer and person who had decided to leave ballet for an academic career. A real 'Team RB' moment that it felt so good to be part of.

A Pandemic Postscript

The sense of community with my Royal Ballet colleagues in July 2021 was the sort of 'high' on which it seemed appropriate to end my journal, especially as I flew away on holiday the following day. But, before doing so, it was impossible not to cast my mind over the past year and a third.

On the one hand, it was (and is) difficult to summarise the whole experience and, yet, at the same time, there are so many words and phrases which convey vividly how it was for me and the whole ballet world: fear, frustration, hope, disappointment, panic, vulnerability, turmoil, impatience, doubt, depression, uncertainty etc. and, then, the same on repeat several times over. For dancers who were members of companies (the lucky ones!) there was practical, financial and mutual support. Nonetheless, there were moments when our livelihoods appeared to be at risk and all of us needed to draw on reserves of mental toughness we might not previously have known we had.

I had not been taking my career for granted but I was moving along a relatively smooth upward path with many of the biggest 'sacrifices' ballet dancers need to make resting in the past and some hopes being fulfilled. Then, suddenly, the routine that had shaped my life for the past 20 years wasn't there anymore and what had felt like a secure existence turned into a very precarious one. If anything, the overall effect of this was to strengthen my ambition and my resolve to find or create more opportunities to be on stage, and to savour every moment – right now, not 'another time'. That meant not only maintaining my fitness and finessing my technique (which was a struggle during the depths of the lockdowns) but also aiming to evolve as much as I could as an artist.

In the middle of all the turbulence I learned quite a bit about myself as well, not least how necessary it is for me as a person to dance, to perform, and to be on stage. Deep down inside, I knew that I was mentally quite resilient and that I had the self-belief, determination and dedication to drive myself through the bumps and bends in the road. But I did have my low moments and mood swings and, although I tried hard not to think too much, I tended to create stress, insecurity and over-expectation by doing just that – about the precious time I was missing from my career, the unpredictability of everything, the inability to plan ahead, the invitations for guest appearances which came to nothing, separation from my family, and what the future might hold in life more generally.

I suppose it's inevitable that such a massive jolt to the world becomes an agent of change. Because of the need to adopt different approaches, the pandemic gave rise to opportunities for ballet to use technology to reach out to people, more people, in ways which might not have been seized quite so quickly otherwise. In consequence, it feels less exclusive and somehow 'modernised'.

At an individual level, while the experience made me cherish what I had, it also caused me to ponder on my life as a whole and, over time, to modify some of my thinking. Of course, in common with many other dancers, I also developed an enjoyable teaching sideline and an expanded presence on social media, as well as starting on this book. And who knows if any of that would have happened, or have happened so soon, in more 'normal' times.

That said, once I knew what it was like to have my career taken away from me, I just wanted it back.

CHAPTER 13

NINE YEARS AND COUNTING

Time has flown! Since my early days with The Royal Ballet, I have reprised many roles, some of them several times and I am conscious that, as I revisit each ballet, much has changed since my first encounter with it – perhaps, especially, me personally.

In order for dancers to achieve what they aspire to, they need a lot of help along the way - from choreographers, designers, stagers, coaches, teachers, partners and colleagues to the pianists, the maestro, the orchestra, the healthcare and fitness teams, the hair and make-up specialists, and the technical crews – and, as the interconnections can vary, the backcloth to a performance is an ever evolving one. Every single person involved is really appreciated, even if it isn't possible to thank them individually, but I would be nowhere without my coaches, the stagers and my partners, all of whom I respect and value so much.

Teachers and Répétiteurs

It goes without saying that the RB has an incredibly strong and diverse group of coaches. Some dancers work with a variety of répétiteurs, as they are called; others tend to have someone with whom they rehearse on a regular, if not exclusive, basis. In my case, this is Alexander Agadzhanov, the Senior Teacher and Répétiteur to the Principal Artists, who has been coaching RB Principals since 1989, including Sir Anthony Dowell and Irek Mukhamedov. As I intimated earlier, Alexander's way of working is fastidious and, for me, his most invaluable advice can often be about breathing and conserving energy to help pace a performance. Initially, I was guided by the much-missed former RB Principal Jonathan Cope and, over the years, I have also had exceptionally valuable input from Kevin O'Hare and Christopher Saunders. Together they, and the stagers I wlll refer to shortly, have not only shaped me but have ensured my continual growth as a performer.

In some countries, there is the tradition that a coach works with a particular dancer throughout his or her career, with the credit for progress and success being very much associated with the teacher. That 'ownership' is less in evidence at the RB but it is obvious that the répétiteurs take pride in the achievements of their charges and that the key motivation of them all is for the dancers to develop and perform to their full potential. They may work in contrary ways but there is a strong sense of everything they do coming from 'a good place'. And, in turn, I want to 'deliver' for them as well as for myself and the audience because what I do on stage reflects their work too.

Approaches to coaching vary widely, sometimes according to the point in the preparation process at which there is interaction with a dancer. At one end of the spectrum, there are répétiteurs who act like a second eye, making suggestions as to how a movement might be presented better or emotions made clearer to the audience. Then there are those who, perhaps on the basis of their own experience in a role, demonstrate the steps, offer help with tricky partnering to make things flow and make suggestions aimed at building the character. In both cases, dancers have the opportunity to talk things through and try out options in a way which brings the artist inside them to the surface. At the other end of the continuum, where coaches go into the fine detail of every moment, dancers may have fewer interpretative choices. Such differences of style and pace are all the more noticeable when, for varying reasons, there might be two or even three coaches for the same ballet – one letting a segment run, followed by discussion and adjustment; one preferring a start/stop approach with corrections enroute; another seeking to pause frequently to explore the storytelling as much, if not more, than the movement.

What I appreciate the most, especially when returning to a role, is being allowed to complete a sequence because that pushes me and enables me find (or exceed) the combined limits of my body, mind and heart. A sense of mutual trust, shared endeavour and encouragement between coach and dancer boosts my confidence (which is everything) and frees me to bring out the character. It doesn't work so well, when I have lived the story or danced an abstract work previously, to be told what to do at every moment. In the latter stages of rehearsal, a 'voice over' can make me feel tense, self-conscious and maybe too careful when I need to be free to be 'in role'. That said, and thinking generally, styles of coaching do seem to be moving away from that of teacher/pupil towards giving dancers more autonomy to find a way of delivering a role in their own distinctive way.

Guest Répétiteurs and Stagers

Often a lot of additional information and coaching comes from guest ballet staff who arrive to stage productions in which they themselves have performed and/or worked with the choreographer. This passing on from one generation to the next is very special as each guest is completely at the service of the ballet. They share stories and offer advice based on their memories of the original.

Working with Sir Anthony Dowell is a particular honour: "Ashton would have wanted...........", he says. "Don't push so much here; just lean into the next step." Invaluable! Donald McLeary makes sure that my Colas has a quite rough persona and, in his solo, just taps the floor and immediately explodes upwards – not, under any circumstances, leaning on his hands for a second's rest. With Irek Mukhamedov, who emphasised to me in *Winter Dreams* that Vershinin had already had many women, it was useful to be able to check that I was managing to express his very real sorrow at leaving Masha. In addition to staging her own production of *The Sleeping Beauty,* Dame Monica Mason is often around offering little gems of advice. For example, the man

226

in *Scènes de ballet* needs to present in a very distinctive, almost impersonal, way. So, after my first performance, she emphasised that I should dance for myself. "Don't ask for attention. Maybe, think of yourself as a decorative teapot which is there to be admired by onlookers," she said.

After a 'Month' De-brief
with Sir Anthony
Photo: Daria Klimentová

Learning, Learning, Learning
from Christopher Carr
Photo: Bill Cooper

Then there is Christopher Carr who polishes the works he is in charge of in such a way as to keep the essence of a ballet as near as possible to what the choreographer intended. He is an exacting taskmaster but everything he gives me in the studio is like a piece of gold and there is something about him which makes it especially fulfilling to please him. When *The Two Pigeons* returned to the rep. Christopher's voice was still in my head to such an extent that he remarked, "You remember everything!" How could I forget? I get so much from him and the former dancers who created roles that I am wanting to soak in all the information to help me deliver my individual interpretation.

It's more testing when a ballet comes back into the rep. and the person staging or coaching it has different expectations about the

Raymonda Solo
Photo: Tristram Kenton

steps and the character from the previous occasion. I have already mentioned *Apollo* as an example of this but that was firstly with ENB and then the RB. I remember as well, when I was rehearsing the cabrioles in Jean de Brienne's Act 3 from *Raymonda* that, in Paris, Irek wanted me to fly across the stage but split my legs only a little whereas Alexander was asking me to travel less but open my legs more. In that instance, there was no problem: they were different productions, geographically apart from one another, and I could comply with both of their wishes.

I don't think that it's giving away any trade secrets to say that perceptions can vary as to the choreographer's intentions. This can be slightly awkward, especially when stagers and coaches are in the studio together. Of course, I want to continue to absorb knowledge from the illustrious teachers but, in such situations, the need to continue to develop a role from inside me comes to the fore and I have sometimes risked saying, "That's a nice way, but I would prefer to do it my way." Or (ssshh!) I might use my own version of compromise and try to please one stager/coach at the first performance and the other at the next.

Partnering

I arrived into the RB in the wake of a period with ENB where I was rehearsing with three ballerinas every day and needing to make adjustments in each session. The learning experience of moulding to each one helped me a lot at the RB where there have been a surprising number of occasions when I have had two or more partners in one ballet usually because, unfortunately, someone has been injured – and that's not counting the repertoire, notably *La Bayadère,* where Solor interacts with two contrasting female characters and *A Month in the Country* where Beliaev dances not only with the leading ballerina (Natalia Petrovna) but also with her Ward and the Maid.

I don't pretend to be an expert but, as I have now had very many partners, my list of 'do's' is a long one – to the extent that I don't think that partnering works, in fact I know it doesn't, unless the man has a particular frame of mind. For a start, he needs to leave his ego behind if he is to respect and respond to what the ballerina wants and absorb corrections, and occasional blame, from her. I have learned to take on board what might be experienced as 'pickiness' and to turn it into a positive which will help me to be a better partner. I also know, from having got it wrong a few times, that it is better to swallow any remark which might go down badly because I don't want to risk changing the atmosphere for the worse. It is for others to say whether I succeed but I do try to be as collaborative, both physically and emotionally, as possible and not impose myself and my own needs too much. I think that my nickname (Vadream) arose more because I was a compliant partner than because I was any kind of ideal.

As regards the nuts and bolts, since it is a major part of my job to present my partner in a way which looks right aesthetically and/ or chimes with the story, I need a lot of practice. The skill of partnering is about providing support and a sense of security to whatever extent it is required and whatever the proportions and needs of the ballerina. Therefore, the only way that the effort can be hidden and the 'workings' appear seamless is through trial and error and much fine-tuning to adjust to the height, weight, grips, speed and individual preferences of one's partner. Whether the choreography is classical, neo-classical or more modern, mastering the very different kinds of lifts – for example, the bent arms of Ashton and the 'over-the man's back' positions in choreography by MacMillan or Cranko – involves a lot of testing before rehearsing full out.

It is quite a challenge to be a trustworthy partner while remaining in character! Staying in role works best for me when my partner 'gives' – not just beautifully executed movement (which is a given for the RB's super-talented ballerinas) but something extra of themselves to help the two of us make a better whole. I guess that that applies equally to an abstract ballet or a classical pas de deux. It also helps me when a partner is not too calculating, especially where linking steps are concerned, when we feel the music in the same way and when the ballerina is able to pull her torso up and 'spring-assist' the lifts (although there are many 'dead' ones where helping the man is impossible).

Although I know that I must put her first, it is obviously more comfortable for me if my partner is temperamentally easy going. Being demanding and needing reassurance are both fine and indicate how much a ballerina cares about her interpretation; but a mind full of a partner's corrections is not the best starting point for a performance. It also suits me better when my partner is willing both to repeat, repeat, repeat and 'run it' in the studio so that we can test our stamina and experience a story in a way which isn't possible if we need to keep stopping. That way we are better placed to have the confidence to 'go for it' on stage.

The word 'chemistry' (or its lack!) is often mentioned when people talk about partnerships, but it's an elusive thing in practice and one which is difficult to define. Obviously, relationships forged in rehearsal (and in life), often over many years, combined with mutually helpful ways of working, contribute much to on-stage rapport, especially if we can laugh together about our struggles and mistakes. Having to wear a mask for so long over the period of the Covid-19 pandemic was an obvious impediment but, strangely, it can sometimes feel as if both my partner and I have some kind of veil which gets in the way of our connecting fully with one another and gelling as a pair. On the other hand, there are partners whom I only have to look at to feel real and, if we are in character, to see who she is being at that moment, not the actual dancer. And if she, in turn, sees only my character in me, something special can emerge which heightens a performance.

I used to feel shy and inhibited with each new partner but I know now that that simply prevents me giving my best to whoever that might be. That's just as well since, even within the RB, I have been paired to varying extents with all the current Principal ballerinas (2022) as well as a Guest Principal, others who have retired, and dancers from every other rank.

Ballerina	RB Ballets We Shared
Claire Calvert	Mayerling (Mitzi Caspar)
Lauren Cuthbertson **	A Month in the Country; Human Seasons; Jewels (Diamonds); Symphony in C; The Two Pigeons
Isabella Gasparini	Mayerling (Princess Stephanie)
Hannah Grennell	Mayerling (Princess Louise)
Francesca Hayward	Alice's Adventures in Wonderland; The Invitation
Fumi Kaneko **	Symphony in C; Two Pigeons (Gypsy Girl); Mayerling (Countess Marie Larisch)
Sarah Lamb **	Afternoon of a Faun; Alice's Adventures in Wonderland; Manon; The Nutcracker; Romeo and Juliet; Raymonda Act 3; Scènes de ballet; The Sleeping Beauty; The Winter's Tale; Winter Dreams
Mayara Magri	Apollo (Polyhymnia); Vertiginous Thrill of Exactitude
Roberta Marquez	Don Quixote (on tour); La Fille Mal Gardée
Itziar Mendizabel	Mayerling (Empress Elisabeth)
Laura Morera	La Fille Mal Gardée; The Two Pigeons (Gypsy Girl); A Month in the Country
Yasmine Naghdi **	Fonteyn Gala (Le Corsaire pas de deux); Apollo (Terpsichore); Romeo and Juliet; Swan Lake; Scènes de ballet (Insight Evening); Mayerling (Baroness Mary Vetsera)
Marianela Nuñez **	Coppélia; Don Quixote; Giselle; La Bayadère (Nikiya); La Bayadère (Gamzatti); La Fille Mal Gardée; Marguerite and Armand; Raymonda Act 3; Swan Lake (2018 production); Sylvia; Symphonic Variations; Tchaikovsky Pas de Deux; The Nutcracker; The Sleeping Beauty; Vertiginous Thrill of Exactitude
Anna Rose O'Sullivan	Apollo (Calliope); A Month in the Country (Vera); Within the Golden Hour
Natalia Osipova **	Don Quixote; La Bayadère (Nikiya); La Bayadère (Gamzatti); Raymonda Act 3; Sylvia

Ballerina	RB Ballets We Shared
Iana Salenko *	Swan Lake (Dowell production)
Akane Takada **	Don Quixote; Onegin (Olga); Swan Lake (Dowell production); The Four Temperaments; The Sleeping Beauty; Vertiginous Thrill of Exactitude
Zenaida Yanowsky	The Invitation (The Wife)
Mica Bradbury	A Month in the Country (Katia)
Tierney Heap	Carmen
Melissa Hamilton	Afternoon of a Faun; Symphonic Variations
Meaghan Grace Hinkis	A Month in the Country (Vera)
Beatriz Stix Brunell	Alice's Adventures in Wonderland; The Winter's Tale (Perdita); Vertiginous Thrill of Exactitude; Within the Golden Hour
Lara Turk	A Month in the Country (Katia)

** Royal Ballet Principals with whom I have also appeared as a guest elsewhere;
* RB Guest Principal

Every one of these ballerinas has been inspiring. In some cases, a similar training or a shared musicality means that we need to make few adjustments; in others, a partner can be so natural in her role that it helps me to respond in a similar way. Then there are dancers whose experience seems to enable them to let the steps take care of themselves and that is very liberating for a male partner.

Different Partners, Different Experiences

I'm conscious that I haven't yet talked about the mutual development of roles within a partnership. In fact, in my case, the interaction about characterisation is often more of a body language conversation than a verbal one. This is possibly plainer to see when the dynamic is altered by a change of pairing because we are both reacting to another personality and a new kind of energy. It's stimulating, of course, to work with different partners as each introduces her own artistry. This can help to give an earlier interpretation a 're-fresh' or to enable something unexpected to develop for one or both of us. I had been looking forward to working with Lauren Cuthbertson on *Month in the*

Country again, but there was an unexpected switch to Laura Morera, who was making her debut as Natalia Petrovna. So I lived the superb Turgenev/Ashton narrative reacting to another character projection. Maybe, together, we illustrated the benefit of 'mixing and matching' partners on occasion.

Equally, there is much to be gained from having established partnerships: frequent joint performances enable both parties to be more 'normal' with one another on stage. With the RB, the ballerina with whom I have been dancing the most is Marianela Nuñez (Nela) and the fact that someone has created an Instagram account - @vadreamteam - reflects the extent to which we are associated with one another in the minds of the audience. I have many special memories of dancing with Marianela, perhaps especially her 20th anniversary performance of *Giselle* and the opening night of *Swan Lake* in 2018, and my career has undoubtedly benefited from her professionalism and popularity.

Much to my surprise, and just as this book was going to press, there was an appreciative feature about Nela in The Times in which she is quoted as saying, "*Vadim is fabulous; we have developed a beautiful partnership. Not only do I feel great dancing with him, but just to see him rehearse is very inspiring. I have never seen him have a moment of frustration, never a diva moment, he's always super calm and funny.*" What can I say except to return the compliment many times over?

For a number of the more dramatic works as well as classical roles, I have also been fortunate to have been paired with Sarah Lamb and to benefit from her knowledge and experience. I remember especially our *Manon* at the beginning of the 2019/20 season because, although we had danced the ballet together in 2014 and 2018, during my third run it felt as though, together, we were able to take our interpretations up another notch. Since then, we have also danced two of the classics, *Raymonda Act 3, The Nutcracker* and, in 2022, *Scènes de ballet*, the last being a debut for me but a return to the work for Sarah after nearly eight years.

While this was more how things were earlier in my career – that is, I was the newcomer benefiting from being paired with an experienced ballerina - more recently, I have sometimes been the one of the pair who has danced a role before and I hope that my partner has found that helpful, especially in the initial rehearsals.

WITH THANKS TO MY MOST REGULAR ROYAL BALLET PARTNERS

Laura Morera
Photo: Bill Cooper

Lauren Cuthbertson
Photo: Bill Cooper

Marianela Nuñez
Photo: Bill Cooper

Natalia Osipova
Photo: Gavin Smart

Sarah Lamb
Photo: Alice Pennefather

Yasmine Naghdi
Photo: Foteini Christofilopoulou

As Time Goes By

Over my eight years with The Royal Ballet I have reprised many roles, some of them several times, and I am conscious that, as I revisit a ballet, my mind set has changed. Part of this is down to a natural career trajectory. Initially, aged 23 to 26, I had the physical and mental freedom of youth; in my later twenties, I was becoming more self-critical while seeking to grow as an artist and person. Now, I feel that I am benefiting from an accumulation of artistic and life experiences while, at the same time, becoming ever more aware of my body's limitations, my inner vulnerability and, if I am to maintain my level, the need to strive for improvement all the time.

For these kinds of reasons, even though I remain positive about my technical capacity and mental will to push myself, my return to a role can be filled with doubt, on occasion going so far as to ask myself, "Can I still do this?" I find it impossible to start where I left off three or more years previously and recapture the dancer and character I was then. That's partly because I have more artistic building blocks – varied stage experience, the confidence

235

to time things more sensitively, improved musicality, and more facets of my personal life - to draw on, help me grow into a role and try to elevate my performances further beyond the steps.

In some cases, a role evolves because I am more familiar with it - for example, I might be better able to 'play' with a solo or get to know a character more deeply, almost as one does with a friendship. Moreover, as I return to some ballets, I am ever more conscious that I am doing so with an affinity which helps me to live a role more completely. For example, with the passing of time, my understanding of the devastating hurt Albrecht's behaviour causes Giselle is very much heightened. Some stories can also resonate in more intense ways. Recently, I became more acutely aware than previously that my Siegfried in *Swan Lake* is trying to escape from the realities of his life by seeking, or dreaming, of an ideal which might never be attainable and mourning something lost and never to be recaptured. Such underlying thoughts and emotions now inform my dancing to a much greater extent than before.

Sometimes, I might not see a role differently but I know that my mood as I approach and perform it has changed. For example, when dancing Beliaev in *A Month in the Country* in 2019, I not only felt his 'innocence' and surprise at the disruptive effect he had on the household but, while I was on stage, I was as happy as Kolia (the son) running around with his kite. Come April 2022, I hope that my Beliaev still came across as young and taken unawares, not least by his own emotions, but I was conscious that some of my own youthful joy had seeped away. I should add that I was thrilled to be cast for the second time, the context had even more meaning for me and I could live the whole scenario with more abandon than three years before.

Having the opportunity to debut in *Scènes de ballet* in the same bill brought its own special challenges. I was getting back under the skin of a known role while becoming acquainted with another, each requiring its own kind of artistic learning and making distinctive demands on one's body. Although one (*Scènes*) appears statuesque and the other (*Month*) has Ashton's signature epaulement, amplitude and much fluid bending, both include very quick steps which test one's feet to the very limit and take some managing twice over.

The resulting schedule of rehearsals was also more taxing than usual for everyone during the lead-in period:

DAY	MORNING	AFTERNOON	EVENING
Tuesday 19th April	Class	Full studio calls for *Scènes de ballet* and *Month in the Country*	Insight evening for *Scènes de ballet* (Linbury Theatre and live relay)
Wednesday 20th April	Class	Stage Call for *Scènes de ballet*	(9.30pm) Stage Call for *Month in the Country*
Thursday 21st April	Class	Stage Call for *Month in the Country*	Pre-General for *Scènes de ballet*
Friday 22nd April	Class	Stage Call for *Month in the Country*	
Saturday 23rd April	Class	*Scènes de ballet* matinée performance	*Month in the Country* evening performance

And on the opening day, just over eight years after I joined The Royal Ballet, I danced in two works on the one bill - another 'first' for me.

Mayerling

Then, at the start of the 2022/23 Season came *Mayerling*, perhaps the biggest challenge of all.

The rehearsal process was long – in my case, from the end of August to nearly the end of October – and, until my debut, was uninterrupted by other calls. That 'total immersion' was hugely beneficial for me and very necessary. Rudolf is a role requiring complete dedication.

Karl Burnett, who stages ballets worldwide but, primarily, Kenneth MacMillan's masterpieces, taught the steps to those of us new to the ballet. And that was almost everyone in the cast where I was Rudolf, including four out of my six partners. Early on, Irek Mukhamedov (one of the greatest ever Rudolfs) was helping with characterisation. It was such a bonus to have him at the RB but he had to return to Paris after only a fortnight because The Paris Opera Ballet, where he is Ballet Master, was also preparing to perform *Mayerling*. It was rather as if the ballet was breaking out all over Europe as I had an invitation to dance Rudolf with The Hungarian National Ballet – but I couldn't envisage doubling my number of partners from six to 12 within a very short time frame.

The Royal Ballet had an amazing team of coaches for *Mayerling* – Edward Watson, another stellar Rudolf, alongside Leanne Benjamin, Laura Morera and Zenaida Yanowsky, all of them renowned occupants of the leading female roles, and Alexander Agadzhanov. They had differing views and suggestions but every fragment of their input was invaluable – about the choreography, the partnering, the interpretation, the timing, the breathing, the pacing. So much to internalise!

My main Stage Call was two weeks ahead of my debut and it was quite hard to keep hold of the essence of Rudolf during the many days back in the studio. My first show (21st October) was actually 24 weeks after my last appearance on the ROH stage (in the special *Swan Lake* for Ukraine) so there were extra nerves jangling – as, indeed, there were on the 11th November after a three week gap and many rehearsals for other works in between.

Everyone describes the role of Rudolf as the Everest of ballet for a male dancer. He is hardly off stage and sustaining the character (and his decline) for nearly three hours is emotionally taxing to the extent that, in performance, one's mind can start to play tricks. For example, in my second show, I was so drained during the Stephanie pas de deux that I felt I wanted to throw her away rather than rape her. Equally challenging is the physicality of the dance movement which itself expresses Rudolf's state of mind so vividly. It draws on the classical vocabulary but goes way beyond that, penetrating muscles, tendons and joints which I didn't know I had until I began to build up the physical stamina necessary to inhabit the role as fully as I could.

But it's the process of discovery, combined with a personal motivation to keep on improving and keep on learning, which continue to spur me on.

MAYERLING MEMORIES

Skull Rehearsal
Photo Andrej Uspenski

Act 1 Stephanie Pas de Deux with (half of) Isabella Gasparini
Photo: Andrej Uspenski

Act 2 Rudolf Alone
Photo: Foteini Christofilopoulou

Act 2 Despair with Fumi Kaneko as Marie Larisch
Photo: Foteini Christofilopoulou

Act 2 with Yasmine Naghdi as Mary Vetsera
Photo: Foteini Christofilopoulou

Act 3 Scene 2 Pas de Deux
Photo: Foteini Christofilopoulou

Act 3 Scene 3
Photo: Foteini Christofilopoulou

Rudolf's Act 3 Solo
Photo: Foteini Christofilopoulou

Final Pas de Deux
Photo: Foteini Christofilopoulou

Nearing the End
Photo: Foteini Christofilopoulou

Final Moments
Photo: Foteini Christofilopoulou

244

PART FOUR

IT GOES WITH THE TERRITORY

Dancing Rudolf Nureyev's Swan Lake in Vienna
Photo: Wiener Staatsballett/Ashley Taylor

CHAPTER 14

HERE, THERE AND EVERYWHERE

Once I had begun to travel – to Lausanne, to London and on tour with The Royal Ballet School – I had dared to hope that my dancing would take me round the world. I was thinking 'sometime in the future' but I didn't know then that Daria (Klimentová) would ask me to be her partner when she was invited to appear abroad. So I started guesting very early in my career and I got a taste for it. Moreover, I had grown accustomed to the pace and the amount of stage time at English National Ballet. It seemed to suit me and I wanted to replicate that throughout the year if I could. Now, I would go so far as to say that performing 'away from home' in both full productions and galas is an essential ingredient in my life.

From 2010 to Summer 2022 (excluding ENB and RB Company tours):

Full Ballets	112	Galas/Soirées	128	Total Shows as Guest	240
Companies/ Promoters	50	Different Partners	51	Partners' Nationalities	27
Theatres/Arenas	76	Locations	52	Countries	32

Why the Wanderlust?

I am, of course, incredibly fortunate to have the status and security which comes with being a member of The Royal Ballet and I cherish every moment of performing with a Company which is so rich in talent. That does mean, though, that a Principal's schedule can involve weeks, or even months, of preparations for just a couple of shows in any one production, some of them one act ballets within Triple Bills. Apart from the fact that, of my own choosing, I am not involved in new works with very modern choreography, my situation is no different from that of any other Principal. It is what it is in the context of a wonderfully strong Company. However, dancing is my passion, performing is what I need to be doing more than anything, and a career in ballet is a short one. So I feel I have to create more opportunities, explore different productions and just be on stage.

In normal circumstances, though, there does need to be a balance and that means declining a number of very tempting offers – for example, *Marguerite and Armand* at The Mariinsky and *Giselle* in Rome. Therefore, although there are annual fluctuations, especially in the context of the Covid 19 pandemic and the seasons since then, the home/away count has hovered around 55%/45%.

Summary (RB Years only)	2014/ 15	2015/ 16	2016/ 17	2017/ 18	2018/ 19	2019/ 20	2020/ 21	2021/ 22	Total
Royal Ballet (Full Productions or Two Acts)	16	22	16	23	18	8	2	12	117
Royal Ballet (One Act and Galas)	7	11	13	5	14	8	21	6 incl. 5th May SL	85
Royal Ballet On Tour (including Galas)	6	3	3	2	4	-	-	-	18
Guest Performances (Full Productions)	13	8	9	15	15	2	2	16	80
Galas/Soirées at home and abroad (as a guest)	18	4	22	18	9	8	8	29	116
Total	60	48	63	63	60	26	33	63	416

But guesting is about much more than numbers or, indeed, any additional income. There is the stimulus of working with, and learning from, different companies and partners, having input from a variety of teachers and coaches and feeling different kinds of energy from the dancers - all of which not only helps me to improve but brings out something different in me. There is another kind of 'feel', including that of being 'free to be Vadim', when dancing outside one home's territory. There is an added sense of achievement, perhaps especially when performing alongside inspirational international stars. There is the honour of being seen in so many countries, of dancing for diverse audiences, and of coming into work and social contact with exceptional artists I wouldn't otherwise meet. A real buzz comes my way from all of that.

My stopovers in any one place may be fleeting and my spare time very limited, but I can experience various cultures and varied attitudes to life and work; stay in every imaginable kind of hotel; sample exotic food; and generally soak up my surroundings.

Before I Go

When I first started guesting on my own, I had either David (Makhateli) or Daria putting out feelers to see whether companies were interested in my dancing with them. But, as time has gone by, I receive invitations quite regularly or I make enquiries myself. The first contact is usually a simple message to sound out whether I would be interested in a particular role or gala on given dates. I used to accept almost every proposed engagement if it seemed feasible. But I've learned to pause to consider my appetite for the role, the production and the place. When it's not a joint invitation (as it often is for galas), I also need to know with whom I will be dancing – a company ballerina or someone they would like me to ask. Then there is the preparation time I would need, depending on my familiarity with the production, my intended partner, and the travel implications (which became more complex during the pandemic and subsequently).

For a gala, it's possible, but not desirable, to: *fly in on the day > do class > rehearse > change into costume > warm up > dance two pas de deux > change into something formal > go to a reception/dinner > sleep > catch a London flight early the following morning > arrive at the ROH in time for morning class with the RB.* I once put myself through something similar for a full length ballet – *a 36 hour fly in > sleep > eat > class rehearse > do the show > sleep > fly back.* But, really, adequate time for rehearsal and, indeed, some rest are a 'must' if I am to meet the challenge of learning a new production or interpreting a familiar role in a different environment. Galas are unlikely to contribute to my dramatic development – in my case, they help maintain my technique - but, even so, it is better to have time to prepare for an occasion where everyone wants to show their very best. It's hard to shine straight off the plane after, say, a 4.00am start from home.

Sometimes, the initial message I receive includes mention of the hotel, subsistence and travel arrangements. It makes a huge difference to guest dancers when everything, including eating after a show, is sorted for them and offers of business class flights are especially welcome as it's very hard to dance on legs which have flown long haul in economy. I then look at my RB schedule to see whether the offer will work for me – not just practically but in terms of doing myself and the audience justice – before I approach my Director. Happily for me, Kevin is always willing to make something happen if it is at all possible in juxtaposition with my Royal Ballet performances and the lead-up to them.

Then there are the contractual arrangements to be agreed. It is normal for dancers from the USA to work through managers and an increasing number of UK-based artists are signing up with agents. I'm not yet one of them as, apart from an early arrangement with David in relation to American Ballet Theatre (ABT) and the rights if I ever produced my own show, I prefer to 'go it alone'. A representative of a well-known dancer I admire once tried very hard to make me to sign with him on the basis that he could squeeze better terms and fees out of organisers and companies on my behalf. But he didn't mention his 'cut' and, when I didn't give in to his pressure, the truth came out, "The trouble is", he said, "that, if you agree to appear for less than X (the international dancer), you get invited more than him. And, because of you, I can't push his fee up either."

There's quite a lot of administration involved: the contract to read and sign; maybe insurance to arrange; sometimes an invoice to submit; visas to be applied for; and travel tickets and hotel booking to finalise, especially if organising the getting there and staying there is down to me. It's only too easy to become preoccupied with the arrangements and forget essentials such as hiring from the RB any extra costume(s) I will need to take with me!

By the time performances are confirmed – and that can take quite a while – I already have the role or my gala choices whirring inside my head alongside other upcoming RB shows. Those preliminaries intensify as the date approaches, especially if I haven't danced a role for some time and I need not only to get it back into my body and but also to test my ability to perform it. For galas where I am booked to dance with an RB ballerina (most often Marianela Nuñez or, more recently, Fumi Kaneko), we tend to choose a pas de deux we have performed previously and rehearse in an ROH studio at the end of an RB day. It is much

more difficult and sometimes incredibly stressful when partners arrive from different countries, having worked on their solos beforehand, and we meet up to rehearse the adagios and codas only hours before the performance. For full-length ballets, I work a lot from videos and go over the choreography again and again so that my body can fully absorb it. This can mean popping

Le Corsaire in Rome

251

into the ROH on Sundays to make the most of the empty studio space. As with galas, I have been lucky and thankful to be able to guest, and therefore prepare with, so many of the RB's beautiful ballerinas. If I am going to partner a dancer chosen by the company I am visiting, I try to 'borrow' someone to help me while I am in the UK. In this way, I can arrive as a guest artist as ready as I can be to begin work.

That need has added significance because, no sooner am I off the plane than I am suddenly transported into a different company or theatre environment with unfamiliar faces, studios (some of them with uneven or raked floors), and schedules. Sometimes there are new costumes to get used to which add extra apprehension into the mix.

'Home'-goings

Over the years, I have guested with the Mikhailovsky, Mariinsky, Kremlin, Kazan, Samara, Almaty, St. Petersburg Ballet Theatre and Stanislavsky Ballet Companies. I have also received invitations from other Directors which I haven't been in a position to accept. However, having a Russian as a guest hasn't seemed to have the same appeal in my native country as someone of another nationality.

There was strong hint of this kind of thinking about me specifically when a recording of The Royal Ballet's *Swan Lake* was broadcast in Russia in 2020. Nikolai Tsiskaridze, Rector of the Vaganova Academy and a former Bolshoi Principal, was shown commenting beforehand. He said that he knew my father, remembered me as a little boy and, in his opinion, I was now one of the best dancers in the world. But he added, "Despite being highly regarded internationally and forging a successful career abroad, Muntagirov does not enjoy the same level of acclaim among Russian commentators." Nikolai added that he didn't understand that. It's hard for me, too, to reconcile that position with the fact that I won the Benois de la Danse twice with Russian judges on the panel. Maybe I was not forgiven for having 'run away'. Now, sadly, as I write, the events of 2022 seem likely to make an early return out of the question.

A Gala Spectre de la Rose
Photo: Andris Liepa Productions

When I have had the chance to appear in Russia, everything seems familiar - like a magical flashback. Having stunning Russian-style classes – for example, from Sergei Vikulov at the Mariinsky - represents a real 'refresher course' for me and working with coaches and dancing with partners who have the same kind of training as me can be very rewarding. Added to that, listening to the dancers' light-hearted changing room talk gives me a shot in the arm. It's all so different from the more intense ballet environment in Europe..

A Bevy of Swans

With ENB, I danced *Swan Lake in the Round* and Derek Deane's adaptation for a proscenium arch stage and, with the RB, I performed in Sir Anthony Dowell's version before it was replaced with the one by Liam Scarlett in 2018. Elsewhere, I have been

Siegfried in no less than 15 productions. Yes, 19 in all, including ones with a happy ending and one Act 2 juxtaposed with a contemporary 'take' on the lakeside scene.

Don't I get tired of it? The thing is that, whenever I hear the music which bridges into Act 2, I get goose bumps.

Wouldn't I prefer to dance something different when I go abroad? No production is the same. The more I dance Siegfried, the more I can get to know him and go deeper into his story. I can also feel freer than is possible 'at home' to find and develop my own take on the role and to play with the choreography.

Aren't I looking for more of a challenge? No matter what I am dancing, every guesting assignment is a challenge.

On several occasions I have performed in versions which closely follow traditional Russian ones, so much so that Von Rothbart gets left with one wing – just as I remember Papa in the role. I personally like the way that some pyrotechnics from the Jester whip things up at the beginning of Act 3 and the Von Rothbart in Riga was leaping around so much that it really was worth defeating him. I wasn't quite so keen on the monster rake on the stage of the Mikhailovsky nor the costume with high-heeled shoes, hat, gloves and cape in which Siegfried dances his Act 1 solo and the White Swan pas de deux. But these hurdles were compensated by the thrill of staying, with Mama, in an apartment in the theatre itself.

Of course, I can arrive with many elements of Siegfried ready to unpack from my suitcase but there is always some additional choreography to learn, generally in Acts 3 and 4, and stage business to get the hang of. Some productions have no soliloquy whereas Nureyev added fiendishly difficult solos and a pas de six right from the start. Which brings me to another huge plus to be derived from guesting – that of being coached by megastars of the wider dance world.

I had watched footage of Manuel Legris dancing Nureyev's *Romeo and Juliet* when I was rehearsing it with ENB and had huge respect for his artistry. Although he was, by then, a Director, Manuel continued to perform at the International Ballet Festival in Tokyo and I think that he must have spotted me there and decided to invite me to dance at his own gala in Japan and with his company in Vienna. Nureyev's incredibly demanding *Swan Lake* was one of the ballets he coached me in. Manuel's approach was exacting, as it needed to be, but he balanced his high expectations with a real concern for my development and many motivating compliments. I hope that my performances repaid his investment.

Swan Lake with Vienna Staatsballett

Assignments such as that one in Vienna are why I continue to add to my *Swan Lake* tally. They can give me so much more than what I go to perform.

And there are numerous instances of this.......

A Substitution in Paris

I have been fortunate to be an occasional stand in for other dancers abroad, notably with the Paris Opera Ballet (POB) in the summer of 2016 when the Director, Aurélie Dupont, put out a call to the RB.

The RB was in full flight with *The Winter's Tale* at the time but I was able to fit in some to-ing and fro-ing between London and Paris for rehearsals and two performances. Fortunately, the POB's version of *Giselle* is quite similar to the RB's and Albrecht was still in my head and body from the RB shows the previous March.

Being in the Palais Garnier surrounded by its history and glamour was an experience to savour in itself and dancing there (with Dorothée Gilbert) was an extraordinary privilege. And the infamous raked stage? [Many older opera houses have these to improve the audience's view where the Stalls are quite flat but, increasingly, it's the seating which is raked rather than the stage.] I think I took the added difficulty in my stride in Paris, along with the 32 entrechat sixes which feature in that production.

But not every invitation to guest culminates in a show........

It's a 'Non' in 2019

Rehearsing with Irek Mukhamedov

Coinciding with the RB's run of *Raymonda Act 3* in the autumn of 2019, I received an invitation direct from the Paris Opera Ballet (POB) to dance the role of Jean de Brienne in the full length version of *Raymonda* which Rudolf Nureyev staged when he was the Director there. This was a fantastic opportunity to perform the whole ballet and the arrangement with the POB required several periods of rehearsals, in both Paris and London with my partner, Valentine Colasante, and our coach Irek Mukhamedov. Irek was expecting to teach me the steps but I had made sure I knew most of the choreography, including the Act I pas de deux, well in advance. I'm not sure whether he was pleased or disappointed because, after watching me for a while, he threw open his arms in his own special way and said, "But you know it already!"

I had really valued working with Irek on *Winter Dreams* the previous Christmas, but our contact had been very brief – too much like "Hello" - correction - "Goodbye". But, in Paris, he was coaching me for something like 90 minutes every day. I suppose the best way of describing what he gave me was encouragement to be more dynamic, to come across as more powerful - probably to be more 'Bolshoi'. I wanted to soak all of that up, not only for then, but also for the future.

Irek also worked intensively on the partnering, not just telling us what to do but mimicking us and doing it all himself as well. That made rehearsals a lot of fun. But it wasn't so amusing when he came into the studio one day with a concerned look on his face, saying, "Bad news!" The nationwide action over retirement ages and pensions had spread into the company and was likely to affect the ballet programme.

And it did! The POB performed only the opening night of *Raymonda* before members of the Company joined in the strikes with the purpose of protecting their traditional rights. For our stage rehearsal, not only were half of the dancers missing, but technicians were absent, the set wasn't being moved, and there was no proper lighting.

On the day of each of my three shows I had to wait until 12.00 noon for confirmation as to whether or not the performance would go ahead. And it was always "Non!" However, an unexpected bonus of the strike for me was that I had Irek to myself for a few days. We would chat, try out sections of different ballets and work on some tricks while, all the time, he was telling me stories and giving little examples, but never promoting himself. He expected a lot but he gave even more. I tried to tell him how much I had appreciated my time with him but he interrupted me to say the same thing back to me. He said that he liked to be with dancers who are keen to work. But, surely, everyone must want to do so when Irek is their coach........

A Note From New York

Among the other inspiring coaches I will remember for the rest of my life, is Kevin McKenzie, the Artistic Director of American Ballet Theatre (ABT) from 1992 to 2022 who, in common with Manuel and Irek, had also been a Principal Dancer. For three summers running (2012 -2014), I had the privilege of guesting with ABT in, variously, Swan Lake (which has a happy ending which I felt matched the 'sunrise' in the music), The Sleeping Beauty and La Bayadère.

Solor
Photo: David Makhateli

With Kevin McKenzie
Photo: David Makhateli

With Hee Seo in La Bayadère
Photo: David Makhateli

When I first went to New York in 2012, it was for a month, including the May season at the Met., and a tour. At that time,

I could feel the energy of ABT's megastars - Angel Corella, Ethan Stiefel and Julio Bocca – hanging in the air. But what was really special was the level of individual, honest attention Kevin afforded me. He let me stay in his flat and, sometimes, I had as many as five rehearsals a day, mainly with him but with invaluable input from Irina Kolpakova (ex Kirov) and Natalia Makarova as well – quite something! I sensed that Kevin and I had a good understanding: I was wanting to absorb and apply all the feedback he gave me and, in turn, he offered me a kind of positive reinforcement which I had not received in quite the same way before.

So much so that I was offered the opportunity to sign with ABT on a rate of salary significantly higher than I was earning at ENB. I was very flattered and very tempted to accept but, after a lot of thought, I decided to stay with ENB and continue to accumulate the years I needed to gain British citizenship, which I did, eventually, in January 2019.

With Another Branch of the RB Family

A fair amount of my guesting has been in countries where I don't understand what people are saying and both ballet staff and dancers are kind enough to use English with me. However, there were no language barriers when I was with Birmingham Royal Ballet (BRB) for two shows of Carlos Acosta's new version of Don Quixote at the Birmingham Hippodrome in February 2022 and it was very much a home from home. The whole company was so extraordinarily welcoming that I felt completely at ease, able to 'be myself' and perform almost without pressure.

It was a very special honour to be invited by Carlos and to have the opportunity to work with him again, including on a new pas de deux he had choreographed for the opening of Act 2. I felt, also, that, in revisiting the work, he was aiming for his characters to be 'more normal' – for example, to have Basilio move around the stage with a balletic walk which was half way between 'toes

Rehearsing with Carlos

down first' and 'heels down first' – perhaps, interestingly, more like the male dancers one can see in very old ballet films. Among the many changes from the version Carlos made for the RB in 2013 was a reorchestration of the score which, to my ears, resulted in Basilio's Act 3 solo having more of an air of Carlos's trademark bravura about it than the music he used originally.

I know that Marianela and I 'took away' two shows from BRB's dancers, but who could refuse an invitation from Carlos and the chance to be coached by him again (more, please!) and it did feel as if we were connecting the two Royal Ballet companies together, if only for a few days. [And that was to continue for me with Swan Lake in March 2023.]

Not Always Alone

As I often guest with one RB partner (as in Birmingham) or on my own, it is really enjoyable to travel and be away as part of a group, such as when I went to Japan with nine other Royal Ballet dancers in January 2020. Hikaru Kobayashi, a former First Soloist with the RB, was producing *The Radiance of the Royal Ballet's Stars*. The performances were at a University

The Group in Japan

rather than at the New National Theatre and I danced the *Sylvia* pas de deux with Lauren (Cuthbertson), the Black Swan pas de deux with Yasmine (Naghdi), and the solo *Dance of The Blessed Spirits*. I felt relaxed, we all talked a lot, we had a lot of laughs in the dressing room, and I liked the feeling of 'dancing for the team'.

Speaking of 'teams', thanks to the cooperation between the Director in Brno, Mario Radacovsky and Kevin O'Hare, Fumi Kaneko (Nikiya – a debut for her), Yasmine Naghdi (Gamzatti) and I (Solor) were able to appear together in *La Bayadère* in February 2022. We rehearsed from a video in London but, once in the Czech Republic, we all needed to become assimilated into an unfamiliar production within little more than 48 hours.

On the occasions I have mentioned in Japan and Brno everything felt equal among the travelling participants and that was uplifting in itself. There have been other times, especially when appearing in galas, when I've been treated as if I was somehow more important than other people and I wasn't comfortable with that. A *Vadim Muntagirov and Friends* type of format where I would be "the one" would not be for me.

People often comment to me. "You're soooo lucky. It must be wonderful to visit all those countries and see all the sights" and, while I might reply, "Yes", I am thinking to myself, "Chance would be a fine thing." Firstly, there is often too little time to rehearse and, secondly, if I am to perform well, I have to save my legs for dancing. I think that my brain plays a bit of a trick and tells me that, if I am walking, I must be tired: it's a kind of self-protection. However........electric scooters are gradually becoming available for hire pretty much everywhere and that's helping me get out and about much more.

I have a growing list of places I would like to return to one day but, on rare occasions, I do manage to stay on after my shows for a few days' break. One such location has been Cape Town where, each time I have been there, I have 'played tourist' for a few days. Of course, the desperate poverty touches every visitor and the crime rate is high but, on the surface, it is bliss. The scenery, the beaches, the climate, the wildlife, the lifestyle of the more well-off population are to die for. And some of that seems to rub off on the members of the ballet company: they work hard but, at the same time, appear relaxed, very sociable among themselves and seemingly able to live a more 'normal' life than many ballet dancers, me included, achieve.

Contrasts in Cape Town - Romeo and Juliet with
Fumi Kaneko and Enjoying the Scenery
R&J Photo: Helena Fagan

Japan

Japan is a unique stop on any dancer's itinerary and it has a special place in my heart. The Japanese people have a real respect for ballet as an art form and hold in high regard the contribution individual dancers make. I suppose that they put us on a pedestal. The country and its culture are unlike anywhere else in so many ways and being there is too. I appreciate the cleanliness of everywhere, the politeness of everyone, and the distinctiveness of everything there is to eat. Because I don't understand any of the language, I can let conversation waft over me. Because people don't make eye contact, when I walk around Tokyo, one of the busiest cities in the world, it's as if I am a ghost – I'm there but not part of anything. I rather like that as there are no real distractions from what I have come to do.

I have toured to the country with both ENB and the RB and, as Vadim, I have danced 23 performances of full length ballets and in 37 galas, including the triennial World Ballet Festival (WBF). For several years, when Noriko Ohara was the Director, I was a permanent guest artist with The National Ballet of Japan to the extent I even had a Japanese 'resident's card'. It was comfortable for me to be able to return to the same studios, dressing room and auditorium and build understanding and trust with my main partner there, Yui Yonezawa.

Two of my visits to dance full length ballets also involved a very familiar face. Wayne Eagling's version of *The Sleeping Beauty* includes a beautiful *Awakening Pas de Deux* to some glorious Glazunov music from *Raymonda*. Then, when Wayne mounted his *Nutcracker* in Tokyo, having been involved in its creation, I was able, in turn, to contribute to the revival process he and Antony Dowson were engaged in with the company dancers. It was similarly rewarding when I danced *Manon*. As I had performed it only a few months previously with the RB, I felt as if I was bringing with me knowledge and experience from where the ballet was born and of having worked with stagers and coaches who had a direct link to MacMillan. The company seemed to want to capitalise on this and it was gratifying to be able make the connection back to my home Company. I had two

shows on consecutive days, but a full stage call the day before actually made it three in a row. It was no wonder, therefore, that, by the last performance, I really felt I *was* the character and, once I had killed the Gaoler, I 'went for it' in the final pas de deux so completely that it felt more real than ever before. I think that that's the best end to *Manon* that I've danced

A full Manon in Japan   so far.

The World Ballet Festival was founded in 1976 by a billionaire sponsor/organiser at a time when it was still quite rare for Principals of different companies or countries to share the stage. The 20 dancers at the first edition included Margot Fonteyn, Maya Plisetskaya and Alicia Alonso and, since then, there have been appearances by virtually all the leading dancers of their time. Although there are now many international galas, there is probably none which gather together as many current Principals and former Principals from across the world as this one. So it's quite something and a huge honour to be included and hosted like a VIP.

The Festival runs over a fortnight in the form of two programmes with four performances of each, all matinées as tends to be the Japanese custom. The dancers who are brought together represent different backgrounds and a wide variety of repertoire and styles. This makes the opportunity to have class and rehearse together, to learn from watching one another's varying techniques and interpretations, and to socialise together very special.

A Manon Pas de Deux with Fumi Kaneko

Performing in that context is also a challenge because, although one might dance only one pas de deux in each show, everyone gives their 'absolute all' for four days without a break. So there is no real 'down time' for the body to recover. Nor can the mind 'calm down' because there are multiple interviews and photoshoot appointments to fulfil. As each show comes to an end with all the dancers lined up on stage taking the applause, it's almost as if there's an electric charge running through us, into the audience and back again.

The appreciation and understanding of ballet which Japanese audiences demonstrate is quite extraordinary and they often go the extra mile to express that. Here is a little of what one man wrote online after a chance encounter with me: *"When I got on the subway of Shinjuku Station, a beautiful young gentleman waved his hand to me in the middle of an escalator. I ran to the bottom, then up again to catch up with Vadim-san who introduced his mother to me…….. I was very moved that I could accidentally meet the real mother of the on-stage prince."* He is not alone in making dancers feel very valued in Japan.

Footnote

I have to admit that the kind of dancing life I've chosen does have its downsides: the hours of often stressful travel for what might be only minutes of dancing; visa complications; changes of time zones which play havoc with one's body rhythm; overwhelming tiredness; the odd stomach upset; a certain amount of loneliness; and a lack of adequate stage time to acclimatise to the floor and the lighting.

Many of these factors came together in August 2021 when I was trying to get to The World Ballet Festival for my much anticipated first galas abroad since early 2020.

Intended journey: 5.00am Chelyabinsk > Moscow/Moscow > Helsinki (extra Covid test)/Helsinki > Tokyo

Actual journey: 5.00am Chelyabinsk > plane struck by lightning > plane lands back in Chelyabinsk > 3 hour wait with little information surrounded by distressed passengers and overwhelmed staff > flight re-booked by Japanese organisers > 12.00pm Chelyabinsk/Moscow > 11 hours in a 'capsule hotel' > Moscow/Tokyo

Entry checks in Tokyo: Tent 1: Covid test [all OK – relief] > Tent 2: visa/passport inspection > Tent 3: other entry papers

In the Airport Capsule Hotel

checked >Tent 4: app. installed on phone to enable official health and location enquiries

Accommodation/Quarantine: all dancers housed in one building together with staff; 3 days of using a 'stretch room' (a bedroom cleared of furniture and equipped with a barre); 13 days of socially distanced queuing for meals and eating our selections in our individual rooms

Class/rehearsals: in timed groups, including the walk or transport from and back to the hotel.

I had another precarious adventure the year earlier when I was invited to dance in Le Corsaire in Slovenia. I had been Conrad before (with English National Ballet) but, in the version by José Carlos Martinez (now the Director in Paris), there is no Ali character, so Conrad gets to dance the whole of the famous pas de deux. I liked that and the Company's work ethic but Covid-19 got in the way. During the stage call in costume, I was really 'going for it' and having a good time. But, at the end of Act 1, I looked at my phone and saw a message which read, "Have you heard the news? After Saturday at 4.00am, you have to isolate for two weeks when you come back. Just announced." I thought, "Oh nooooooo!!!" The rehearsal continued until quite late and, in contrast to my fretting about the need to book a return flight urgently, the Director was very calm and invited me for a drink. The Slovenian company didn't change my tickets until the following morning but I still caught the 12 noon plane to London. I had escaped in time to beat the deadline. So no Conrad for me then after all; although I did get to dance him in Rome in May 2022.

But, whatever the hurdles and the inconvenience, the change of scene and the experience of dancing elsewhere give me contrasting sensations which alter my frame of reference and, importantly, also make me appreciate 'home' that much more on return. I come back to London thinking, "Mission accomplished" and walk into the ROH feeling refreshed, somehow more alive, and energised for my next RB role.

CHAPTER 15

TEACHING IS LEARNING TOO

Along with many current dancers, I am not a trained teacher. I am just someone who tries to use his experience of being taught and coached himself and of performing to pass on what he can to students whose foundations (the hardest bit) have been laid in their regular classes.

Prague Masterclasses

I suppose that there had been times when I had tried to help fellow dancers with particular moves, but my first foray into any more formal teaching was at The International Ballet Masterclasses in Prague in 2013.

The Masterclasses were started in 2003 by Daria (Klimentová), as the Artistic Director, and Ian Comer as the Administrator. Their vision was to enable students and young professional dancers to be taught intensively by leading dancers of the day while, at the same time, visiting the beautiful city of Prague alongside their peers from all over the world. So I knew that I would be teaching in the footsteps, on the male side, of Irek Mukhamedov, Jan-Erik Wikström, Julio Bocca, Nicholas Le Riche and Tamas Solymosi among many other stars. Very hard acts to follow!

The invitation took me by surprise and I protested, "But I'm too young; no one will listen to me." "The earlier you start, the easier you will find it later," countered Daria, adding, "It will be good for you in many ways, you'll see." Daria explained that she didn't want the teaching to mirror that in ballet schools but to be more challenging, with daily classes conducted as if they were company classes. "No stopping," she said. "When they're professionals, any corrections will be given as the class goes along. They need to get used to that." So, once the ENB season had ended, off I went to Prague, feeling nervous and holding onto the advice I had been given about explaining clearly and throwing my (quiet) voice in the studio so that everyone could hear me and I would come across as authoritative.

The norm is for guest teachers to give three (mixed) classes a week (the Masterclasses run over a fortnight). I like to stretch the students with combinations which might be unfamiliar to them. For the men's solo sessions, the teachers' choice is influenced by what has been coached in recent years as some participants go to Prague several times and repetition is best avoided. If at all possible, I prefer to select repertoire which the students might not have encountered before and which will extend them, whatever their level. For example, in 2020, I worked with them on the male variation from the pas de cinq in Act 1 of Rudolf Nureyev's *Swan Lake*.

My starting point for the solos especially is to connect with the students, ensure that the sessions are enjoyable and try to transmit my love of ballet. I try to focus on different students to make them feel included and show respect for their efforts but I know that, in the space of a week, or even a fortnight, I am not going to be able to transform anyone's technique. However, I can try to problem solve with them, give them some extra tools and help them polish their presentation. I want them to think for themselves too.

My approach is to show the solo, teach the choreography and, then, to try to offer the students an awareness of how to *perform*. Therefore, there comes a point (actually, quite quickly) where I won't necessarily correct the steps but, rather, concentrate on some performance essentials. For example, they need to learn how to breathe in a way which assists their movement, where it is essential to relax their muscles to help them 'get through' a solo, ways of interpreting the music, and how to 'present' with an awareness of the audience. It is even more important to get across to the students that they have to make the choreography speak the story.

Of course, what I am able to offer is very dependent on the level individuals are at when they come to Prague. "Show me Prince," I might say if they are coming on as if they are going shopping. "You are village boy," I might call out if their body language is too stiff. My instinct is to encourage 'quality' more than 'show off' and it's very rewarding to see tips about even the smallest fragments consolidate into real improvement over the course of a week.

Teaching at the Masterclasses in Prague
Photography by ASH

I think - I hope – that I have got better at being a masterclass kind of teacher as time has gone on, but working with students on pas de deux (which I was asked to do subsequently) took me longer to grow into. Perhaps, in part, that was because there were two teachers in the room and both female and male roles needed to be worked on. But I came to enjoy it – as long as I could arrive in Prague with my body sufficiently rested to be able to demonstrate the essentials of partnering many times over, not just with my fellow teacher but also intervening to lift students myself when a 'boy' can't 'get it'.

I'm not the only one who can get a bit fatigued. The students are very keen to learn but sometimes find that the pace of so many classes a day (they do contemporary as well) combined with being a tourist and living in a lively group proves a little too much for them. Therefore, let me put this kindly, by the time it comes to the end of the solos or during the afternoon, some of them are beginning to wilt. That makes it all the more vital that both teacher(s) maintain their own energy levels for the pas de deux. In other words, with the responsibility firmly on me, my own tiredness cannot show – as it can't in a performance.

Teaching Over the Airwaves

Not long after the first 2020 'lockdown', I was approached from a number of directions about teaching via Zoom. For example, Andrew Ward's Dance Forward asked if I would join a roster of dancers whose class or coaching sessions could (for a handling fee) be booked via their website. There were terms to be negotiated, a price to be set (I was very wary of over-valuing myself), and a 'hello video' to be made. Then, suddenly, bookings were open.

In entering into that formal arrangement alongside several of my RB Principal and Soloist friends, I was conscious of the risk of taking on more than would be manageable further into the future. But the offers kept on coming from individuals, families, schools abroad and UK organisations such as Danceworks and, with severely curtailed opportunities to perform, I was glad to be occupied and to try to buoy up trainee dancers at that very difficult time.

The somewhat experimental coaching I did with just one 14 year old student over several months on Zoom was surprisingly fruitful. The main focus in this instance was preparation for a competition and, although my ability to illustrate my corrections via demonstration was very limited, the student had the technical base and understanding to apply my advice and improve session on session. In a one to one situation, it is possible to go beyond recognising that something worked - the "Nice; well done" response - and discuss why it worked and how it felt when it worked. Also, throughout, I was trying to instil the need to 'perform', emphasising that good pirouettes and jumps alone are not art. I think that this student was receiving me: he won a medal!

The hardest form of online teaching proved to be that involving small, mixed ability groups of boys aged between nine and 17, mostly coming from different schools. Experimentation soon taught me that I needed to pitch the class to the younger members and be very clear in what I was asking them to do and why. But, then, I had concerns about giving all the attendees value for money, especially when the more advanced among them had to wait while a basic technique was broken down in detail for the others.

All the boys wanted to try solos – often in confined domestic spaces which made me fearful for their safety – but many didn't really have sufficient grounding to attempt that, even when I tried to teach each one of, say, six on an individual basis. Sometimes, all I was able to offer, based on what I could see on my screen at home, was feedback about what went well for them, followed by a reined in demonstration from me to reinforce the point I was making. Corrections needed to be adjusted to individual capability and balancing corrections with praise – I seemed to be saying, "A little bit better" many times over – was essential in maintaining momentum and motivation.

I wanted very much that every member of these groups would gain from their participation, even if it was simply that I wasn't their usual teacher but a dancer they had heard of. Of course, I originally thought that these were 'emergency measures' and that one-off group sessions or a short series which usefully filled a gap during the pandemic may not be altogether suitable for the longer term. But I was mistaken and I am continuing to receive requests for masterclasses from as far afield as China.

An Online/In Person Mix

A Danceworks Poster
Photography by ASH

Hybrid teaching, with students attending both via Zoom and in person, seems to have become the norm. The ongoing Masterclasses organised by Danceworks, firstly streamed only and later offered live in the studio as well, can have around thirty students actually present and any number online. The sessions attract mainly female students of mixed age and experience. Many are doing ballet for fitness and/or fun so the class for them needs to be pitched at the easier end of the spectrum. But I mustn't neglect the many, including those physically around me and the group of youngsters from the *Leap of Dance Academy* in Nigeria attending on line, who need more challenge.

With those kinds of numbers, the teachers, including some of my RB colleagues, are necessarily peering at the monitor and making generalised corrections. It takes a bit of mind-juggling and head-twisting to attend to the participants in the studio as well as those on screen participants but it can be done and I enjoy it. A minute or two of what I say might sound something like this: "UUUUUUUUUUse your upper body; juuuuuuuuicy plié; very good; faaaaaster; puuuuull up (like someone pulling up your ears); breeeeeathe; well done". Once the students are away from the barre, whatever the movement, it's good for them to imagine that someone is watching then and that they are presenting "to yooooooou"; "and to yooooooou"; and "to the cat" and to smile in such a way as to sell their dancing as something incredible. It's really interesting what a difference that mindset can make.

A Little Too Young For Me

While working on this book, I have been picking up on the kind of occasional sessions with mainly younger students I had taught before the pandemic. Managing a group of up to 40 young men at a time (as in Prague) isn't easy but teaching children aged, say, 9 – 12 is equally testing, especially when the groups are small, as in both the UK (with Dance Forward) and Japan (where Daria introduced a second Masterclass initiative in 2017). I have sought advice from Papa, based on his work with children, and I have also watched school videos so that I can decide on the most appropriate content and level for my classes.

When I was their age, no one in my year group was thinking seriously about ballet but it seems different with the new generation, especially in Japan. Boys as young as nine really seem to 'want it': they listen attentively and they try, try and try again so much that a teacher doesn't need to urge them on. I appreciate that ambition and I enjoy seeing their faces when I have helped them master something. But I am always left feeling that I ought to give more. Unfortunately, real and lasting progress takes years rather than days and I think that I am probably better suited to teaching at a more advanced level.

A Variation on a Theme

Early in 2021, I was also invited contribute, under contract, to balletclass.com. This commercial brainchild of Xander Parish (formerly of The Royal Ballet and the Mariinsky) involved prominent dancers creating and demonstrating a class, giving a coaching session or teaching another ballet-related specialism. Each of these is then recorded to be made available on the website for purchase on subscription – for both dancers and people who just wanted to watch.

As is often the case with a novel idea, this generated a fair amount of scepticism with some people questioning my involvement. A bit of, "No one knows this brand" and "You don't

Working for
balletclass.com

need to do that kind of thing" came my way. But I wanted to help Xander and I thought that, even if the scheme didn't take off, I would retain copies of the footage I had recorded. What's not to like about that?

After my first, four hour shooting of a full class had been captured by Andrej Uspenski (@dancersdiary), Xander ordered more segments from me for his online 'shop'. So I filmed some solo coaching of Siegfried's Black Swan Solo, Florimund's Act 3 solo from *The Sleeping Beaty;* and Albrecht's Act 2 variation from *Giselle*. The routine was to introduce myself, say what Xander had scripted (that was the hardest bit), work on/demonstrate each section (not just the technical side but also setting the scene and the mood), and perform the solos myself. Both Xander and Andrej seemed surprised that I had so much to say but I really felt in my element and wanted to give Xander's customers as much as I possibly could, perhaps even more about the reasons behind what the character is expressing through the steps than the steps themselves.

Two Way Traffic

As I have illustrated, the Covid-19 pandemic gave rise to many and varied teaching opportunities over and above what I expected to be doing at that point in my career. Since then, I have tried to retain a sense of proportion - after all, performing is my current priority.

Nevertheless, I have found myself liking teaching, especially coaching, more and more. It is satisfying to help students, even if it can be only a little bit, and it really does enable me to learn as well. Dancing and teaching are two completely different skills but, when I am watching someone's technique really closely, my brain is also giving the dancing Vadim important reminders of what *I* might be neglecting. A simple example is that, when I say to students, "Hold your back", the correction stays with me and I apply it to myself.

The coaching I have given in Prague is no less applicable to me. For instance, the manège with which Prince Florimund ends his Act 3 solo in *The Sleeping Beauty* should show a distinction between the first half – all smooth-looking – and the more exhuberant coupés-jetés en tournant. What can happen is that the dancer uses up his energy too quickly and there is no noticeable change in the dynamic. So, when I say to the students, "Ah – but you have to pace yourself to start with and then drive yourself to show the difference," it serves as a prompt to me too.

Learning from teaching can extend to characterisation as well. When I was recording for Xander's balletclass.com, I found myself explaining that, in his Act 2 solo, where Albrecht has Myrtha on one side and Giselle on the other, his doubles assemblés need to show the malevolent pull of the Queen of the Wilis but, at the same time, his yearning to be with Giselle. The jumps should be used to continue the story, to show the grief and physical suffering, not as a display, and 'letting go' rather than being 'in control' of one's body reinforces the narrative. More reminders to me too for whenever I 'dance to the death'.

I like the fact that the benefit can be two-way and that I can share with students how much I am continuing to learn as well. It is important, I think, to 'give back' as much as I can now rather than wait until I'm older. But I also hope that the various kinds of teaching and coaching that I have been engaged in since my early twenties, and latterly online, will equip me to be a company répétiteur one day. But that is for my second career, if people will employ me, not in the middle of what should be my best dancing years.

CHAPTER 16

BEYOND THE STAGE DOOR

Ballet dancers live two lives up to the age of 40 or beyond – one within a tightly knit and highly focused professional world, the other within the more 'normal' context of family and friends, pursuing different interests and getting out and about. The dancer and person which audiences see on stage may be moulded, in part at least, by the life outside dancing but that isn't normally something which is in the public domain. There is, however, a third dimension – that where the two worlds interconnect - and that creates its own agenda.

Being Interviewed

Nothing in one's training prepares one to field questions of every kind which come one's way quite soon in a career. Over time, I have been interviewed, face to face or via video link, for ballet students, as part of the ROH's Insight programme, by ballet appreciation groups, in connection with guest appearances or specific events, for specialist magazines, for 'dancers' chats' (fun to do), for people who blog, and for specific broadcasts or films - as well as talking to camera in the context of performance relays or World Ballet Day streamings.

At first, I was very diffident about being asked questions at all, let alone in public - why would anyone be interested in me? what would I say? – and I needed the interviewer to take a strong lead. But I can only be myself and, over the years, it has become easier to let the answers flow naturally and honestly. If there is an 'elephant in the room', I would rather raise that myself than leave the question hanging in the air.

Of course, the audiences for interviews vary quite widely in every sense, including their nationality and, for that reason, some adjustment is necessary each time. Therefore although, generally speaking, I would want to be upbeat about my profession, when talking for students I also need to leave them in no doubt about the hard work which lies ahead and how important it is for them to take responsibility for their own improvement and career progress. It helps if there can be laughter while getting such messages across, but I remember one year in Prague when the amusement went over the top because all the clips of me dancing were reproduced sideways and everyone was twisting their heads to watch them.

After I had filmed a conversation for The Royal Ballet School in 2020, many compliments appeared online afterwards, some of them saying that I was an inspiration. I am very appreciative that anyone feels that way, of course, and it makes me feel very humble, but I can't quite connect with the fact that it's me who is being talked about. It surely has to be someone else? After all, I am trying to improve myself all the time – just like the students are. Maybe, when I'm very old and sitting in a chair thinking back, what all those young dancers were saying, and the fact that they were saying it about me, will finally sink in.

Some interviews are quite narrowly focused and relate to an upcoming performance here or abroad. A few connected with guesting overseas take place online or via voicemail beforehand; others can catch me with a microphone just as I am going on stage to warm up for the show. It isn't always the case that the person posing the questions has been briefed beforehand and it isn't easy to reply when something doesn't make sense in terms of the particular production I am dancing in. I just have to go for a general answer and hope that it suffices. Other conversations are of a more general nature and I think that I have been taken through my training and career to date dozens of times. I hope that this doesn't come across as too repetitive to those who are listening – it did (somewhat) to me during the earlier stages of the Covid 19 pandemic when I felt that I was becoming more of a chat show guest than a dancer.

A Filmed Interview   The Result of Interviews in Japanese Print

Many interviews have been via Zoom but, more usually, there is a live audience ready to ask questions at the end. The most frequent are: "What are your favourite ballets?" And "Is there a ballet you haven't danced which is on your 'wish list'?" My replies to both of these inevitably change over time although *Swan Lake, Month in the Country, Manon,* and *Giselle* will always be 'up there' in my top ten. Then there is: "Who do you like dancing with the most?" – to which the only possible answer is a general one (!) and, also, "How is it that you haven't been injured?" I have had physical problems during rehearsal periods and illnesses which have kept me off the stage; but I want to cover my ears and say to the questioner, "Please don't ask me that; you are tempting fate!"

Where 'in person' interviews or interpersonal contact (such as that at books or DVD/BluRay signings) are concerned, people are usually kind enough to steer clear of enquiries or comments about my life beyond ballet but the boundaries are much more blurred online.........

Signing Copies of Bill Cooper's Wonderful Book of Swan Lake Images

Social Media – the Upside

It's difficult to believe now that Instagram didn't exist when I first turned professional but it seems to have become the (current) medium of choice for dancers, no doubt because it is primarily visual. Social media may not always reflect reality but it is helpful for thanking people, recognising a special occasion and generally saying, "I'm here". I don't post every day, partly because it's all too easy to come across as self-centred but mainly because I'm no good at doing so 'on demand'. However, there were a few occasions during 2020 and 2021 when I said to myself, "Well, if I can't be on stage with a real audience, I will just have to perform for a virtual one." So I did. More normally, there is either a recorded sequence made initially for my parents which I decide to share or an idea can suddenly come into my head when Instagram is the last thing I'm thinking about. I suppose the outcome is that I express different sides of myself as a person, not just as a dancer, and anyone who cares to take a look can see that I enjoy life, play the piano (not very well), and appreciate the things and beauty around me:

SOME CONTRASTS FROM INSTAGRAM

There seem to be other Instagram accounts which have adopted versions of my name or are fan sites but I'm not (yet) into advertising any products, although that seems to be the direction in which Instagram is pointing for many dancers. Someone commented on one of my posts that social media had changed people's perception of dancers from the 'distant beings' of bygone eras to artists who are more accessible. That's so true, and welcome, but I am still reluctant to share some of the more personal aspects of my life. Nevertheless, during 'lockdown', I knew that I was opening my home to 'the world' and needed to remember to tidy the throw and cushions on my sofa rather more than usual. I was also really pleased that the ROH reproduced one clip where I was poking fun at myself because it showed people who were accustomed to me being serious on stage that I also have a sense of humour.

And the comments I get? I do read the ones on my own feed and everyone is usually very generous with what they say (some phrases are really beautiful) or the emojis they put up. That's nice for me to see because I'm happy that people are smiling with me or that something strikes a chord for someone. Indeed, on balance, I guess that I get more 'public' feedback about my Instagram posts than I do for my dancing! Also, during the pandemic, I felt that it was a way of connecting with people outside my small world. It kept me in touch with family, friends and audience members, almost to the extent of its being a form of mutual support. To have people say, "This is what inspiring social media looks like" and "Your content is the best thing to come out of quarantine" meant a lot at that particular moment.

Another growing dimension of dancers' social media is its use to share photoshoots, including fashion and other kinds of modelling, but that isn't really for me.

The ROH account advertises upcoming shows or events and all of the RB Principals will feature on the official feed at some point or another. For example, when the RB was ready to reveal that there would be a Gala evening in October 2020, the online publicity included a photo of me – or, rather, as someone put it, my bottom, from my solo of the 20th June. As importantly, the fact that numerous dancers re-posted the 'advertisement' racked up the excitement about being able to perform again and, hopefully, helped to sell the Live Stream.

I once managed to get into trouble because I put up a clip from the studio on Instagram a day before that was officially allowed and felt very foolish when this was pointed out to me. On that occasion, I wasn't up to date with the guidance which has been changing in some respects over time but, importantly, dancers cannot include anything played by ROH musicians, and photos taken by the official photographer need to be properly credited along with members of the hair and make up teams and anyone else appearing in an image.

So far, so good but............

Social Media – the Downside

As in the rest of society, there is the risk of dancers' lives being portrayed with such a glow of perfection as to cause others to become dispirited. There is also the expectation on the part of some supporters that dancers are available to chat online and, unfortunately, it's just not possible, timewise, to engage in that way. Then there is online harassment........

I have been in two minds about whether or not to mention my experience here because I don't want to exacerbate the situation by giving it 'air time'. Equally, though, I feel that it's important to bring it out into the open to show that anyone can be subject to cyberbullying and that change is needed in how the law is applied to this kind of crime.

It was obvious that something wasn't right in 2020 when someone reproduced some of my holiday shots, but I thought it best to ignore it at first – as one does. It then became apparent that a series of accounts was being set up, seemingly with the sole purpose of bullying me. Each account would first draw attention to itself by commenting on one of my posts or hashtagging me before putting up threatening images, making accusations, some of them libellous, and messaging me in a menacing way. It was worrying personally (and professionally) but, at the same time, I felt concerned for the perpetrator(s) as they were obviously in a very upset state of mind and feeling vindictive towards me. Whatever it was, despite all advice to the contrary, it was difficult not to put blame on myself.

I took the action that victims of this kind of online behaviour are supposed to – all to no avail because the fake accounts continued to multiply. I decided not to follow the recommendation to withdraw from social media entirely because maintaining an online profile felt right in a professional sense. I tried to turn detective but, apart from finding out where the images being used (including one of a man being murdered) were being sourced from, I was unable to uncover the originator of the problem. But I am now well-informed about VPNs (Virtual Private Networks) and other methods of disguising IP addresses.

After another burst of hostile activity towards me early in 2021, I thought, "This has gone far too far" and decided to submit an online report to the Metropolitan Police. However, to cut a long story short, there was no real investigation. Instead, the Officer assigned to the case rang me to say that the Met. was unable to approach Instagram for information and they were therefore closing the file. That was it!

This was very frustrating and not really acceptable, so I went back to the Met. with a complaint, attaching additional information and trying to get across that, over the preceding six months, I had been subject to a range of malicious activity from someone or some people who appeared to be totally invested in a 'campaign' against me and others around me. I also tried to explain the kind of psychological stress that this induces, the reputational risks involved and a very real fear for personal safety. The Officer investigating the complaint was very thorough. Having requested summaries of the incidents (by that point there were around 70) and sample screen shots, he came to the conclusion that "there had been no meaningful (police) investigation of the case or attempts to solicit assistance from Instagram". He listed a number of areas where police practice had been at fault and recommended that the case be re-opened. But it wasn't.

Most of the malevolent posting directed at me tailed off in 2022, but there must be thousands of people in the same kind of situation as mine, or far worse, who are not protected by the weak procedures of the social media giants and cannot obtain the help they need from the police.

Moving on from social media, there is the altogether higher league of official recordings.......

Cinema Relays and Streaming

I think that every dancer is thrilled to be told that their performance will be filmed for the cinema or streaming but that news gives me an added bounce because it means that my family might be able to see me dance, especially if a recording ends up as a DVD/BluRay disc. A company's right to feature their dancers is enshrined in the terms and conditions of employment but, in the case of guest appearances, the option to record, reproduce and distribute film can form part of the contract signed with the organisers.

I have been exceptionally fortunate to appear in the following:

RB Performances filmed for Streaming [in date order]	RB Cinema Relays leading to DVDs/BluRays
Dance of the Blessed Spirits	*Afternoon of a Faun* (Lamb)
Don Quixote Pas de Deux (Nuñez)	*Coppélia* (Nuñez)
Tchaikovsky Pas de Deux (Nuñez)	*Giselle* (Nuñez)
Le Corsaire Pas de Deux (Nuñez)	*La Bayadère* (Nuñez/Osipova)
The Sleeping Beauty Act 3 (Nuñez)	*Manon* (Lamb)
Within the Golden Hour (O'Sullivan)	*Raymonda Act 3* (Osipova)
Scènes de ballet (Lamb)	*Symphonic Variations* (Nuñez)
	Swan Lake (Nuñez)
[Abroad]	*The Nutcracker* (Nuñez)
Giselle (National Theatre Ballet, Prague) (Klimentová)	*The Sleeping Beauty* (Nuñez)
Manuel Legris Gala (Japan) (Nuñez)	*The Two Pigeons* (Cuthbertson/ Kaneko)
Swan Lake (Japan) (Yonezawa)	*Within the Golden Hour* (Stix Brunell)
The Nutcracker (Naples) (Takada)	*The Art of Vadim Muntagirov* (Box Set)
Marguerite & Armand (Nureyev Gala Vienna) (Nuñez)	
Manon (Japan) (Yonezawa)	**ENB TV Documentary**
Le Corsaire PDD (Centenary Gala Finland) *(Baranova)*	*Agony and Ecstasy* [ENB]
RB Streamed Insights/ World Ballet Day Relays	**ENB DVD**
Don Quixote Solo	*Le Corsaire (Cojocaru)*
Don Quixote Pas de Deux (Takada)	
La Fille Mal Gardée (Nuñez)	**Separate TV Programmes**
Swan Lake Act 4 (Nuñez)	Series about Ballet [Czech TV] (Klimentová)
Tchaikovsky Pas de Deux (Nuñez)	*Men at the Barre* – Documentary (RB)
Scènes de ballet (Naghdi)	*The Royal Ballet All Star Gala*

The Box Set of Coppélia, Giselle, Manon and The Sleeping Beauty

At the RB, preparatory filming of rehearsals and mini-interviews by the in-house team happens during the weeks preceding a screening. With that enjoyable activity done, there is little (apart from more natural face make-up) to distinguish a filmed performance from any other – except that, no matter how hard I try not to think about it, the presence of cameras backstage for the presenters makes it impossible for me to convince myself that everything is normal. The pressure remains very much 'on' despite the comfort of knowing that I will be consulted as to which of the two captures of my solos should be included in a DVD/BluRay version.

A commercially produced disc is there for ever and it's humbling to know that one's performance might be watched way into the future. But, because interpretations of a role develop – Des Grieux comes to mind especially - I have occasionally wished that there was a magic way of updating a recording! Second 'goes' are pretty much unheard of, I think, and there are some ballets which have so far 'got away from me' in terms of filming: *Apollo; Don Quixote; Month in the Country;* and *Sylvia.* Maybe one day........?

In addition to streamed performances, the whole of Marianela's and my rehearsal the *Tchaikovsky Pas de Deux,* where we 'ran' the piece, was shown on World Ballet Day (WBD) in 2020 – followed by a short Q&A when we were both almost too breathless to speak. My first ever WBD (in 2014) was a studio call with Carlos Acosta for Basilio's solo from the *Don Quixote* pas de deux. It doesn't get much better than that.

In common with World Ballet Day, the team which came into the ROH before Christmas 2019 to follow male dancers at work posted details of what they would be filming during each session. The resulting TV programme entitled *Men at the Barre: Inside The Royal Ballet* by Richard Macer was shown on BBC4 at the end of May 2020 when we were all in lockdown and there have been a number of repeat showings since.

The crew had shadowed me quite a bit, filming rehearsals, performances, mini-interviews, and informal conversations where other people were talking about me. It was a very enjoyable process. What's not to like about that level of attention? Except that the commentary which implied that I was "the best" was accompanied by a clip which, in my view, did not back up that claim. I wish that they had let me choose! I was rather hoping, also, that they might include the occasion when my coach was not giving me corrections after my show but, instead, along with Marianela, was being really complimentary about me to my face. There was a brief snippet of that but, unfortunately, the nicest words had long since hit the cutting room floor.

I know that they wanted that TV programme to show what the life of a male dancer "was really like" and that there were a lot of dancers involved, which was how it should be, but having so many themes must have made the project difficult for the film-maker. I think that we would all have liked there to have been more than one programme so as to give adequate space to the varied aspects of being a male dancer that they wanted to cover and be able to spend more time on each of the featured dancers – an obvious example would be Valentino Zucchetti developing a successful parallel career as a choreographer. But I guess that ballet isn't sufficiently popular in the UK for them to risk a whole series. That was shame as it might have been an opportunity to draw viewers in through a slightly different gateway to ballet – not tutus! However, at an individual level, I valued the relationship I had with Richard during the filming – I suppose that one of the skills of documentary-makers is to win their subjects' confidence – and I wasn't alone among my colleagues in wishing that there could be a reason to work with him again sometime in the future.

Reviews

Another area where the dance and 'real' worlds interrelate is in the written reviews of performances in the press and online and the comments posted by individuals who have seen a show. I'm afraid that I don't read what is being said about me unless something is specifically put under my nose. That is not out of disrespect to the authors but mainly because it doesn't sit easily with me to see that someone might be saying nice things about me when my own perception is that a performance could have been better. Perhaps I have problems with praise while also fighting shy of seeing anything negative which might dent my confidence?

But it feels somehow different when the critics or audience members take a collective view..........

Awards

I know that awards for dance are sometimes knocked on the basis that there are 'political' considerations in play, But there's no denying that to be nominated or to 'win' in a performance category or overall makes one feel very valued at the time and extra motivated to keep working and improving the next day. Being named as a permanent guest principal or being appointed an 'ambassador' are also honours to be treasured.

Season/Yr	Award/Nomination/Position	Awarding Organisation
2009/10	**Outstanding Male Performance (Classical) Award** for Prince Siegfried in English National Ballet's *Swan Lake*	National Dance Awards
2011/12	Best Male Dancer Nomination	National Dance Awards
2012/13	Best Male Dancer Nomination	National Dance Awards
2012/13	**Prix Benois de la Danse** for Prince Désirée in English National Ballet's *The Sleeping Beauty*	Benois de la Danse
2013/14	Best Male Dancer Nomination	National Dance Awards
2013/14	Outstanding Male Performance (Classical) Nomination for Conrad in English National Ballet's *Le Corsaire*	National Dance Awards
2013/20	**Permanent Guest Principal**	National Ballet of Japan
2014	**Bright Past Award** (in recognition of citizens' achievements)	City of Chelyabinsk
2014/15	**Best Male Dancer**	National Dance Awards
2014/15	Outstanding Male Performance (Classical) Nomination for The Royal Ballet's *Symphonic Variations*	National Dance Awards
2015/16	Best Male Dancer Nomination	National Dance Awards
2017/18	**Best Male Dancer**	National Dance Awards
2018/19	Best Male Dancer Nomination	National Dance Awards
2018/19	**Prix Benois de la Danse** for Prince Siegfried in The Royal Ballet's *Swan Lake*	Benois de a Danse
2018/19	**Positano Premia la Danza Award**	Positano Premia la Danza Léonide Massine
2019/20+	Best Male Dancer Nomination	National Dance Awards

Season/Yr	Award/Nomination/Position	Awarding Organisation
2019 >>	**Permanent Resident Guest Artist**	Ballet of the National Theatre, Brno, Czech Rep.
2020	**Dancer of the Year** (voted by Readers)	Dance Magazine Shinshokan (Japan)
2021	**Dancer of the Year** (voted by Readers from nominations by Critics across Europe)	Dance Europe Magazine
2021	**Dancer of the Year** (voted by Readers)	Dance Magazine Shinshokan (Japan)
Dec. 2021	**Ambassador of the Rudolf Nureyev Foundation**	Rudolf Nureyev Foundation
2021	Outstanding Male Performance (Classical) Nomination for the title role of Apollo with The Royal Ballet	National Dance Awards
2021	Best Male Dancer Nomination	National Dance Awards
2022	**Dancer of the Year** (voted by Readers)	Dance Magazine Shinshokan (Japan)

Photo: Andre Uspenski   Photo: Foteini Christofilopoulou

And I Got my British Passport the Same Day!

Dance Europe Cover Image
December 2021/January 2022 Edition
Photo: Emma Kauldhar

Three Years in a Row with the
Dance Magazine (Japan)
Photo: Dance Magazine

And Finally……..

The magazine features, DVDs, statuettes and certificates chart the passage of time in my career to date in a tangible way. However, everything now seems so fluid with ever-changing values affecting, or needing to be reflected in, the ballet world that it is difficult for individual dancers to envisage how their futures might pan out.

For some time, there has been concern about the lack of diversity among dancers and ballet audiences combined with disquiet as to how various groups are portrayed in ballet. This has led to a range of initiatives and to some ballets being refreshed, adapted or withdrawn from repertoires. It doesn't seem all that long ago that I was tentative about holding a girl's leg; now dancers are able to say if they feel uncomfortable about physical contact and new choreography is being mindful of that and of audience sensibilities. I began dancing within a training system where obedience was everything and into a profession where dancers were usually very compliant. Now, rightly, schools are ever more concerned to nurture individual students as people; in companies, dancers not only have a voice but what they put forward is discussed and acted upon; and, at an individual level, admitting to having problems is no longer taken as a sign of weakness. At times also, it feels as if the very nature of ballet will soon be unrecognisable compared with where it was when I joined my first class not much more than 20 years ago. Nothing can stand still, of course, but it would be very sad if classical ballet was to be allowed to 'disappear'.

World events are being represented increasingly and movingly in new work. But these are unusually challenging and anxious times. And whatever stands are taken or statements made, the world of ballet seems to be largely on the receiving end of what is happening outside. The scars are also impacting on individual dancers.

I am, of course, fortunate compared to many others. However, the fact that Mama spent weeks in intensive care as a result of Covid-19 thousands of miles away from me in London, the pandemic itself, the hurt when some people appear to condemn all Russians on account of their nationality alone, and other aspects of normal life have, in combination, affected me deeply as a dancer as well as a person. I will remember for ever the night in 2022 when I was told two hours before my show that a close relative, my childhood playmate, had died. One moment I was preoccupied with the usual physical aches, the next I was facing the far greater emotional pain which real life can bring.

There was nothing I could do then except go on stage. More generally, like most artists, I throw all that I have into what I'm doing and try to remain focused. For the eleven years or so when I lived alone, ballet was my everything. But, now, I am more aware of, and sensitive to, what is happening beyond that world.

Recently, I have also become less nervous and less hard on myself. It is almost as if I have had a re-boot for what I hope will be a long second half of my career – one where I will keep learning (from life as well as ballet), absorbing feedback and drawing on the support of family and friends to help me bring more to the stage each year that goes by.

And maybe, one day, Papa will get to see me dance live for the first time.

Printed in the USA
CPSIA information can be obtained
at www.ICGtesting.com
LVHW021552181223
766789LV00027B/184/J

9 781803 813851